rejection of the structural framework and thematic concerns of the "realistic" novel. He analyzes these novels in a context that includes the ebb and flow of critical opinion. Mellard expertly relates his thesis to the analytical works of such noted critics as Fowler, Frye, Iser, Kermode, Tanner, Scholes, Jameson, and Graff, and explains their varied responses to the modernist trend. Mellard shows us how and where the modernist American novel has arrived and suggests answers to the question: Where does the novel go from here?

"This is a very fine work. It is written with clarity and grace; its structure is logical, firm; it shows sound and extensive scholarship in its field; its thesis, controversial as it may prove, is useful and defensible; its discussion of particular texts is scrupulous and illuminating." —Ihab Hassan, author of *Paracriticisms* and *The Right Promethean Fire.*

JAMES M. MELLARD is chairman of the department of English at Northern Illinois University and author of *Four Modes: A Rhetoric of Modern Fiction.*

The
Exploded
Form

The Exploded Form

The Modernist Novel in America

James M. Mellard

University of
Illinois Press

Urbana

Chicago

London

Library of Congress Cataloging in Publication Data

Mellard, James M
  The exploded form.

  Includes index.
  1. American fiction—20th century—History and
criticism. I. Title.
PS379.M399   813'.03   79-25993
ISBN 0-252-00801-4

FOR MY FATHER,

MY MOTHER,

AND

MY WIFE, SUE

Contents

Preface

The modern age, as many recent scholars contend, began with the crisis that occurred when the world moved inside man. In modern literature, the modernist element has been associated with those philosophical positions identifying human consciousness as the basis of the external world's meanings, if, indeed, not of its actual being. This modernist theme has emerged in the broad reaches of Western philosophy, but it has also penetrated the farthest realms of Western science. Modernist philosophy has been aided by major concepts in twentieth-century science, for when evolution, entropy, relativity, discontinuity, and indeterminacy are projected into metaphysics, they further establish man at the center of his universe. Like modern philosophy, modern science has lost its naive objectivity, at first replacing it with critical empiricism or pragmatism, later replacing these with a more sophisticated, personalized, and subjective epistemology.

The problem we call *modern* is mainly this: the external world can only mirror the internal. This peculiar problem is compounded in the novel as a literary genre, for the novel-as-novel has never been oriented that way. Its orientation has been just the opposite: in the novel, the ground of authority has been the external world, so for the genre to follow the epistemological and ontological paths of philosophy and science is simply for it to enter a world turned upside down. The fiction we call *modernist* has followed the sciences and philosophy into the open, exploded universe, only to discover (or reconfirm) that man's own intellectual and imaginative resources have had to provide him with the authoritative groundings once provided by the now-discredited world outside. The novel-as-genre had been comfortably situated in Sir Isaac Newton's stable, mechanical universe; the modernist novel entered the universe of Albert Einstein, where both knowledge and being became defined by their own modalities, not by permanent essences. The movement resulted in the exploding of the traditional form, the monolithic novel-as-genre, and began the recreation of the "novel" as modes-of-the-novel, novels as models of a world that is itself comprised only of models constructed by science, philosophy, and—so be it—by literature.

In the age of the modern, fiction and history are subject to the same sense of indeterminacy as reality itself. This means that our histories, like our fictions, are just as much creations from human resources as the models of the world created by philosophy and science. It is just as pointless to search for a single "true" narrative of how a genre changes as it is to search for the one truth about the origins of wars and other complex human events. We have learned, however, that narrative archetypes or formulae are basic features of man's intellectual and imaginative resourcefulness. Though we do not always know their origins (and may not need to know, in fact), we nonetheless find them satisfactory in perceiving, discovering, or creating coherent, patterned temporal relationships. For a modernist thinker, one of the most useful formulae is the pattern of the dialectic. It is the dialectical pattern of destruction and reconstruction I wish to call attention to in the history of the traditional/modernist novel. But the essential feature of the pattern is an additional dialectic overlaying the modernist phase. Extrapolated from theories of Alastair Fowler, Northrop Frye, and Thomas S. Kuhn, this dialectic is powered by authorial responses to the modernist form and is identified in paradigmatic attitudes I shall describe as *naive, critical,* and *sophisticated.*

In this study the terms *naive, critical,* and *sophisticated* organize the narrative development of the modern novel. By naive, I identify those innovative authors who create many effects, using quite radical techniques, but who at this stage have no clear, conscious awareness of all they are doing; in the language of psychology, their works are the manifest contents of complexes about which they are not yet conscious. By critical, I mean a middle stage in which the same writers become conscious of the manifest contents and act on the knowledge; the term also applies to their imitators who analyze the innovators' accomplishments and, often, erect credos upon the originators' purely objective achievements. By sophisticated, I wish to suggest the stage of consciousness at which critical understanding becomes separated from belief in its objectives; this is the final stage before new paradigms emerge to change consciousness into new manifestations of unconsciously originary themes—a new stage of naive experimentation. Although these adjectives are sometimes used to label phases of an author's career, their primary use here is to identify the three phases of the history of the modernist novel.

The modernist "novel" is really a galaxy of modalities exploded from the once nuclear form. The modes constituting modernist fiction, as a generic construct, belong to the historical mode/epoch Frye identifies as "ironic," and the metaphor "exploded form" fits the genre because it seems congruent with the historical epoch's dominant philosophic foundations. The metaphor seems appropriate, as well, because by the time of the sophisticated phases, the energy of the modernist modes has begun to run down, portending a new historical phase as yet unidentifiable.

Much of the history of the novel is a product of the influence of world hypotheses or of metaphors from science and theology/philosophy upon the mimetic premises of the genre. Two main themes are the idea of nature and the form of the novel, from the emergence of the genre in the seventeenth and eighteenth centuries to its transformation in the twentieth century's exploding universe of modern astrophysics. From Melville, James, and Twain, who exemplify the late phase of the traditional form of the novel in America, specific developments can be traced that saw the exploding of the unitary genre, particularly by the later Henry James, Gertrude Stein, Sherwood Anderson, Ernest Hemingway, F. Scott Fitzgerald, and William Faulkner. Faulkner's *The Sound and the Fury*, my major paradigm for the naive phase of the modern American novel, provides a focus for analysis of modal fragments in a single work that in itself is a textbook of modernist practices.

Applying Thomas S. Kuhn's concept of scientific paradigms to the growth of critical knowledge in modernist literature produces a new perspective from which to extrapolate again the phases of naive, critical, and sophisticated modernism, dwelling particularly on the critical phase and the triumph of existentialism as a mode of thought to express it. Ihab Hassan and Nathan Scott, Jr., two critics of rather different persuasions, provide explanatory paradigms of that triumph.

Critics such as Hassan, Jerome Klinkowitz, and Philip Stevick insist that we are now clearly into a post-modernist epoch, but I feel that what they call "post-modernist" remains largely only third-phase, sophisticated modernism. Though I take particular issue with Stevick, one aspect of his description of our present epoch is appropriate, namely the concern of so many of our current novelists with the concept of *game,* a concept which must be distinguished from the related idea of *play.* As I see it, two strains of modernism originally competed for dominance early in the epoch: the objective, iconic, print mode (Eliot and Joyce), and the performative mode (in the fiction of Hemingway and in the poetry of Robert Frost, Wallace Stevens, and William Carlos Williams). The performative mode survived, and is being renewed in the late-modernist fiction of Kurt Vonnegut, Jr., Richard Brautigan, Jerzy Kosinski, and others. To understand this phenomenon requires explanation of the ways certain features of modernist aesthetics—including performance— answer the perennial questions of belief, of ultimate *authority.* In a very real sense, modernism devolves to this one question: On what ground does knowledge of our being exist? Different modes of the modernist novel—the lyrical, the dramatic, the oral narrative— answer in different ways, but the main answers—consciousness, self, language, myth, history—become the most important authorities of modernist thought.

The problem that many perspicuous critics regard as the most pressing is simply that of realism (new or old). Many would argue that this problem is solved in some of the modalities of modern or putatively post-modernist fiction—including "antifiction," the "nonfiction novel," "superfiction," "surfiction," and "metafiction," to name just a few rubrics given to various forms. My view is that all these competing paradigms for the post-modern's genre simply point to the crisis that exists, and they do not yet provide us with a satisfactory answer to the question about an adequate *novelistic* realism for an age beyond the modern. A truly adequate new realism, which must come with a new cultural epistemological framework, must acknowledge two conditions of our contemporary existence: that consciousness and its governing structures are inextricable aspects of any human "reality," and that any "reality" we therefore define is provisional and, finally, indeterminate. Given these conditions for a new realism in the novel, the most recent fiction that makes any claims toward realism might best be described by Ihab Hassan's term *indetermanence.* Although I do make an attempt to look into the future, surely Hassan is right when he says that even the present, to say nothing of the future, "remains always concealed from us; and true prophecy requires madness, unseemly on this [or any] occasion."

I admit that one is about as likely to find a single, continuous thread of argument in *The Exploded Form* as to find a single, continuous plot in Faulkner's *Absalom, Absalom!* I cannot apologize for its absence since I believe that the gains more than balance the losses in my method. New criticism and formalism, if they have had no other effect, have made us skeptical of the broadly diachronic view, and when we find unified historical narratives we must realize that critics, too, have been forced to construct them for themselves. Our position as critics today, when faced with a discontinuous field, is analogous to that of the reader of a modernist novel of the naive phase such as *The Sound and the Fury* or one of the sophisticated phase such as *Trout Fishing in America.* Even where we have been given the data—as found in collections of essays by single or diverse authors—we still lack an adequate metaphor. In *The Exploded Form*, what I have tried most persistently to do is to ground synchronic depth analyses of just a few paradigmatic works in a unifying metaphor that explains and, perhaps, determines the relations among many dozens. I have tried to give a modernist form to the subject of the modern novel in America.

Acknowledgments

I wish to thank the editors of *Bucknell Review* and *Studies in American Fiction* for permission to reuse in a slightly different form materials originally published there as an essay on *Catch-22* and a review of Nathan A. Scott, Jr.'s *Three American Moralists: Mailer, Bellow, Trilling,* respectively.

I also wish to thank those colleagues and friends who have helped me work out some of the ideas in this book. Though I cannot name them all, I feel compelled to mention at least these: Richard Finholt, Gregory Galica, and Glenn Meeter.

Finally, I wish especially to thank Charles W. Hagelman, Jr., for spiritual encouragement, professional counsel, and scholarly judgment he has given me over the years.

Introduction

I The Critical Paradigm

Broadly speaking, a model is a symbolic representation of selected aspects of the behavior of a complex system for particular purposes. It is an imaginative tool for ordering experience, rather than a description of the world.

Ian G. Barbour
Myths, Models and Paradigms (1974)

Man lives in two worlds, the world of nature which forms his external environment, and the constructed world of civilization and culture which he has made himself because he wants to live in such a world. The mythological universe is a model of the latter world: it is usually believed to be, at least in its earlier stages, the structure of the former world also, but it is ultimately not a proto-scientific construct, even when it develops or tries to develop a science. It is a world built in the image of human desires and anxieties and preconceptions and ideals and objects of abhorrence, and it is always, and necessarily, geocentric and anthropocentric, which the actual environment is not.

Northrop Frye
"Expanding Eyes" (1975)

In order to talk about the movement of a literary period or genre, historical critics must establish two bases: they must determine a set of aspects of the subject considered and create a metaphoric or "proto-metaphoric" paradigm. They do the first to generate a subject and the second to generate a narrative of the temporal relationships among those aspects. In this process, however, the historical critic must always remember that, ultimately, all he creates is a fable, an idealized abstraction. And we know now that the methods of any historian are not greatly different from those of the fiction writer. The novelist and the historian share an achievement; when their works are deeply rooted in our experiences of the world and the literary texts, they both may assume an ontological status of their own. Both narratives begin as modes of knowing, but they end—in the best fiction and the best historical criticism—as modes of being. *The Virgin Land, The American*

Adam, Love and Death in the American Novel, The Machine in the Garden, Radical Innocence, and other critical histories have achieved an ontological status in themselves. That status does not reside in their existence merely as books: the "realities" they create now exist apart from the texts themselves.

In "Towards Dialectical Criticism," in his *Marxism and Form,* Fredric Jameson explains some of these matters usefully. He points out that historical studies are necessarily dialectical, that in turn dialectical studies must be diachronic, and that in either case the subject one sees is a result of the author's original, determinative choices of the "key factors" that will provide the "dominant categories of the work."[1] This means, says Jameson, "it may be claimed that no matter how genuinely temporal or historical in character . . . a diachronic sequence is bound to remain an abstraction, inasmuch as it is nothing but an ideal cross section of the existential density of concrete history itself—the isolation of a single plane or level of reality, where the latter is understood both as the ideal sum of all such levels and as that ultimate, unthinkable totality which can never be thus additively reconstructed through the operation of pure thought alone."[2] Jameson's comments here make clear how evanescent may be the efforts of literary critics who engage in historical studies of either a genre or a period. But his strictures are not meant to discourage them from diachronic, historical analysis of literature. They are meant only to clarify the method and its intellectual discipline. Against such a background, then, it is possible to erect one's own system for analysis. I shall proceed along two lines. The first involves a "proto-metaphoric" paradigm identifying the perspectival aspects of modernist fiction; the second involves a metaphoric narrative model. The one represents what has happened to authors' attitudes toward their genre's form, while the other represents what has happened to the form itself.

The model I use for studying both epoch and genre as they are joined in one concept—the modern "novel"—rests upon Jameson's principle that "movement" or change in a genre within an identifiable diachronic period ordinarily must be described in a dialectical sequence. The model here employed has both a "proto-metaphorical" and a metaphorical base. One is abstract, the other concrete. I have constructed the proto-metaphorical base from similar models created by two quite different critics, Alastair Fowler and

Northrop Frye. In his essay "The Life and Death of Literary Forms," Fowler outlines a dialectical model based upon the sequence *primary*, *secondary*, and *tertiary*.[3] Fowler says a genre, by which he means almost any identifiable form of presentation, evolves through a primary stage in which the form emerges, a secondary stage in which artists base their creations consciously on the newly emergent form, and a tertiary stage in which the established form is itself used in a new way, usually through a parodic or antithetic formula that may readily initiate a new dialectical sequence. "Perhaps," says Fowler, "the sequence of phases is best described as a sequence of relations between genre, mode, and abstract formulation. At the primary stage, no equivalent mode or critical description of the genre as yet exists: following its requirements is a matter of unconscious obedience to the extrinsic type, or of imitation in the common sense. With the secondary phase, criticism begins: the genre is labelled and its requirements are understood so abstractly that a modal form separates out. . . . During the tertiary stage, criticism may recognize variations of genre. . . . Now conscious modal innovations proliferate."[4] Of his most concise formulation of the dialectical principle, Fowler says, "This restatement suggests a general hypothesis: namely that genre tends to mode."[5]

Any set of metaphorical or proto-metaphorical terms used to identify the abstract paradigm with which one is dealing in dialectical criticism will have limitations, but the set one uses ought to suggest the relative bases inherent in the *mythos* of periodization. Fowler's sequence as it is described seems legitimate enough, but these ordinal terms fail to suggest a closure, that is, a *telos* or necessary end to the sequence. A useful *mythos* might have been suggested better in actual metaphors, for example, of birth, maturity, and death (terms which the title and some discussion in his essay suggest); creation, consolidation, and decline; or primitive, civilized, and decadent. In fact, there is a set of proto-metaphorical terms embedded in Fowler's description of the dialectic. They are "unconscious obedience," "critical understanding," and "conscious innovation," terms that indicate much more clearly than primary, secondary, and tertiary both the narrative configuration and Fowler's real base of periodization. That base lies in a hypostatized author whose consciousness of his genre grows within a closed pattern. For Fowler, the ideal of an epochal, mythical author's shifting orientation to a specific genre is what actually defines dialectical sequences in the history of that genre. My paradigmatic authors, therefore, are only symbols of phases undergone by a *Weltanschauung:* Modernism.

In *Anatomy of Criticism* and elsewhere, Northrop Frye applies to authors a dialectic that suggests more clearly and more concisely the perspectival relation of author to generic form. The terms Frye uses are "naive," "sentimental," and "sophisticated," which bring a rich critical heritage that Frye both explains and adds to in the first essay of *Anatomy.* "The word naive," he says, "I take from Schiller's essay on naive and sentimental poetry: I mean by it, however, primitive or popular, whereas in Schiller it means something more like Classical."[6] Frye also alters the meaning of Schiller's "sentimental," for while it suggests in Schiller a level of self-consciousness not present in the "naive" (or "natural") author, it is used by Frye to indicate a degree of literary self-consciousness, to refer, that is, to "a later recreation of an earlier mode. Thus Romanticism is a 'sentimental' form of romance, and the fairy tale, for the most part, a 'sentimental' form of folk tale."[7] Frye uses the term "sophisticated" throughout *Anatomy;* by it he means something that takes in much of what Schiller had meant by "sentimental," but he also pushes the term beyond Schiller's usage to suggest the phase that begins to move away from the conventional base established by the truly naive and consolidated by the sentimental. At the dialectical extreme from the "naive" is the "sophisticated" phase, where "we have the pure variable, where there is a deliberate attempt at novelty or unfamiliarity, and consequently a disguising or complicating of archetypes."[8]

As Frye uses the terms, they afford a paradigm that can be used to cut across any level of literary criticism, any aspect of the literary "field" defined by the parameters of author, work, "context," and audience.[9] One change is needed, however, for Fowler's sense of the "critical" nature of the author's attitude toward form in the second phase is perhaps a more accurately descriptive term (certainly less confusing) than is "sentimental," so the three terms I use will be *naive, critical,* and *sophisticated.* Any item in the "field" can be identified as naive or critical or sophisticated depending on its relation to other items in a hypostatized series. But there is nothing inherent in these terms to suggest a diachronic sequence along with the synchronic paradigm, although clearly the major problem of literary history is the shift from one of these axes to the other.

INTRODUCTION

My discussion of the modernist novel in America begins with the assumption that modernist fiction is a tertiary, sophisticated phase of the genre of the novel. But in the history of the genre itself it is possible to recognize that in a sequence which includes Bunyan, Defoe, and Richardson, we are moving from naive, to critical, to sophisticated practitioners of the genre. In a sequence that includes *Pamela, Tom Jones,* and *Tristram Shandy,* we again are clearly moving from naive, to critical, to sophisticated exemplars of a generic form. Shifting to literary historical epochs, we see that the same sorts of applications of the terms are possible. The romanticism of Wordsworth has been considered naive, the later romanticism of the Victorians can be labeled critical, and the romanticism of modern literature can be called sophisticated (probably terminal-phase) romanticism. The point here is to clarify my stand that the models we propose for historical study are hypostatizations of an abstract dialectic and are problematic in themselves. And these problems are compounded when we take the next necessary step and move from the synchronic to the diachronic aspects of the models.

In order to move from the synchronic axis to the diachronic, I rely upon the model Frye provides elsewhere in the first essay of *Anatomy of Criticism.*[10] The dialectical terms already adapted from Frye may also be seen as aspects of a historical schema embracing five basic modes: myth, romance, high mimesis, low mimesis, and irony. The schema offers a mixture of synchronic hypostatization and diachronic observation, and may be, as its detractors contend, a "utopian" history pieced together upon a mythic framework of fall, quest, and redemption.[11] Be that as it may, the schema works as a synchronic "model" when it deals with myth and romance, and as a reliable diachronic "history" when it treats the mimetic and ironic modes. Fowler's dialectical theory presents a synchronic model, but suggests little possibility of a historical context. Frye's historical schema is much more useful in suggesting how a literary genre can be related to an epochal world view. The novel, for Frye, is a narrative form typical of a specific historical mode, an epochal way of doing and thinking. His view is readily borne out in a multitude of studies showing how the novel as a genre resulted at a particular historical moment only after many determinative factors coalesced: the development of print technology, the rise of an individualistic, literate middle class, the growth of an empirical science amidst an emblematic or figural and providential conception of nature in Puritan religion, and the emergence of three-dimensional, representational, pictorial art along with Cartesian models of philosophy and psychology.[12]

II The Narrative Metaphor

The spectra of the spiral nebulae have revealed facts which appear to show that they are travelling outwards from a common centre, and this has resulted in the theory that the physical universe originated at a date not infinitely remote in the past, in something resembling an explosion of energy which at once began time and began, in time, to generate space.

R. G. Collingwood
The Idea of Nature (1945)

Modern science . . . maintains on the one hand that nature, both organic and inorganic, strives towards a state of order and that man's actions are governed by the same tendency. It maintains on the other hand that physical systems move towards a state of maximum disorder. . . . Is one of the assertions wrong?

Rudolf Arnheim
Entropy and Art (1971)

I shall discuss modernist transformations of the generic form by seeking a metaphor congruent with the modernist cosmology. Frye's schema has another advantage over Fowler's here: it permits me to trade abstract, proto-metaphorical terms for more energetic, metaphorical ones. Frye's conception of historical modes indicates that both traditional and modernist forms are rooted in historical contexts and, moreover, that each comes with typifying, characteristic metaphors which allow us to see the transitions that occur.[13] Throughout *Anatomy of Criticism*, Frye suggests that an epochal mode is known by the metaphors it keeps. The shift from novel-as-genre to modernist modes of the novel, therefore, can be observed in a shift of metaphor. The habitual metaphors of the "low mimetic historical mode," Frye says, characterize the triumph of the novel-as-genre; those of the "ironic historical mode" characterize the triumph of the modernist forms. The low mimetic mode projected, says Frye, a philosophy of generation and organism, and these made the concept of evolution the basis for the nineteenth-century novel's conventional critical metaphor. Authors felt they saw the genre approaching maturity at that time, so evolution—one aspect of the organicism of low mimetic thought—provided an excellent model not only for regarding the content and philosophy of novels, but also for viewing the developing history of the genre itself. But even the metaphor of evolution has a life-cycle.

Though providing very problematic ideals, Darwin and Spencer gave the age metaphorical plots of triumph, or growth, or progress, and authors easily associated the novel in its defeat of rival genres with man's evolutionary triumph over other organisms. Such became the power of the metaphor of evolution that by the century's end the metaphor had become literal, part of the fabric of reality itself. Late in the century, just before the breakup of the monolithic novel form, for example, one finds Hamlin Garland calmly preaching the gospel of the novel and the norms of the low mimetic mode, and using the concept of evolution less as metaphor than as an established fact of life. Says Garland, 1893:

> Evolutionists explain the past by means of laws operative in the present, by survivals of change. In an analogous way, we may infer (broadly, of course) the future of society, and therefore its art, from changes just beginning to manifest themselves. . . .
>
> Fiction already commands the present in the form of the novel of life. It already outranks verse and the drama as a medium of expression. It is so flexible, admits of so many points of view, and comprehends so much (uniting painting and rhythm to the drama and the pure narrative), that it has come to be the highest form of expression in Russia, Germany, Norway, and France. . . .
>
> Taking it as it stands to-day in America, the novel not only shows its relation to the past and the present, but it holds within itself prophecies of impending change. No other medium of art expression is so sensitive to demand. Change is sure. What will it be?[14]

Garland proceeds to outline what the changes will be in the novel, and though very little he specifically predicted came to pass, most of us would nevertheless agree with virtually everything he says of the novel as a form. He did not realize, though he himself contributed to it in a small way in *Main-Travelled Roads*, that a new epoch, with a new reality, and thus with a new form, expressed through new metaphors, was about to begin.

The modernist novel emerges with the historical mode Frye calls *irony*. Since this new ironic epoch projects a philosophy not merely different from, but totally alien to the traditional novel's, the old generic form was necessarily warped out of shape, much as traditional verse was reshaped in the movement from high mimetic neoclassicism to low mimetic romanticism, or as a low mimetic "epic" poetry such as *Song of Myself* was re-shaped by an ironic "epic" such as *The Waste Land* or Pound's *Cantos*. And as the genre's form goes, so go its themes and values. Where the traditional novel had fostered growth, attachment, assimilation, and integration (low mimetic values, Frye suggests, as much of Walt Whitman as of George Eliot), the modernist novel reverses these and presents decay, detachment, alienation, disintegration, what generally has been summed up as "nihilism." For the novel, as the world goes so goes the form itself: as the world proposed by twentieth-century science "explodes," so explodes the novel. And a new metaphor is born to replace the old.

The shift of epochal metaphor, however, was not necessarily from evolution to explosion. As many recent novelists and critics now fully realize, the metaphor for novel and cosmos might have gone from evolution to entropy. The problem for metaphysics, once the primordial astronomical explosion became a given, was no more authoritatively answered by the biological than by the thermodynamic metaphor. But given the conservative aspect of the novel-as-genre and the readily appropriable, optimistic potential of biological evolution, the metaphysical system erected on it was infinitely more attractive as a world than one erected on the equally available base in physics. The potential shift can be seen in the differential between the cosmic model of evolution as propounded by Herbert Spencer and the metaphysic based upon the thermodynamic concept as it had stood since the work of Clausius and Rankine, and publicized by William Thompson (later Lord Kelvin) in the early 1850s, before Darwin's *The Origin of Species* (1859). The persistent optimism of the nineteenth century and the novel-as-genre is reflected in the essentially low mimetic aspects of evolution; the regnant pessimism of twentieth-century modes of the novel is reflected in the decidedly ironic features associated with the Second Law of Thermodynamics. The contrast is explicitly put by P. B. Medawar, in the essay "Herbert Spencer and the Law of General Evolution": "By the end of the nineteenth century the philosopher could choose between alternative doctrines of world transformation, the one apparently contradicting the other. The principle of General

Evolution spoke of a secular increase of order, coherence, regularity, improbability, etc., and Spencer's own derivation made it appear to follow from physical first principles; while the Second Law of Thermodynamics, suitably generalized, spoke of a secular decay of order and dissipation of energy."[15] Though Medawar points out that Spencer's own later thought was "darkened" somewhat by the spectre of universal entropy as the *telos* toward which the cosmos was moving, evolution itself persisted as a metaphysical concept well into the second phase of modernism, largely because the vision of a primal universe in explosion simply overwhelmed modern thought for many decades, though evolution conceivably is explained by the explosion's energy.

Consequently, if we now were to return to a proto-metaphoric dialectic, we might see that in the development of modernist literature, *explosion* becomes a middle term, situated between *evolution* and the present-day catchword, *entropy*. John Barth has legitimized the critical aspect in the well-known essay, "The Literature of Exhaustion," and Tony Tanner has raised it to a virtual methodology in *City of Words*, his study of American fiction since 1950. Nonetheless, fiction and criticism both have lagged behind science and metaphysics in grappling with the implications of the concept. Authors concerned with *Naturphilosophie*—including figures such as Whitehead, Weyl, Collingwood, von Weizsäcker, and Teilhard, at least from 1925 with *Science and the Modern World*—made early attempts to reconcile themselves to the dilemma of universal organic evolution leading to cosmic entropy.[16] Only now are contemporary novelists attempting reconciliation. Though now we can see "entropy" imaged in *The Waste Land*, *The Great Gatsby*, and many other works, not until the 1950s and 1960s was there any truly conscious treatment of the notion in fiction itself. This apparent anomaly proves the rule when it comes to the treatment of historical context in the development of the novel. Only those ideas of nature or reality widely acknowledged can exert a problematic force upon the form of the novel. Recent works by Thomas Pynchon, William Gaddis, John Barth, and even John Updike and Saul Bellow—along with the interesting book *Principles of American Nuclear Chemistry: A Novel*, by Thomas McMahon—are finally catching up to science fiction and metaphysics. These novelists' reconciliations of entropy and art are now deliberate; moreover, as novels like Gaddis's *The Recognitions* and Pynchon's *Gravity's*

Rainbow attest, their efforts are quite sophisticated. Still, these works would not have emerged, in all likelihood, had not Whitehead and others prepared the way. It is not so much that novels imitate life, as that novels as such represent the metaphysics of a dominant intellectual class in a given historical epoch.

III The Modernist Novel in America

> . . . we attribute to the world what really belongs to the "log-
> ical projection" in which we conceive it. . . . Many issues
> that seemed to concern the *sources* of knowledge . . . now
> appear to turn partly or wholly on the *forms* of knowledge, or
> even the forms of expression, of symbolism. . . . The recog-
> nition of the intimate relation between symbolism and ex-
> perience, on which our whole criticism of traditional
> problems is based, is itself a metaphysical insight. For
> metaphysics is, like every philosophical pursuit, a study of
> meanings. . . .
>
> Susanne K. Langer
> *Philosophy in a New Key* (1951)

> . . . all communicable speech acts, written or spoken, belong
> to a limited number of genres. Now, a genre is a kind and
> shape of utterance whose norms and conventions have been
> partly fixed through past usage. Every communicable utter-
> ance belongs to a genre so defined, and in communicated
> speech there can be no such thing as a radically new genre, for
> so-called new genres are always, by linguistic and social
> necessity, extensions and variations of existing norms and
> conventions.
>
> E. D. Hirsch, Jr.
> *Validity in Interpretation* (1967)

> . . . as the archetype is the communicable symbol, arche-
> typal criticism is primarily concerned with literature as a
> social fact and as a mode of communication. By the study of
> conventions and genres, it attempts to fit poems into the
> body of poetry as a whole.
>
> Northrop Frye
> *Anatomy of Criticism* (1957)

The novel always has depended upon those concep-
tions of nature, reality, and the world given the highest credibility in
any epoch, so the genre has been particularly susceptible to what
Northrop Frye terms "cultural aging." That is, it has markedly
reflected the shifts in ideology—especially in metaphysics—that
have occurred with transformations within our culture. Such transformations are not matters of "decline" any more than of "prog-

ress," but only of "a certain range of imaginative possibilities" exploited and exhausted, according to Frye.[17] Major ideas of nature, reviewed in the next section herein, have given the novel its range of imaginative possibilities, each in turn exerting an effect on the form and its possibilities, bringing us to the point of crisis at which emerges the possibility of the peculiarly modernist novel. That crisis, involved in what Erich Kahler identifies as the "inward turn" of narrative, develops because the metaphysics of both Newton and Darwin are incapable of accounting for the novelist's "world" in the twentieth century. "We have long since weathered," insists Frye, "the Newtonian crisis separating mythological from natural space, and the Darwinian crisis separating mythological from natural time. A third crisis, more difficult and subtle, is succeeding it: the distinguishing of the ordinary waking consciousness of external reality from the creative and transforming aspects of the mind."[18] It is this third crisis that gives us the modernist novel, a phase of the genre that persists into the present, though amidst signs that it, too, will pass.

The aspects that make the novel in this century *modern* are found, then, in novelists' expressions—usually unconscious—of notions from various disciplines aggrandizing the importance of subjectivity, of consciousness, in an atomistic, indeterminate, exploding universe. As various conceptions of relativity and indeterminacy—expressed or exemplified in writers ranging from Henry Adams, John Dewey, and William James, to Joyce, Pound, Eliot, and Yeats—were gradually introduced into the novel-as-genre, either as elements of form or of theme, they could only (we can see now) explode the monolithic nineteenth-century form. As A. Walton Litz says of an important modern text, for example, "*Ulysses* may be viewed as a two-part performance in which the modern novel is built up and then disintegrated into its original components."[19] Another text, Faulkner's *The Sound and the Fury*, based on the same principle, reverses the order, disintegrating the generic form and then progressively reconstructing it. But both texts finally come to this: their locus is no longer the world but the human consciousness, which also must bear the burden of hermeneutic determinacy.

A modernist metaphysics generated subjectivistic fictions of consciousness and open, indeterminate forms. Writers in the twentieth century were thus forced to identify "authority"—their textual validations and determinations—elsewhere than in the traditional figural, emblematic monism upon which the genre had been based; but when they did so, nothing remained available to them except *modes* of the novel.[20] One development is that the epistemology underlying any one of the available fictional modes might, for a specific work or author, exhibit a sanctioning authority, or what Frye might call a "spiritual authority." Though no epistemology has been able to equal the philosophic base on which the traditional genre rested by the time of its late phase, the triumph of philosophic existentialism in the middle third of the twentieth century and its alliance with the historical mode of irony have nonetheless legitimized fiction's disparate modes, allowing each a heuristic status such as Wittgenstein permitted the modes of discourse in language.[21] So, despite the exploding of the generic form, the modalities of the modern novel resume their legitimacy by persisting in their imitation of models of the world—albeit an exploded world.

The modernist novel in America, rooted in Melville, Twain, and James, begins in the essentially naive-modernist works of Gertrude Stein, Sherwood Anderson, F. Scott Fitzgerald, Ernest Hemingway, and William Faulkner; it develops into the critical consolidations of the modern in such authors as Saul Bellow, Ralph Ellison, Norman Mailer, Bernard Malamud, Joseph Heller, John Updike, and William Styron; and it culminates in the sophisticated-modernist innovations of John Barth, Donald Barthelme, Richard Brautigan, Robert Coover, William Gass, Kurt Vonnegut, Jr., and many others. These names do not include all the novelists one would consider "modern" or "modernist"; they are simply among the most important or the most representative: this criterion of representativeness is by far the most determinative in any selection of authors in the critical and sophisticated phases.

The different phases of the modernist novel do not necessarily exclude the appearance of "traditional" novels. But their appearance does raise questions about an author's attitude toward his traditional form: does he "believe" in it or does he accept it provisionally, as a mode only, one of many possible modes? In modernist fiction's naive phase, during which the form was emerging, many novelists, including Willa Cather, Ellen Glasgow, Sinclair Lewis, and Edith Wharton, retained at least a critical faith in the traditional "mode" of realism, and yet others, such as Theodore Dreiser, James T. Farrell, John Dos Passos, John Steinbeck, and Thomas Wolfe kept faith in the genre by working in realism's extension, the "mode" of naturalism. Even during the critical phase of modernist consolidation we still find naturalistic novels naively projected as other than a mode in, for instance, Richard Wright's *Native Son*, Norman Mailer's *The Naked and the Dead*, and James Jones's *From Here to Eternity*; and in the works of Louis Auchincloss, J. P. Marquand, John O'Hara, and the novelists of manners we find a relatively naive realistic form. But modernism teaches us this: modes, metaphors, *mythoi*—all may persist after origination and, after epochal "old age" or "death," may thrust forth again, sentimentally, at any historical moment.

In the naive beginning, the different modes modernists such as William Faulkner seem to have isolated intuitively were actually the most basic ones of fiction. These were the epistemological modes of presentation related to techniques, and the ontological (or hermeneutic) modes of narrative related to *mythoi* or "worlds" or "hermeneutic systems." Dealing with the naive modernists, therefore, one may focus on a rather limited number of concepts, ones usually related in some way to generic concepts such as *drama*, *lyric*, *epic*, and *novel*; or *romance*, *tragedy*, *irony-satire*, and *comedy*.[22] Beyond the early naive stage, however, it would not be practicable to limit consideration in these ways, for after the 1920s, once the American novel had been exploded by modernist attitudes and experiments, modes not habitually associated with fiction, such as the pastoral and the elegiac, became as important as any others to novelists.

Why are so many different concepts of mode necessary to the phases of the modern? Because, by thrusting the authority not only for meaning, but also for synthesis and organization upon the reader, indeterminate forms thrust authority increasingly upon conventions of every sort. In the traditional novel-as-genre, the relationship among author, text, universe, and audience was quite different: authors through novels imitated the world, and readers tested them against that world. "That texts have contents, which in turn are carriers of meaning, was until the arrival of modern art an almost uncontested assumption," writes Wolfgang Iser. "Therefore interpretation was always legitimate if it reduced the text to meaning. The advantage of this was that meanings could be generalized, that they represented established conventions, and that they brought out accepted or at least understandable values."[23] According to Iser, for the modernists the ontological being of a work stands, not between text and world, but in the gap between the author's text (which has projected a consciousness) and the reader's consciousness; and while texts have always "had to be seen in the context of what was already familiar or comprehensible to the reader,"[24] it is also true that "the more texts lose their determinacy, the more strongly is the reader shifted into the full operation of their possible interpretations."[25] In the traditional novel-as-genre, the gap between text and reader was filled by conventions associated with an extrinsic spatio-temporal reality; in the modernist modes of the novel, that same gap is filled by literary conventions, which are intrinsic to both text and reader, however objective their heuristic being. The situation can be summarized thus: if the novel is an ontological object, as modernist criticism says, and if, as says modernist philosophy, our only knowledge of objects is subjective knowledge, then the only knowledge of form that readers of novels can have is subjective—thus generic, modal, or archetypal—knowledge. This is a position that both E. D. Hirsch, Jr., and Northrop Frye, from their different theoretical stances, would accept along with Iser.[26]

The gap in modernist literature, between the undetermined text and the reader's determining imagination, has been the focus of most of our acceptable definitions of modernism itself, for critics have tried to find bridges across it at the same time that authors have tried to widen it. Maurice Beebe, for instance, has explained the period in terms of its formalism, irony, myths, and reflexiveness:

First, Modernist literature is distinguished by its formalism. It insists on the importance of structure and design—the esthetic autonomy and independent whatness of the work of art—almost to that degree summarized by the famous dictum that "a poem should not mean but be." Secondly, Modernism is characterized by an attitude of detachment and noncommitment which I would put under the general heading of "irony" in the sense of that term as used by the New Critics. Third, Modernist literature makes use of myth not in the way myth was used earlier, as a discipline for belief or a subject of interpretation, but as an arbitrary means of ordering art. And, finally . . . Modernist art turns back upon itself and is largely concerned with its own creation and composition. The Impressionists' insistence that the viewer is more important than the subject viewed leads ultimately to the solipsistic worlds-within-worlds of Modernist art and literature.[27]

From the point of view of formalist critics such as the Russians— who had already created a "modernist" criticism by the time most

American writers were beginning production of modernist texts—or a critic such as Frye, this definition is merely a projection into the undetermined historical "field," itself made up of undetermined texts, of the principles of formalist criticism. But this has also meant that the characteristics of the texts—their formalism, detachment, use of myth, and artistic autonomy—have pushed readers to the employment of the mode of archetypal criticism, where meaning or significance is dealt with "in terms of the generic, recurring, or conventional shape indicated by . . . mood and resolution, whether tragic, comic, ironic, or what not, in which the relationship of desire and experience is expressed."[28] While such criticism may have been "reductive," a lowering of fiction to least common denominators, it has also had a positive social effect by making even the most difficult text potentially available to every reader, as, by "the study of conventions and genres, it attempts to fit poems into the body of poetry as a whole."[29]

The maturation of modernist American fiction beyond the naive phase, then, is achieved in a second generation's explorations. Their explorations transformed the solar world of the conventional novel-as-genre into a galaxy of modes. The modes themselves had been created by isolating traditional techniques and then projecting them into metaphysical principles beyond aesthetics, as, for example, in Hemingway's dramatistic objective "world," Anderson's oral traditional, yet subjective, one, and Faulkner's pluralistic objective and subjective ones. All the main modalities are seen in *The Sound and the Fury*, even traditional mimesis. Writers effecting a critical consolidation—Bellow, Ellison, Malamud, Hawkes, Styron, Heller, Updike—apply a consciously critical understanding of the narrative paradigms introduced by the naive authors. Though authors of the critical phase are now sometimes identified by use of the term "contemporary," they are nonetheless preoccupied with "projects" early modernists had begun. Within the limits set down for them by the masters, the second-phase novelists continue to explore the new worlds of consciousness, particularly those identified with Faulkner and British authors such as Woolf and Joyce; in the process, they have become aware of myth, the archetypal unconscious, history, and language, just some of the authorities underlying naive paradigms. They have been especially persistent in the use of myth or patterns of archetypal imagery to provide controlling meta-structures for modernism's ironic, disjunctive worlds. Heller's

Catch-22 offers an exemplary manifestation of these features of the critical phase.

Among writers whom I would label *sophisticated* are Barth, Barthelme, Brautigan, Coover, Gass, Kosinski, Pynchon, and Vonnegut. They belong to this phase because they have begun to lose faith in the now-conventional—however relative—modalities of the modern. Loss of conviction has led them to analyze their own roles as authors of novels, since the genre is meant to have something to *do* with reality, even a pluralistic reality. Their knowledge now extends beyond simple awareness of the modes and authorities available to fiction. They have become *self*-conscious and self-questioning, as well. They are threatened—as Barth suggests powerfully in *Lost in the Funhouse*—by the paralyzing burden of their knowledge, by historicity and self-awareness. Having lost an ability to "believe" in modernism's modes, these sophisticated practitioners have increasingly stressed the "playful" activity of novel-writing. For them, the act of writing becomes the "reality" imitated, rather than any conventional objective reality. As performance becomes a modernist mode of reality, the rituals of authorship and storytelling become "authorities," as well as content, and the modes of Stein, Hemingway, and Anderson have thus regained status they had lost while subjectivity reigned after Faulkner. The primary authority of sophisticated writers has become the authorial role itself, and their fictions become, often as not, reflections upon themselves or upon novel-writing, or both together in the act of imagination, which in Brautigan, Pynchon, and others is self-consuming as it materializes. Such sophistication has become the focus of the "metafiction," "surfiction," "superfiction," or even "antifiction" identified by "post-contemporary" critics.[30] Brautigan's *Trout Fishing in America* is a surprisingly sobering exemplum of the themes and forms of the third phase of the modern American novel.

The late phase of the modern novel is difficult to analyze. As Alastair Fowler says, a "surviving modal abstraction is capable of a variety of applications, which may result in new genres distant from their original both in quality and in degree of sophistication."[31] Fowler illustrates what can happen in a late phase: a gothic novel or romance such as *The Old English Baron* might yield a more permanent gothic mode that could then be "applied to forms as diverse as the maritime adventure (*The Narrative of A. Gordon Pym*), the psychological novel (*Titus Groan*), the short story (Isak Dinesen) and the detective story, not to mention various science fiction genres (not wholly unpredictable, these last, in view of Mary Shelley's *Frankenstein*)." What is more, Fowler suggests that a mode such as the gothic could also be crossed with a variety of social or political ideas to complicate the form even further. "In gothic science fiction," says Fowler, "the politics are often quite conscious. So too the mode abstracted from satire proper (Juvenal, Horace) was applied to other genres to generate the satiric mock-epic (*Rape of the Lock*), the satiric travel-book (*Gulliver's Travels*), the satiric novel (*Catch-22*) and many other forms not easy to refer to their origin."[32] So too, I should add, the mode abstracted from pastoral by Anderson, Hemingway, and Faulkner generates all sorts of curious modal combinations in the works of Malamud, Updike, Vonnegut, and Brautigan. One can become lost in the murky byways of various modal and generic permutations in this late phase, but the difficulty of analysis should not obscure this thesis: in the modern period, the novel-as-genre fragments into constituent, elemental modes that, in the process, at the hands of Anderson, Faulkner, Bellow, Malamud, Heller, Updike, Vonnegut, Brautigan, and numerous others, begin to fuse with modes and themes outside the conventional genre of fiction. The history of the modernist novel in America, in short, is the history of that seemingly ever-accelerating movement away from the exploding center of the traditional form.

The central metaphor around which the narrative of *The Exploded Form* is organized is one with which modernists are familiar. Astronomers, cosmologists, and physicists have concluded that the universe "as we know it" began in an unimaginably violent explosion of condensed matter, and all its millions of galaxies are still riding the thrust of that explosion. But these same authorities in the diverse sciences now suggest that the universe is running down, that the law of entropy is abrogating the other relevant physical laws, and that the process of the cosmos will end up in simple stagnation. Now, they tell us, it all will run down after about 14 billion years or so (depending upon whose numbers one accepts). There is hopeful speculation, however, that the process overall is more cyclical than linear, and so after a time it will reverse itself and start over again. As far as the novel-as-genre is concerned, I believe this last speculation about the future applies—though on a much more intimate time scale—just as readily as the metaphor of the original explosion. For I think it is likely that the novel's primal form, modified as it must be by the vicissitudes of history, will return to a central place in the poetics of the near future, though that form never again can be as "innocent" as it once was.

The mode of the post-modern "novel" will probably be a new realism. This realism will be taken less in a special sense than is the romantic or epistemological realism of modernist fictions. David Goldknopf's *The Life of the Novel* has suggested some of what I wish to discuss here.[33] Modernist fiction's fusion of novel and romance brought together the two basic conceptions of reality ordinarily found in the larger construct called "prose fiction." One conception—found in the tradition of the novel—is "reality as a hard-rock donnée." The other conception is the sense of reality as a projection of the fabulistic or fantastic imagination of the romancer. As we draw near the end of the sophisticated phase of modernist fiction, however, neither of these conceptions appears adequate for our sensibilities. Our communal sense of reality has now encompassed and will surpass the once-radical conceptions of the naive modernists. What will this new realism look like? Perhaps like Robert M. Pirsig's *Zen and the Art of Motorcycle Maintenance*, or Saul Bellow's *Humboldt's Gift*, or young Tim O'Brien's *Going after Cacciato*.

It may well be, as many estimable critics now contend, that modern literature has already become a *post*-modern literature, though I do not feel that such is the case. By the end of the twentieth century we probably will be able to say with some certainty that our now-contemporary fiction writers are of a new literary epoch, but we are still too close to the phenomena at present to see clearly the broader historical outline. One can merely speculate briefly on the turn that a post-modernist *ethos* might take toward a new realism, a new mimesis. Modernist American fiction, in any case, has reached the terminal generic stage Alastair Fowler calls "conscious *innovation*," and even when radically different writers in the sophisticated phase such as Vonnegut, or Barthelme, or Brautigan show their debts to a convention of the naive phase, they do so in ways that make us aware the tradition of the modern has actually reached the end of the line.

Notes: Introduction

1. Fredric Jameson, *Marxism and Form: Twentieth-Century Dialectical Theories of Literature* (Princeton, N.J.: Princeton University Press, 1971), p. 311.
2. *Ibid.*, p. 312.
3. Alastair Fowler, "The Life and Death of Literary Forms," *New Literary History: A Journal of Theory and Interpretation,* 2, no. 2 (Winter 1971): 199–216, 213–14. The term *proto-metaphor,* which was drawn to my attention by Victor J. Vitanza, comes from Robert Zoellner, *The Salt-Sea Mastodon: A Reading of Moby-Dick* (Berkeley: University of California Press, 1973), pp. 4–5.
4. "The Life and Death of Literary Forms," pp. 213–14.
5. *Ibid.*, p. 214.
6. Northrop Frye, *Anatomy of Criticism: Four Essays* (Princeton, N.J.: Princeton University Press, 1957), p. 35.
7. *Ibid.*
8. *Ibid.*, p. 103.
9. For a fine discussion of the objects inhabiting the literary "field," one that encompasses the presuppositions of M. H. Abrams's "Introduction" to *The Mirror and the Lamp: Romantic Theory and the Critical Tradition* (New York: Norton, 1958), pp. 3–29, see Hayden White, "The Problem of Change in Literary History," *New Literary History: A Journal of Theory and Interpretation,* 7, no. 1 (Autumn 1975): 97–111. I rely heavily on Abrams's conception of the coordinates of literary criticism throughout *The Exploded Form,* particularly in the discussions on the "Sophisticated Phase."
10. Fowler, in "The Life and Death of Literary Forms," casts occasional aspersions upon the historical sequence Frye outlines in *Anatomy,* but it seems to me that when Fowler makes his most explicit charges— such as ". . . schematic classifications have often been devised, by writers as disparate as Aristotle and Scaliger, Hobbes and Frye. But all seem more or less simplistic and unconvincing" (p. 209)—they are made against chimeras in Frye of Fowler's own creation. Fowler's comments are directed toward the first essay in *Anatomy,* but that is not the essay dealing with genre criticism. For that, one ought to go to the fourth essay, "Rhetorical Criticism: Theory of Genres," pp. 243–347. There Frye defines genres in ways that permit them to be construed both synchronically and diachronically, and Frye's treatment of a specific genre (the four are lyric, *epos,* drama, and prose fiction) follows a cyclical pattern imposed upon a historical sequence. I do not find the problems in Frye that Fowler does, nor do I see any reason not to meld the two models at points where they usefully converge.
11. Angus Fletcher's "Utopian History and the *Anatomy of Criticism,*" in *Northrop Frye in Modern Criticism,* ed. Murray Krieger (New York:

Columbia University Press, 1966), pp. 31–73, is the source of this epithet, though Fletcher is not, as he makes clear, a detractor; Fowler calls this essay a "desperate defence of Frye against charges of unhistorical schematicism" (p. 209n). In a more recent essay, "Northrop Frye: The Critical Passion," *Critical Inquiry*, 1, no. 4 (June 1975): 741–56, Fletcher rejects the epithet and the bias it permitted others to project into it. For a response to Fletcher's essay and an explanation of his own historical underpinnings, see Northrop Frye's "Expanding Eyes," *Critical Inquiry*, 2, no. 2 (Winter 1975): 199–216. The distinction Frye makes between the narrative modes (*mythoi*) and the historical modes has caused a great deal of confusion in discussions of his theories by critics such as Robert Scholes and Tzvetan Todorov. One way to explain the difference is to suggest that the narrative modes are essentially synchronic, the historical modes essentially diachronic. Thus, while there is a relation between some of the terms involved in each concept, as there is between the aspects of language known as *langue* and *parole*, there is no necessary identity. The historical mode of irony, for example, includes the synchronic narrative mode of irony-satire. But the specific work in the synchronic narrative mode has no special authority until it is matched up with the historical (diachronic) mode of fictional naturalism. The synchronic mode seems to encompass all reality when the literary philosophy of naturalism takes over as a world-metaphor. Its values are congruent with those of irony-satire, as both see an undesirable, repugnant, deterministic system as identical with reality itself. It is possible, conversely, to have an ironic plot (usually a subplot dealing with lower-class, i.e., "low mimetic" or "ironic," modalities of characters) in the midst of a narrative that belongs to both the *mythos* of romance and the historical mode of romance. Frye suggests, in his discussion of the historical modes, that the "center of gravity" of literature has, historically, moved inexorably downward; this is also to say that the historical development of literature, especially of the branch known as prose fiction, has seen the rise of realism. While a work like Erich Auerbach's *Mimesis* suggests that the literature of the Western world has "progressed" toward representational realism, Frye's *Anatomy* would suggest that only our points of view have changed. Our relative valuations of myth, romance, fabulation, realism and the like have shifted from epoch to epoch, but their absolute meanings have not.

12. Most of the developments I allude to in this sentence are well known; see, for example, Ian Watt's *The Rise of the Novel*, Marshall McLuhan's *The Gutenberg Galaxy*, and, more recently, J. Paul Hunter's *The Reluctant Pilgrim: Defoe's Emblematic Method and Quest for Form in Robinson Crusoe* (Baltimore: Johns Hopkins University Press, 1966), and Wolfgang Iser's *The Implied Reader* (Baltimore: Johns Hopkins University Press, 1974).

13. I am aware that I lay at Fowler's door the same charge of a lack of historical perspective that he levels at Frye. The problem is not that either critic is actually without historical awareness, but only that to talk about genre and modes of a genre always involves definitions that are in themselves static, so synchronicity must normally appear to be predominant. The same type of problem recurs in linguistics, in the difference between *langue* and *parole*, and in interpretation, in the

INTRODUCTION

"gap" in the hermeneutic circle. An immensely important work on hermeneutics and genre, which Fowler discusses (pp. 200–201), is E. D. Hirsch, Jr., *Validity in Interpretation* (New Haven, Conn.: Yale University Press, 1967).

14. Quoted in A. Walton Litz, *Modern American Fiction* (New York: Oxford University Press, 1963), p. 27.

15. *The Art of the Soluble* (London: Methuen, 1967), p. 51.

16. Some of the texts relating to the subject of science's relation to philosophy, literature, and art include: Alfred North Whitehead, *Science and the Modern World* (New York: Macmillan, 1925), Hermann Weyl, *The Open World* (New Haven, Conn.: Yale University Press, 1932), R. G. Collingwood, *The Idea of Nature* (Oxford: Clarendon, 1945), C. F. von Weizsäcker, *The History of Nature* (Chicago: University of Chicago Press, 1949), Pierre Teilhard de Chardin, *The Phenomenon of Man* (New York: Harper, 1959), Werner Heisenberg, *Physics and Philosophy* (New York: Harper, 1958), and Rudolf Arnheim, *Entropy and Art: An Essay on Disorder and Order* (Berkeley: University of California Press, 1971). Tony Tanner, in *City of Words: American Fiction 1950–1970* (London: Jonathan Cape, 1971), discusses the theme of "entropy" in the chapter entitled "Everything Running Down," mentioning that many different novelists—Sontag, Mailer, Bellow, Updike, Barth, Percy, Elkin, Barthelme—use the word in their works, but few actually treat the concept as an important theme in the way Thomas Pynchon does in *V*, *The Crying of Lot 49*, and *Gravity's Rainbow*.

17. "Expanding Eyes," *Critical Inquiry*, 2, no. 2 (Winter 1975): 209.

18. *Ibid.*, p. 211.

19. "The Genre of *Ulysses*," in *The Theory of the Novel: New Essays*, ed. John Halperin (New York: Oxford University Press, 1974), p. 116. In connection with my argument, also see in this collection of essays Alan Warren Friedman's "The Modern Multivalent Novel: Form and Function," pp. 121–40, and Max Schulz's "Characters (contra Characterization) in the Contemporary Novel," pp. 141–54.

20. Edward W. Said, in *Beginnings: Intention and Method* (Baltimore: Johns Hopkins University Press, 1975), offers a fruitful consideration of the problem of authority in fiction in the chapter "The Novel as Beginning Intention," pp. 81–188. Said's *Beginnings* provides a radically philosophical study of modernism's various "great prior" realities (p. 73), though focusing particularly upon the priority of language observed in most structuralist thought, and I heartily commend it to anyone interested in the groundings of contemporary art.

21. Wittgenstein was caught up in the same problems that beset the modernist novelists, and the shift from the realist position of the early *Tractatus Logico-Philosophicus* (1922) to the linguistic naturalism of the later *Philosophical Investigations* (1935; rev. 2nd ed. 1958) is essentially the shift undergone by the novel-as-genre when it becomes decentered modes-of-the-novel. For a concise explanation of this shift, which is at the heart of modernism, see David Pears, *Ludwig Wittgenstein* (New York: Viking, 1970), pp. 1–35, esp. pp. 3–5.

22. See Frye's *Anatomy of Criticism* for discussions of these concepts, the first four of which include what Frye calls "genres," the second four, "pre-generic narrative archetypes." See also the discussion of genre and other conventional forms in Hirsch's *Validity in Interpretation*. In

order to consider the shifting centers of fictional authority in specific novels, I frequently employ Frye's notions of the generic types, for it seems to me that the shift from a realistic, universe-oriented fiction to a lyrical, subject-oriented fiction involves a radical shift in authority along with the shift in form. The same holds true—with appropriate modifications—when one shifts from, for example, a romance plot to a tragic or a comic or an ironic plot.

23. "Indeterminacy and the Reader's Response in Prose Fiction," in *Aspects of Narrative: Selected Papers from the English Institute*, ed. with a Foreword by J. Hillis Miller (New York: Columbia University Press, 1971), pp. 1–2.

24. *Ibid.*, p. 2.

25. *Ibid.*, p. 6.

26. Hirsch begins the first chapter of *Validity in Interpretation* (p. 1) with an epigraph from Frye that Hirsch then takes issue with, but, nonetheless, it seems that Frye's basic position with regard to conventions is not really different from the one Hirsch elaborates. For an authoritative work that begins to move modernist thought toward a less grimly existential view of subjectivity and knowledge, see Michael Polanyi, *Personal Knowledge: Towards a Post-Critical Philosophy* (Chicago: University of Chicago Press, 1958).

27. "Introduction: What Modernism Was," *Journal of Modern Literature*, 3, no. 5 (July 1974): 1073, quoted by Beebe from his own *"Ulysses* and the Age of Modernism," *James Joyce Quarterly*, 10 (Fall 1972): 175. This issue (3, no. 5) of *JML* is devoted to "From Modernism to Post-Modernism."

28. Frye, *Anatomy of Criticism*, p. 105.

29. *Ibid.*, p. 99.

30. In the first section on the sophisticated phase, I take up the problem of critical terminology in the discussion of modernism. David Daiches identifies "the modern" in fiction in *The Novel and the Modern World* (Chicago: University of Chicago Press, 1939). Ihab Hassan's *Radical Innocence: The Contemporary American Novel* (Princeton, N.J.: Princeton University Press, 1961) applies the term "contemporary" to those writers I call "critical" and whose careers began after 1940 or 1945. Though Hassan was not consciously employing the epithet as an epochal label, since then it has become one, thus permitting "post-contemporary" as a term for the authors of the late 1960s and the 1970s in Jerome Klinkowitz's *Literary Disruptions: The Making of a Post-Contemporary Fiction* (Urbana: University of Illinois Press, 1975). In many respects, Daiches, Hassan, and Klinkowitz are critics of modernist fiction who form the same dialectic of *naive, critical,* and *sophisticated.* Daiches remains "naive" about the modern novel, for in "What Was the Modern Novel?," *Critical Inquiry,* 1, no. 4 (June 1975): 813–19, he suggests that Bellow, for example, belongs to a different mode from the modern (cf. p. 818).

31. Fowler, "The Life and Death of Literary Forms," p. 214.

32. *Ibid.*

33. David Goldknopf, *The Life of the Novel* (Chicago: University of Chicago Press, 1972), pp. 192–93.

INTRODUCTION

Phase One   The Naive

I "Nature" and the Novel

> . . . the mentality of an epoch springs from the view of the
> world which is, in fact, dominant in the educated sections of
> the communities in question. There may be more than one
> such scheme, corresponding to cultural divisions. The vari-
> ous human interests which suggest cosmologies, and also are
> influenced by them, are science, aesthetics, ethics, religion.
> . . . But each age has its dominant preoccupations; and
> during the [last] three centuries . . . the cosmology derived
> from science has been asserting itself at the expense of older
> points of view with their origins elsewhere.
>
> A. N. Whitehead
> *Science and the Modern World* (1925)

> The astronomers have lately been making us familiar with
> the idea of a universe which for the last few thousand million
> years has been expanding in galaxies from a sort of primordial
> atom. This perspective of a world in a state of explosion is
> still debated, but no physicist would think of rejecting it as
> being tainted with philosophy or finalism.
>
> Teilhard de Chardin
> *The Phenomenon of Man* (1959)

> . . . the vast changes in the modern novel . . . [are] the
> consequence of a process that has been at work throughout
> the whole history of Western man. That process is the
> transformation of man's reality, of which the transformation
> in the forms of art is one expression. If we wish to understand
> what has happened to the novel, we must grasp both the
> transformation of our reality and the transformation within
> man's consciousness.
>
> Erich Kahler
> *The Inward Turn of Narrative* (1973)

Whatever else in its history it may have been, the novel
is a mimetic form. Traditionally, its orientation has been not toward
the author, the work, or the audience, but toward the universe that
exists beyond author, work, audience. As a form governed by principles of mimesis and resistant to the idealism of the prose romance,
the novel has inevitably been at the mercy of any spiritual agencies
in human culture powerful enough to define—or redefine—nature,

reality, the world, the cosmos. The genre happened to have begun at a time when the basic trinity of spiritual authority—religion, philosophy, and science—were in harmony about man, nature, and his relationship to it.[1] "The Protestant Calvinism and the Catholic Jansenism," says Whitehead, "exhibited man as helpless to co-operate with Irresistible Grace: the contemporary scheme of science exhibited man as helpless to co-operate with the irresistible mechanism of nature. The mechanism of God and the mechanism of matter were the monstrous issues of limited metaphysics and clear logical intellect."[2]

Thus, the centers of defining authority at the time of the emergence of forms we now would call novels or "proto-novels" agreed completely on the crucial issues that could make novels. But during the course of the genre's history, Newtonian science, Augustinian theology, and rationalist philosophy have encountered other powerful movements with which the novel—because of its mimetic base—has had to cope. In turn, rationalist empiricism gave way to romantic idealism, deterministic theology gradually yielded to theological existentialism, and Newtonian mechanics has been displaced by Einsteinian relativity and quantum physics. The novel remained relatively stable through the trends in thought until the last one, for as long as it could count upon the changelessness of nature as viewed by empirical science, it had an authority that could counter any combination of the other modes of thought. But when the new science exploded the world, it exploded with it the novel as well.

The formal problem of the novel, therefore, has persistently been to find ways to imitate a world that is continually being redefined by theology, philosophy, and science. Wolfgang Iser, in *The Implied Reader*, suggests that the genre grew out of theological concerns, the interests of the Puritans in discovering their relation to God through the world's emblematic symbology. The "world" is thus very much with *Pilgrim's Progress*, because its hero, Christian, can identify his spiritual condition—the state of his soul—only through his relation to external reality. To illustrate this new situation, Iser contrasts the novel as a genre with two of its narrative predecessors. "The epic and the allegory of the Middle Ages were firmly based," says Iser, "on what Lukács called 'God-given security'; Bunyan's *Pilgrim's Progress* arises out of the total withdrawal of such security." But the shift is not totally bad, for the "loss gives human existence an unexpected significance, because only through self-observation was it possible to attain any degree of assurance." The doctrine of predestination consequently added to man's valuation of his experience, the very province of the novel as a genre. "In a 'God-forsaken' world," says Iser, "it offers the one chance of human self-understanding. Through it, the self and the world can be reconciled in a new way, but since there can be no paradigmatic, universally applicable reconciliation, literary fiction can only offer situational answers to each of the historical problems that need to be solved. The history of these problems and answers constitutes the history of the novel."[3] *The Pilgrim's Progress* to many literary historians is not acceptable as a novel, but the attitude toward the world embodied in Bunyan's work is also similar to one J. Paul Hunter has demonstrated as operative in later texts—prose narratives by Defoe such as *Robinson Crusoe*—which are almost universally regarded as novels or "proto-novels." The intended application of such works of Bunyan and Defoe may have been theocentric, but the form itself was as anthropocentric and experiential as one could possibly expect of any novel.[4]

If, as Iser suggests at the end of his chapter on Bunyan, "literature counterbalances the deficiencies produced by prevailing philosophies,"[5] then the next major historical problem to beset the novel was created by the Newtonian, Puritan, and rationalist objectivism that underlay the novel's empirical realism. Such objectivism was not sufficient to satisfy the demands created by the other half of the basic dichotomy of the thought of Western man. Opposed to any fatalistic determinism, the second half includes the conception of both man and nature as freely developing organisms in time and space. For satisfaction of this insistent demand one must look not toward science or theology, but toward popular thought, in the directions of humanistic ideals handed down from ages past. "When we leave apologetic theology," says Whitehead, "and come to ordinary literature, we find, as we might expect, that [even] the scientific outlook is in general simply ignored. So far as the mass of literature is concerned, science might never have been heard of. Until recently nearly all writers have been soaked in classical and renaissance literature."[6] It is from Greek and Renaissance cosmologies that post-Newtonian literature gets its organic concepts of nature. Classical and Renaissance ideas of nature and the world diverged in ways that resulted in the science of Newton and the philosophy of the rationalists. The Greeks had regarded the world as an organism permeated by a mind. During the Renaissance, Copernicus, Telesio, and Bruno developed an opposite, mechanistic view. According to R. G. Collingwood, "The Renaissance thinkers, like the Greeks, saw in the orderliness of the natural world an expression of intelligence: but for the Greeks this intelligence was nature's own intelligence, for the Renaissance thinkers it was the intelligence of something other than nature: the divine creator and ruler of nature."[7] The pivotal term linking the Greek and Renaissance conceptions of nature, therefore, is "mind."

It is the phenomenon of mind—the varied activities of the human psyche—that the materialism of traditional science left out as it set man's observational powers outside and against nature, separating him at the same time from the nature he studied, separating as well his body, which dwells in nature, from the mind that dwells in the body. "Just as the fundamental axiom of Greek thought about mind," says Collingwood, "is its immanence in body, so the fundamental axiom of Descartes is its transcendence. Descartes knows very well that transcendence must not be pushed to the point of dualism; the two things must be connected somehow; but cosmologically he can find no connexion short of God. . . ."[8] The philosophy of romantic idealism, therefore, was able to restore an important dimension missing in the more empirical tradition of fictional mimesis, the dimension of holistic unity. "It is the defect of the eighteenth century scientific scheme," writes Whitehead, "that it provides none of the elements which compose the immediate psychological experiences of mankind. Nor does it provide any elementary trace of the organic unity of a whole, from which the organic unities of electrons, protons, molecules, and living bodies can emerge."[9] The poetry and the fiction of the romantics—a poetry largely British and European and a fiction largely American and Germanic—thus rectified this imbalance: by putting mind in nature, they were able to put man back into it, and if they were so inclined they could put God back into Nature, too, though not so much "out there" as in man himself, giving us, in Carlyle's phrase, the special authority of a "natural supernaturalism."[10]

The emblematic tradition of Puritanism, which made it obligatory for man to study nature in order to understand God's relation to himself, gave the novel as a genre an exploratory task in relation to man's experience analogous to the chosen task of traditional science. But the idealism of the romantics redefined the world and changed the novel's task, even threatening the life of the genre itself, as narrative poems of self-exploration such as *The Prelude* and *Song of Myself* encroached upon the novel's traditional experiential base. M. H. Abrams explains the relation of such poems to the Christian tradition from which romanticism adopted its crucial metaphoric models: "The tendency in innovative Romantic thought," says Abrams, "is greatly to diminish, and at the extreme to eliminate, the role of God, leaving as the prime agencies man and the world, mind and nature, the ego and the non-ego, the self and the not-self, spirit and the other, or . . . subject and object."[11] What results is a new sense of ontological dimension, for "this metaphysical process does not delete but simply assimilates the traditional powers and actions of God," along with the narrative shape of Christian history. Now, Abrams says, "subject and object, in their long interworking, are adequate to account for the whole story, from the metaphysical equivalent of the creation, through the fall and redemption, to the apocalyptic consummation at the end of the providential plot."[12] For the romantic poet, the Christian quest has been absorbed by human consciousness.

The "plot" of *The Prelude*, about which Abrams is here concerned, in its charting of the spiritual quest, is thus quite analogous to the plot of Bunyan's expressly Christian allegory, but there is a vast and symptomatic distance between the objectives of the two works, romantic versus Puritan. Including elements of the prose traditions established in Germany as the *Bildungsroman* and the *Künstlerroman*, *The Prelude* records the growth of an individual's mind at the same time it records the "history of a *Poet's* mind." So the *telos* toward which Wordsworth's poem moves is not the revelation of God's grace, but the revelation of man's—a single man's—self, the immanence in himself of his being and destiny. Such self-containment results in an autotelic form represented in the circularity of *The Prelude* itself. According to Abrams, it recounts two major revelations—"Wordsworth's discovery of precisely what he has been born to be and to do" and of a knowledge of "the union between the mind and the external world"—and it ends by being about itself: it "is about its own genesis—a prelude to itself. Its structural end is its own beginning; and its temporal beginning . . . is Wordsworth's entrance upon the stage of his life at which it ends."[13] Thus, whereas the novel as a genre had begun with man's trying to know a self through the emblems of a world that might lead him to God, the romantic avatars of the novel—in verse, as well as prose, narrative—attempted to contain the world and God (if posited at all) in the operations of the human mind. That change meant, finally, that "reality" and its spiritual authority had moved inside man.

The reflexiveness of the romantic imagination has had important consequences for the genre of the novel. Conceptions of nature—of reality and the world—before the romantic idealists had always located it outside man's mind, even though an ordering principle of mind had been identified in nature by both the Greek and the preromantic philosophers: in the former, upon the analogy of the individual human being, as the relation of the self-conscious, rhythmic, vital organic microcosm to the macrocosm of nature; in the latter, upon the analogy of the "human experience of designing and constructing machines,"[14] as the relation of the creative handiwork of man to God's creation of self-consistent mechanisms. But the direction of romantic idealist thought led more and more to the conception of nature not just as something analogous to man's mind or even as the projection of the mind of God, but to the conclusion that "nature is, so to speak, a by-product of the autonomous and self-existing activity of mind."[15] "Hence," writes Northrop Frye, "in Romantic poetry the emphasis is not on what we have called sense, but on the constructive power of the mind, where reality is brought into being by experience."[16] Consequently, the shift from rationalist empiricism to romantic idealism offers no immediate bargain to the novel. As Frye says, "Romanticism is difficult to adapt to the novel," which "demands an empirical and observant attitude; its contribution to prose fiction is rather, appropriately enough, a form of romance," which "attempts to maintain a self-consistent idealized world without the intrusions of realism or irony."[17]

Romanticism and the romance, by the middle of the nineteenth century, had thus pushed the novel into a philosophical corner: the genre, on its scientific authority, could continue to represent to us the objective world, and many of our greatest novelists continued the empirical tradition during the century. But the authority of romantic philosophy had made the external world considerably less important than the subjective world of human consciousness. Though the novel has been a hardy genre, it has found difficulty in surviving without both science and philosophy/theology behind it.

34

The "death of God" in the nineteenth century thus might well have resulted in the demise of the novel, for that deity who in the Puritan epoch had helped create the authority for the novel itself had also stood behind and/or was manifested in the empirical reality in which even scientific man dwelt. "Writers of the middle nineteenth century," says J. Hillis Miller, "tend to accept the romantic dichotomy of subject and object, but [they] are no longer able to experience God as both immanent and transcendent."[18] By 1859, these writers had been confronted by two ideas—evolution and entropy—that would lead to major crises in metaphysical thought, and had begun to move into the radically a-theistic cosmos of objective modern science—the cosmos built by Darwin and R. J. Clausius (who formulated the Second Law of Thermodynamics), and by Michelson and Morley, and eventually monumentalized by Einstein. There is not much necessary difference between the external universe known by the Victorians and the universe of "modernism" finally and fully unveiled by the theory of relativity. But there is some difference, for though "God" remained an important concept to the Victorians, both evolution and entropy had led to major metaphysical consequences. "God seems to Tennyson, to Arnold, or to the early Hopkins to have withdrawn beyond the physical world," Miller says. Thus, while God may still exist for these authors, "He is no longer present in nature." What is more, since they are unwilling to concede authority to the inner Being of Self in the way the earlier romantics had, that which "once was a unity, gathering all together, has exploded into fragments. The isolated ego faces the other dimensions of existence across an empty space."[19]

By the latter decades of the nineteenth century, the intense subjectivity of idealist philosophy had created an even more pressing problem for the genre of the novel, not an ontological or metaphysical problem, but an epistemological one. As Collingwood writes, "The question at issue was a very far-reaching one: under what conditions is knowledge possible?"[20] The question had not been foremost in Greek, Renaissance, or romantic philosophy, for while it was assumed that nothing could be known unless it was unchanging, there was always assumed to be an unchanging substance (matter) or an unchanging substratum ("laws," "thought," or "forms") beneath the appearance of change in nature. The novel and its narrative congeners, even the prose romance, are all based upon such preconceptions, so that regardless of their specific underlying philosophic differences, the novelist, like the romancer, could believe that his "instrument" of knowledge—the form itself—was capable of presenting, representing, or imitating nature, the world, reality—however it was construed: as matter, as social structures, or as ideal forms.

Although most critics, at first glance, would not agree with such a comment about novel and romance, the case is made securely enough by C. C. Walcutt's *American Literary Naturalism: A Divided Stream*, a major study not of the two genres, but of a mode of the novel alone. According to Walcutt, naturalism in American fiction—and, by extension, even in European fiction—is a result of romantic transcendentalism. "American transcendentalism," Walcutt says, "asserts the unity of Spirit and Nature and affirms that intuition (by which the mind discovers its affiliation with Spirit) and scientific investigation (by which it masters Nature, the symbol of Spirit) are equally rewarding and valid approaches to reality."[21] As Walcutt presents his argument, then, the difference between novel and romance is not epistemological, for both the empiricism of the former and the idealistic intuition of the latter permit the author and his mode to get at knowledge of the world, of nature itself. The difference between the two becomes, for Walcutt, primarily matters of tone and affect. "When the mainstream of transcendentalism divides, as it does toward the end of the nineteenth century, it produces two rivers of thought. One, the approach to Spirit through intuition, nourishes idealism, progressivism, and social radicalism. The other, the approach to nature through science, plunges into the dark canyon of mechanistic determinism. The one is rebellious, the other pessimistic; the one ardent, the other fatal; the one acknowledges will, the other denies it."[22] Though Walcutt, who is not dealing specifically with the romance tradition here, attributes the differences to something in romantic transcendentalism itself, he is unable to make clearly the point I would make, even while using his thesis: it is no longer only the problem of reality that besets fiction—realistic, naturalistic, or idealistic; it is also the problem of how to know a reality that seems to recede farther and farther from both science and philosophy. It may have taken a century, but the romance—which, because of science and philosophy/theology, split in order to develop the novel—reconverges with the novel in the epistemological crisis of modernist thought.

For the novelist and the romancer, as for Plato, Aristotle, Descartes, Spinoza, and Hegel, "The question was: How are we to find a changeless and therefore knowable something in, or behind, or somehow belonging to, the flux of nature-as-we-perceive-it?"[23] But in the new world of post-Darwinian and, particularly, post-Einsteinian cosmology, nothing could be regarded as changeless, neither the farthest reaches of the astronomical universe, nor the smallest unit of subatomic physics. In Collingwood's words, "It comes to this, that physics now finds that it has no need for the conceptions of absolute rest or absolute motion: all it needs is the conceptions of relative rest and relative motion."[24] Consequently, our knowledge can only be relative, provisional, situational, and temporal.

So it is, then, that one as percipient—even prescient—as Henry Adams could lament for men of science in the year (1905) of Einstein's revelation of the specific law of relativity: ". . . it seemed in their minds a toss-up between anarchy and order. . . . In 1900 they were plainly forced back on faith in a unity unproved and an order they had themselves disproved. They had reduced their universe to a series of relations to themselves. They had reduced themselves to motion in a universe of motions, with an acceleration . . . of vertiginous violence."[25] Adams is responding to the nineteenth-century explosion of energy and consumption of energy; in the twentieth century, whose "education" he is attempting to outline, energy becomes known as matter and the physical universe of space-time has lost the authority of Deity and infinity, for now it is also regarded as having "originated at a date not infinitely remote in the past, in something resembling an explosion of energy which at once began time and began, in time, to generate space."[26] But even to Adams, just before the start of the modernist epoch, it was clear that man's knowledge was less a moment of "truth" than a "provisional step to the next synthesis."[27]

It is at this critical juncture that the conditions emerge for the *modernist* novel, for not even the historians—and Adams was both a historian and a novelist—can any longer argue for ultimacy, permanent syntheses, final truths. Nature has now become historical, but historians, too, have become relativists. They and the novelists—whose fictional form had begun as an analogue to history—are now committed to the provisional, modal, paradigmatic nature of their enterprises, so that in place of speculative theory and metahistory we now find that the most important aspect of modern philosophy of history is the critique of its methodology.[28] In the same way, in place of mimetic representations of the objective universe, we now find in the novel that the most crucial emphases are on consciousness and its epistemological problems, its ways of knowing. The typically representational aspect of the modern novel, therefore, is concerned with the critique of knowledge rather than of being, though clearly being will remain linked to our forms of knowledge.

As Wolfgang Iser says, the twentieth-century novel is concerned with "the functioning of our own faculties of perception."[29] This concern in turn has meant that we become aware of the nature of our faculties, of the reader's "own tendency to link things together in consistent patterns, and indeed of the whole thought process that constitutes his relations with the world outside himself."[30] Among other things, this modernist concern has meant that "the novel no longer confines itself to telling a story or to establishing its own patterns, for now it also deliberately reveals the component parts of its own narrative techniques, separating the material to be presented from the forms that serve its presentation in order to provoke the reader into establishing for himself the connections between perception and thought."[31] It has further meant that the sense of indeterminacy the modern scientist, historian, or novelist must feel can be transmitted to the reader in his relation to both text and world. "Then the reader realizes how far short of the mark are his attempts at consistency-building, since he has had to ignore so much of the potential content of the text in order to formulate his restricted interpretation."[32]

And such a realization—which has been reached by both modern science and philosophy—brings us to the issues that today appear most prominently in modernist thought: the roles of modes, models, and paradigms, including such literary concepts as genres, types, and archetypes. In Iser's words, the reader of the modern novel "is forced to discover the hitherto unconscious expectations that underlie all his perceptions, and also the whole process of consistency-building as a prerequisite for understanding. In this way he may then be given the chance of discovering himself, both in and through constant involvement in 'home-made' illusions and fictions."[33] Thus, one is prepared to say that the "reality" of the modernist novel is a consequence less of what is objective than of what is subjective, and subjective is rather exclusively a consequence of the genres, models, and paradigms provided to us by our various imaginative activities—the "worlds" of theology and science, philosophy and the arts.[34] Fragmented into a multitude of modes, the novel can no longer be the monolith it once was.

Ironically, the modernist novel again will find its validation in science, the same authority that, with providential Christianity, had originally validated the genre itself. But twentieth-century relativity and quantum-physical models serve to reverse the old Newtonian, mechanical, solid-state-physical models in much the same way that, in literature, an ironic mode will reverse the nineteenth-century low mimetic. The modernist novel, which seems to be coexistent and, perhaps, coterminous with the historical epoch of irony, is, then, the corollary of an exploding universe, of pluralism, of relativism, and of indeterminacy. Though conscious exemplars who are European (regardless of birthplace) such as Pound, Stein, Eliot, and Joyce appeared by 1920, America's early-modern novelists in the beginning were scarcely conscious of the shift from a universe in evolution to one riding the shock waves of explosion, however much their work registers the tremors of value shifts. Apparently, as Marshall McLuhan suggests of media environments, awareness of mythopoeic governing metaphors develops fully only at points of crisis, where we ourselves are prepared to move into another epoch, another metaphoric environment—or another paradigm—as Thomas Kuhn's *The Structure of Scientific Revolutions*[35] would express the matter as it pertains to the closely analogous field of science. It may have been in largely covert ways that modernist concepts in science and philosophy supported a fiction of modernism, but they nonetheless helped to accelerate those changes in it that led to a manifestly modernist form (although, if Fowler is right, the shift may have occurred regardless). Still, we must not misconstrue what, from our vantage points, looks like an inescapable reality when science's metaphor, of an exploding universe subject to the law of entropy, corresponds with literature's fragmenting genres of poetry, drama, and fiction. The modernist experiment that exploded fiction's unitary world, replacing it with a multitude of models, now seems only a phase in a continuous historical cycle. And that cycle portends now the deconstruction of the very aesthetic that had made possible modernism's distinctive pluralism. The modernist American novel, in short, seems at its entropic edge, awaiting a renewal of energy in its own exhausted forms or—more likely—in a new mode of fictional realism energized by the traditional novel-as-genre.

II From Genre to Modes

A novel is a picture of life, and life is well known to us. . . .
Percy Lubbock
The Craft of Fiction (1921)

The novel ended with Flaubert and James.
T. S. Eliot
"Ulysses, Order, and Myth" (1923)

Once the world had become subjective and relative, the novel had to become subjective and relative, too, or disappear as other genres had disappeared. Once the world had become such that it could be represented only provisionally in models, then the novel could represent the world only through models identified with the different modes incorporated in the traditional novel's form. The various modes of fiction involve distinctive perceptual and valuational orientations. The traditional novel-as-genre, however, has always rested upon the assumption that these different orientations fused at a given point. The easiest way to identify this point is to call it the perspective of the genre itself—the formal perspective of the novel, a God-like comprehension, by any account. The modernist novel begins when this formal perspective explodes.

The novel as we know it from the practice of the great nineteenth-century authors—British, European, and American—involves a unitary conception of the two modalities implicit in any literary work that establishes a relationship to the world. These modalities, to the extent they can be distinguished, are the epistemological and the ontological; they include the ways an author presents his "world" and organizes its meanings. The epistemological modes include the techniques by which an author permits a reader to know the contents of the world, and the ontological modes include the formal patterns which become an author's hermeneutic systems. The novel-as-genre, an omnivorous form, has taken specific techniques of both modalities. Its epistemological modes, for example, have been assimilated from both verbal and nonverbal arts: its origin lies somewhere in the mode of oral, formulaic narrative, but it has borrowed a dramatic mode from the drama, a pictorial mode from the nonverbal medium of representational painting, and a lyrical mode from poetic expression. Its ontological modes are more conventionally literary, for meaningful patternings of worlds can only be identified with specific narrative types (or *mythoi*) such as romance, tragedy, irony, and comedy.[36] The novel-as-genre of the nineteenth century rested on the assumption that the epistemological and the ontological modes were congruent, not only with each other, but also with the world. Indeed, what established this type of fiction as a genre was its triumphant assumption that the ways we can know the world in that type are a function of what we can know; what we can know, a function of the ways known.[37] The presumptions of this tidy congruence between fiction and the universe have been destroyed by "modernism," and the conflict between *how* we are permitted to know and the form of *what* we have been permitted to know has become the preoccupation of the modernist novel in America.

Such nineteenth-century works as Herman Melville's *Moby-Dick*, Henry James's *The Portrait of a Lady*, and Mark Twain's *The Adventures of Huckleberry Finn* all embody the unitary conception of the novel-as-genre. *Moby-Dick* includes a whole range of specific modes of presentation—oral narratives, lyric meditations, pictorial representations, dramatic encounters—but the narrator at the center (whether Melville or Ishmael makes little difference since the form fuses them) assumes their ultimate unification. *The Portrait of a Lady* is less sweeping in its presentational modes than the anatomy form of Melville's work, but it too melds at least three epistemological modes—the pictorial, the dramatic, and, briefly, the meditational—through the central consciousness, Isabel-James. *Huckleberry Finn* does the same thing: it is much closer to the oral-narrative origins of fiction than are the other works, but it nonetheless draws together pictorial techniques and lyrical techniques (as Leo Marx demonstrates in *The Machine in the Garden*), as well as dramatic conventions. The narrator stationed at the center of these novels, regardless of whether identified *with* or *as* the author, operates upon the assumption that the world can be known and communicated, its wholeness represented. And that assumption determines the ontological modes of these fictions: they will be comedic if the protagonist is successful in his quest for that available knowledge; they will be tragic if he is not. Between author and reader, therefore, a single vision is assumed possible in these works, even if it is not achieved, and, as different as they are in many particulars, they remain similar in this one important respect. Moreover, arranged on a vertical scale, with Melville at the top (moving toward romance) and Twain at the bottom (moving toward naturalism), they can adequately represent the traditional novel-as-genre out of which the modes of the modernist novel in America emerge. Because of his centrality and his articulation of the principle aesthetics of the generic novel, James is the focus of concerns we may legitimately call "pre-modern."

The preoccupation with technique one finds in James provides a grounding for the conflict between presentation and interpretation in the modern novel. By putting so much emphasis on point of view, on the controlling role of a dominant central consciousness, James inadvertently isolated the divergent concerns of the epistemological and the ontological modes. As one critic argues in a recent essay,[38] a logical extension of the concept of point of view would suggest that if no objectively real world exists in fiction outside a subjective consciousness, then there can be in fiction only *views* of the world. The development of James's aesthetic and, especially, of his practices gradually reveals this philosophic underpinning. In the early stage, James had to argue for the validity of his realism; in the middle stage, his practices and those of the then-dominant realists seemed to confirm that aesthetic; in the third, last stage he began to question the validity of the model he had taken so long for granted. This development represents a gradual philosophical shift to the modernist philosophy that is inherent in the theory from the outset. In the late-middle phase of James's career and in the final, "major" phase we thus find James's fictions themselves beginning to undermine the earlier sense of congruency between realism's techniques and reality itself. In the works of this phase—*The Spoils of Poynton, What Maisie Knew, The Sacred Fount,* and the late novels, beginning with *The Wings of the Dove*—we find that the epistemological modes begin to create what Frank Kermode calls "hermeneutic gaps" and what Wolfgang Iser calls "gaps of indeterminacy."[39] To close these gaps—whatever one calls them—a reader is forced into active participation in the place of the once-mediating author. As Kermode writes: "The confounding of simple expectation—the *not* telling us what it was that Maisie knew—is a way of stimulating the

42   PHASE ONE

reader to a fuller exercise of his imagination: to make him *read* in a more exalted sense (*not* 'devour'). Consequently the *affair* will not be grasped, even in its ambiguity, without many readings, and those readings will find senses which remain inexplicit."[40] When a reader is himself forced—by James or any other author—to close hermeneutic gaps created by epistemological indeterminacy, he must turn to other, more familiar determinants. In general this means he turns to the archetypal, ontological modes, the narrative *mythoi*, that he knows implicitly from his experience of reading fiction. In James, then, the tension between presentation and interpretation becomes as well a tension between author and reader.

By returning to one of James's earlier works, *The Aspern Papers* (1888, rev. 1908), perhaps we can see more clearly what James is beginning to do to the genre of the novel.[41] While he does take an important step toward Joyce, Woolf, Faulkner, and the modernists, James still retains a firm grip on his text and thus upon his reader's imagination. But his practice in some works suggests why the modal imagination of the reader will later become so crucial to modernist fictions, for by James's placement of point of view and the absorption of its epistemology by a particular ontological mode of imagination he shows us *how* to read his later, "modernist" fictions at the same time he creates gaps which, Kermode says, can only be "gloried in." James, in *The Aspern Papers*, reaps the benefits of the enormous gap created between the ontological structures of myth and romance when they are displaced toward the realism embraced by his own aesthetic. Northrop Frye calls this "modal counterpoint" when it refers to the antitheses of historical modes, but the concept may also include any contrast of modes, epistemological or ontological. Exploited in its full range by moderns like Joyce and Faulkner, modal counterpoint permits James to relate, through the language of his central epistemological consciousness, antithetical ontological modes: the romantic (including the broadly "mythic") and the realistic. The narrator, who is bent upon gaining possession of the papers of the dead poet Jeffrey Aspern, by any means, fair or foul, fuses the details of the real task with the mythic structure of the heroic quest or perilous journey. In this fusion of epistemology and ontology, the narrator becomes the hero, Aspern becomes a dead god, the papers become relics, and the women—especially the old one, Juliana—become witches, except when his plotting requires the younger one—Tina—to become the innocent maiden whom the hero would rescue with the boon and eventually wed after returning to the real world.

When James turns over his report on the world to a character, he raises many crucial questions for modern literature. The disparity—the hermeneutic gap, if you will—between the language and structure provided by the narrator and the language a discerning reader would use to describe and structure the same experience calls into question the validity of the report. That is as it should be: that is the point of James's irony. But if one can question the narrator's report, might one not go back to the traditional authorial report and question it, too? Thus, James here begins to undercut the authority of *any* narrator, any epistemological mode of presentation. At the same time one questions the report, one must begin to question the "world"—the experience—upon which the report focuses. If the world is not what the narrator says it is, then we must decide for ourselves what it is. But are we never mistaken, our views similarly canted? James here begins to drop us into an indeterministic, relativistic universe, where epistemological perspectives become the ways to know and, since perspectives are always contained by subjects, subjectivity necessarily becomes the ontological object to be known. By raising these issues, which were inherent in his aesthetic philosophy from the beginning despite his assumption of a unitary genre and a monistic universe, James began to split the genre of the novel; by turning the novel's varied techniques into epistemological modes, and, similarly, turning its structured interpretations into ontological modes, he also began to split the world.

While James seems to have meant the counterpointing of different modes to remain a means of authorial control, in the end he actually draws the reader more insistently into the narrative, for when the unnamed narrator of *The Aspern Papers* loses his *author*-ity, he becomes just another reader of his experience, no more authoritative than any of us. In confronting us with the problems of indeterminacy and the potential solutions for it found by modernist authors and readers, James becomes thus a precursor of the modern and remains important to us in ways the naturalists and other realists between 1880 and 1920 do not. The naturalists, as had Howells and the other conservative realists, generally accepted the view in which James had begun, but these writers, with the possible exception of Stephen Crane, continued to operate on James's middle, "sentimental" assumption that the techniques of the novel-as-genre were

44

adequate to represent the world. While James was moving toward indeterminism in form and philosophy, the naturalists, especially, persisted in their belief that their more pessimistic, deterministic philosophy could be represented in determined forms that truly embodied the world. Consequently, their frequently immense works are interesting to us, but they seem more the relics of extinct dinosaurs than missing links to the modern.

Gertrude Stein is our American version of Laurence Sterne, for she has seemed at the same time a pre-modernist, a modernist, and a post-modernist. There is no question that Stein is an important figure in the development of modernist fiction, American and European. But, appearing to be everything at once, she seems to have no real definition; instead, she seems to be struggling toward definition, specific shape, form, configuration. However important she may be, she is simply not looked back on as a writer of fiction in the way that James, and later Woolf, Joyce, Faulkner, and others have been. Rather than a novelist, she was an experimenter, albeit one whose experiments evolved fiction toward modernism. "She was one of those rare artists," says David Lodge, "whose work was 'experimental' in a sense genuinely analogous to scientific experiment: a series of artificial and deliberate experiments designed to test some hypothesis about language, or perception, or reality, or about the relations between these things."[42] Such an approach, finally, is quite different from that of those authors we actually still think of as novelists. Lodge is right about her work, one feels, when he adds: "Its interest and value is therefore largely theoretical, rather than particular and concrete, and can best be appreciated in the context of her own theoretical glosses upon it, in essays and lectures."[43] If she is a modernist, then, she certainly is no modernist in the naive phase of the dialectic, for she is entirely too conscious and articulate (in her own fashion) to be put in company with such naive giants as Anderson, Hemingway, and Faulkner. Still, one can easily see why many estimable critics regard *Three Lives* (1909) as perhaps our first truly modernist novel. With its colloquial style, its fusion of "biographies" as if together they constituted one novel, and its pervasive sense of indeterminacy, *Three Lives* clearly bridges the gap between Twain and Anderson's *Winesburg, Ohio*.

Winesburg, Ohio (1919) is a most effective exemplar of those characteristics associated with fiction of the naive modernist phase. As Ellmann and Feidelson suggest in their preface to the comprehensive collection of materials in *The Modern Tradition*,[44] a major theme of the modern justifying those hermeneutic gaps seen in the later James and Stein is discontinuity itself. The modern is a world in which humanity seems separated from all around it. The human sciences everywhere had made the message clear: in biology, Darwin's theory of evolution severed the biblical cord linking man and God in Genesis, and "Social Darwinism" pitted one human against another in a battle of "survival of the fittest" based upon a premise of "natural selection," thereby separating person from person. Modern pyschology, developed and typified by Freud, separated man from himself, as it envisioned an ego constantly doing battle with a primordial id and with a culturally conditioned superego. Even modern physics figuratively separated man from an ideal long cherished, for Einstein's theory of relativity separates man from previous ideas of nature by creating a disjunction between our ordinary perceptions of the world and the new relativity model. Man thus seems to the modern temperament to be separated from God, from nature, from other men, and, ultimately, even from himself. A modernist rubric for this new condition is "alienation," and one of Anderson's achievements in *Winesburg, Ohio* is the exploration of some of the forms of our human alienation. He suggests, for example, alienation from God in the episodes called "The Strength of God" and "Godliness," alienation from nature in "A Man of Ideas" and "Sophistication," from other persons in "The Untold Lie" and "Loneliness," and from oneself in "The Teacher" and "Mother." But Anderson's most important achievement for the modern American novel is his creation of a discontinuous fictional form that would embody the theme of alienation.

As Ellmann and Feidelson suggest, even among the most "liberated or alienated" modernists, experiment is always played off against conventions and traditions from a relevant past. Anderson's is no different from others. Hamlin Garland's *Main-Travelled Roads*, Stein's *Three Lives*, Edgar Lee Masters's *Spoon River Anthology*, and Joyce's *Dubliners* all gave Anderson models for developing stories identified with a particularized locality, *ethos*, or social stratum. They gave him, moreover, types of stories generated from brief episodes or epiphanic perceptions, forms that normally would be relegated to oral tradition or to the intenser modes of lyrical poetry. But Anderson, working even more in the manner of the lyric poet than did Joyce in *Dubliners*, while

PHASE ONE

maintaining the oral-traditional elements of Twain and Stein, incarnated his modernist theme by selectively precipitating the once-stable, bonded elements of that unitary, molecular fiction of the nineteenth century. Like e. e. cummings, who created new poetic forms simply by isolating the most basic units out of which poetry is made, Anderson created a new form of the novel by isolating those elements that make fiction: *character, incident, symbol,* and *theme.* Any one of these in *Winesburg, Ohio* might at any time become the only important focal point for one of his "stories." Isolation of focus, rather than unification, becomes the essence of his impressionistic epistemological modes of presentation. *Winesburg, Ohio,* thus made up of four distinctly different types of form, simplifies local presentation, but considerably complicates the interpretation of the whole form. The conventions of linear, uniform, continuous fiction, the fiction of Hawthorne, Melville, Howells, and James, sought in style and structure to meld fictional elements as they bridged the gaps between man and nature, self and other, subject and object. This tradition exerts a tremendous influence on any writer, and, in the end, no more than James could Anderson give up every linear pattern. Thus, in order to counter a tendency toward total fragmentation he had to introduce another technique in *Winesburg, Ohio.*

Perhaps the most innovative unifying device he employed was not the single, nearly continuous setting: after all, Garland, Masters, and Joyce in different ways had tried that; it was the recurrent, nearly continuous presence of one character in many of the separate stories who would eventually emerge as the "hero." It is usually around a hero that a hermeneutic fictional pattern develops, for his movements—metaphorically "up" or "down" or "cyclical"—define the meanings of the fictional universe. Thus, the role of George Willard is ontological, not epistemological. George Willard is not the personal, individual hero of traditional narrative; he becomes a typal, a generic, hero, and he puts Anderson's novel in touch with the archetypal rhythms of myth and romance. As a typal hero George suggests that despite alienation and discontinuity there remains something permanent in and about man that he can turn to for meaning. Not by the argument or frequently comic bombast with which one sees Walt Whitman creating his typal hero, but by weaving the story of George Willard across the truly individual stories of the town of Winesburg, Sherwood Anderson touches the order that the rhythm of age-old patterns can bring into man's life. Anderson may have undercut the deterministic form of the traditional novel, but his impulse to achieve unity suggests that he was no more comfortable in an indeterminate universe than anyone else.

Between Anderson's *Winesburg, Ohio* and Faulkner's *The Sound and the Fury* (1929) stand two important works that contribute to our sense of a developing modernism in American fiction. *In Our Time* (1925), by Ernest Hemingway, is very much in the mode that Anderson established, with one "story" ("My Old Man") reading virtually as a parody of, for example, "I Want to Know Why." A "novel" comprised of separable stories and "chapters," *In Our Time* is almost completely in an objective epistemological mode. Stories such as "The Three-Day Blow" are about as close to a true fictional "drama" as fiction is likely to come, and though many of the "chapters" that precede the stories are in a first-person mode, they nevertheless incline to the extreme objectivity of most of the longer stories. At the most basic level of fictional creation Hemingway was, he said, simply trying to write "one true sentence," but like the stories in *Winesburg*, the different narratives of *In Our Time* also show Hemingway experimenting with the elements of fiction—character, event, dialogue, description—rather than attempting to blend those elements as they are found in the traditional novel or story. So, like *Winesburg, Ohio*, *In Our Time* remains an exploratory, improvisatory manipulation of the elements of narrative. Out of his experiments—influenced by Gertrude Stein, as well as by Anderson—Hemingway eventually found the epistemological mode, the objective, dramatic, externalizing formula, for which he is known, though his later mode is more insistently *epos* than drama.

Fitzgerald's novel *The Great Gatsby* (1925), the other major work, is in the tradition of the middle James. Fitzgerald, too, uses a technique of counterpoint, and, as James had in *The Aspern Papers*, he places his narrative in a created character. Fitzgerald even creates the possibility of counterpointing two ontological, hermeneutic modes—a tragic, narrative construct around Gatsby and a comic construct around the narrator himself.[45] But there are important differences between Fitzgerald and James that suggest how far the later novelist has inclined to modernism's indeterminacy of form. In James it seems enough simply to decide that the narrator is "unreliable," but in Fitzgerald even if we say that Nick Carraway is unreliable we do not solve the central problem, the unreliability of the world itself. Nick's view of Gatsby admittedly becomes just one of many perspectives, from each one of which he means something a little different. Not even the consolidating perspective of the narrator is able to blend those meanings into one homogeneous meaning. Thus, while *The Great Gatsby* is not totally modernist in its impulses, it nevertheless forces upon readers the task of putting its nominal hero together from a multitude of perspectives: Nick's, Nick's reports of the views of Jordan Baker, Daisy, Tom Buchanan, Myrtle Wilson, Wolfsheim, Owl Eyes, Gatsby's guests—the "guest of Trimalchio"—and the father of James Gatz-Jay Gatsby, in addition to Gatsby's own view of himself, offered, retracted, modified. Gatsby becomes Fitzgerald's golden bowl, and the novel more modernist, even Faulknerian, than we might suppose.

In American fiction, William Faulkner finally exploded the genre of the novel so completely that its elements could return only as modes. Faulkner tears apart all the techniques—both epistemological and ontological—conventionally associated with the novel-as-genre. The epistemological problems are the most baffling at first in a novel such as *The Sound and the Fury*. In the book's first section, presented through the idiot, Benjy, one jumps immediately to the other side of the universe from the world of the novel-as-genre. Benjy presents "content" not only in an extreme version of Hemingway's objectivity, but also through clusters of narrative fragments that might once have been speech, gestures, and acts from ritual dramas. Though Benjy's section explodes the traditional novel, the other sections seem to represent Faulkner's efforts at putting it all back together. The Quentin section, while it offers a demanding lyrical mode of presentation, returns considerably closer to fiction's norm. The Jason section offers a mode of presentation that is extremely close to the primal base of fiction in oral formulaic narrative, so it moves even closer to the generic norm. The final section, presented from a traditional authorial perspective, returns us to the middle-Jamesian model with which the modern had begun. The effort Faulkner seems to be making here is to restore the traditional epistemology of the novel, but having once exploded it he can only fail in the effort. Instead, he convinces us how truly relative our epistemologies in fiction have become. This work, like Joyce's *Ulysses*, fragments the novel-as-genre into the elemental modes of the novel.[46]

In *As I Lay Dying* (1930), Faulkner takes up the epistemological problem again, but he takes it up here as thematic content rather than presentational technique.[47] In this novel, which immediately follows *The Sound and the Fury*, he treats the modes of perception as philosophical themes by making major characters focal points for ontological or metaphysical philosophical perspectives. The main issue Faulkner forces us to join in *As I Lay Dying* is the one of how we know: what are the grounds of our knowledge, the objective realm of actions and matter or the subjective realm of language and ideas? Addie Bundren, for example, espouses in her language and attitudes, if not explicitly by overt allegiance, a doctrine of nominalism; while her own mode of presentation is not dramatic, her philosophy supports the objective epistemology of the dramatist, or the epistemology that underlies Benjy's section and much of Hemingway's fiction. Addie feels that in order for existence to prove itself, for her *self* to prove its own existence, it must impinge upon someone's senses. Addie elevates acts, but derogates words. Her son Darl is an idealist: he puts most of his faith in those words his mother feels are empty of real existence. As a consequence of his philosophy, the base for Darl's knowledge *and* reality, like that of Quentin's section and of lyrical fiction in general, becomes language, concepts, ideas; indeed, in one of the novel's cruel ironies, at the end as Darl looks out through the bars of a mental institution he seems to have dissolved into a mental construct. The eldest son, Cash, apparently represents a middle ground. His is a philosophically realistic position: he seems to affirm the material world just as staunchly as his mother does, though without her monomania; at the same time he affirms Darl's idealism, though without his brother's total separation of reality from ideas. Though the operational potency of the two other philosophical modes interests Faulkner enormously, his own position seems finally to lie with Cash's. Faulkner questioned intently the relation of man and man's mind to the world, but he finally seems to have backed away from either an extreme idealism or an extreme materialism.

As I Lay Dying takes up a theme related to the epistemological modes of presentation seen in *The Sound and the Fury*. *Go Down, Moses* explores another aspect of the relation between fictional content and reader's interpretation suggested by the same novel.[48] *The Sound and the Fury*, while evolving through a succession of modes of presentation, is also drawing a reader through a succession of narrative modes of *mythoi*. If the hermeneutic systems are not clear in themselves the reader is obliged to make them clear for himself. The way he does this is becoming one of the most crucial aspects of contemporary criticism, which is trying to catch up with the practices of the novelists. The German critic Wolfgang Iser contends that the reader bridges the gaps of meaning in the fictional worlds through an archetypal imagination. Iser uses the following comment of Northrop Frye in order to explain how readers close gaps of indeterminacy: "Whenever we read anything, we find our attention moving in two directions at once. One direction is outward or centrifugal, in which we keep going outside our reading, from the individual words to the things they mean, or, in practice, to our memory of the conventional association between them. The other direction is inward or centripetal, in which we try to develop from the words a sense of the larger verbal pattern they make."[49] As the reader is drawn back into the work in the space, the gap, created between the author and his work, the reader is forced to create his own work, as it were. He will do so—Frye and Iser, as well as Claudio Guillén, suggest—by resorting to the conventional modes of ontological organization associated with genres, or what Frye would call *mythoi* or modes of narrative.[50] Thus, the conventions that become most useful for modern readers, precisely because authors seem not to be concerned with them, are the modes of plot Frye calls archetypal, pre-generic *mythoi*. Readers can turn the perceived realities of undetermined fictional structures into one or another of the only four types of plot that exist. Depending upon how one's imagination can arrange the details, the types of plot or *mythoi* one will identify are romance, tragedy, comedy, or irony. That is Frye's view, and for practical purposes I will share it.[51] Without arguing the issues here, I will say that the four modes of ontological, hermeneutic organization of *The Sound and the Fury* are, in succession, romance (pastoral and elegiac), tragedy, irony-satire, and comedy.[52]

In *Go Down, Moses* Faulkner is more concerned to work along the lines of the ontological modes manifested in *The Sound and the Fury* than its manifested epistemological modes, though in one chapter ("The Bear") the lyrical epistemological mode does present severe reader challenges.[53] If we imagine, as Frye does in *Anatomy of Criticism*, all four of the narrative modes as existing at once in a total order of words, belonging, that is, to one giant, anagogic form, then we can see how in *The Sound and the Fury* Faulkner has exploded narrative itself. In *Go Down, Moses* we can see Faulkner putting narrative back together, and he does so in the pattern of the

Bible, the one revelational work his readers will know that is vast enough to contain the disparate modes an anagogic narrative must contain. The meaningful form of *Go Down, Moses* is founded upon the narrative rhythm of the Bible. That rhythm is split into two phases, Old Testament and New Testament, and permits Faulkner to deal with sequences of plot that concern both "old times past" and the more immediate present. No one can be sure that Faulkner intended such a reading, nor will all readers read in the same ways, but it can be shown that there are two concentric cycles of narrative in the work: the first cycle moves from romance, to comedy (mixed), to irony; the second cycle moves from romance, to tragedy (mixed), to irony, and finally to comedy. Faulkner not only gives two cycles, but he also makes it possible, through details, imagery, and allusions, for us to project them upon a screen with which we are all implicitly familiar. Seen in its biblical rhythm, *Go Down, Moses* is clearly comedic.

Perhaps the most complex experiment among these remaining works takes place in *Absalom, Absalom!* In this novel, which rivals *The Sound and the Fury* as the most important multi-modal form Faulkner created, the narrative modes—that is, the hermeneutic systems—the different narrators create manifest different modes of narrative imagination. Northrop Frye, in his discussion of historical modes in *Anatomy of Criticism*, isolates the modes Faulkner must employ in his most historically conscious work. Frye suggests that literary narrative begins in the historical mode of romance (which is a displacement toward realism of the structural principles of the pre-literary historical mode of myth), goes to high mimesis, then to low mimesis, and ends in irony. In *Absalom*, Faulkner begins with the narrative presentation of Miss Rosa Coldfield; her highly imaginative account of Thomas Sutpen is a narrative in the historical mode of romance (the gothic, more specifically). The narrative of Mr. Compson is tragic in the historical mode of the high mimetic. The narrative of Quentin Compson, a "chivalric romance," is also high mimetic tragedy. Finally, Faulkner presents narratives by those nearest and farthest from the central Sutpen story. Thomas Sutpen's own story, only briefly observed in details presented through Mr. Compson from General Compson, is essentially low mimetic, is quintessentially novelistic, a story of the journey of a young man from the provinces through innocence to experience; the Canadian Shreve McCannon's version of the Sutpen story is ironic and satiric, a grotesque tall tale of a dirty old man who, bargaining for life and immortality, merely reveals his mortality.[54] *Absalom*, in short, recapitulates the history of narrative as Frye conceives it, at the same time that it illustrates Fowler's model of the evolution of a genre. If this work were typical of the century it spans, the inchoate "I-narrative" by Thomas Sutpen would have constituted its epistemological and hermeneutic center. Instead, as it must be in a modernist text, it is merely a momentary node in an expanding historico-fictional universe.

The novels of William Faulkner show what happened to the modernist American novel. Even more energetically than James Joyce, Faulkner seems to have tried out for himself most of the potential combinations of the novel's basic epistemological and ontological modes. Besides the experiments we have considered already, there are other experiments in *Light in August, Absalom, Absalom!, The Unvanquished, The Wild Palms, Intruder in the Dust, A Fable*, and *The Reivers*. (Even the conventional novels of the Snopes trilogy, *The Hamlet, The Town*, and *The Mansion*, suggest an important point about the modern novel: it still remains possible, as novels by Bellow, Mailer, Joyce Carol Oates, Roth, Updike, and others also suggest, to write conventional, nineteenth-century-style novels as one of the modes of the novel.) In *Light in August* and *The Wild Palms*, for example, Faulkner counterpointed two distinct narrative *mythoi*, the tragic and the comic in the former, and the ironic and the romantic in the latter; in addition, in *The Wild Palms* Faulkner employed radically different styles in a basic narrative mode of presentation. In *Intruder in the Dust*, Faulkner yoked together a content—the conventional realism associated with the novel-as-genre—and a popular form, the detective novel, which Faulkner admired. In both *A Fable* and *The Reivers* Faulkner constructed essentially realistic plots against archetypal frameworks of event and language, making one a version of the Christ story and the other a version of the romantic rite of passage.

III Faulkner's *The Sound and the Fury*

> Q. What symbolic meaning did you give to the dates of *The Sound and the Fury*?
>
> A. Now there's a matter of hunting around in the carpenter's shop to find a tool that will make a better chicken-house. And probably—I'm sure it was quite instinctive that I picked out Easter, that I wasn't writing any symbolism of the Passion Week at all. I just—that was a tool that was good for the particular corner I was going to turn in my chicken-house and so I used it. . . .
>
> William Faulkner
> *Faulkner in the University* (1959)

The period of crisis in fiction from about 1880 to 1919 revealed those gaps in the traditional novel's foundations that made possible—even inevitable—the cataclysm of the modernist novel. But it was the period from 1920 to 1940 that saw the real emergence of "modernism" in the American novel. Modernism—as a period concept—has its base in the changing knowledge of man's condition in his natural and self-created environments—the physical universe as it was being redefined by science; and history, art, and literature as they were being redefined in light of modern physics, psychology, linguistics, and other disciplines. In fiction, this changing knowledge has taken what cultural historian Erich Kahler calls "an inward turn." "The transformation of man's consciousness," says Kahler, "and the transformation of the reality that this consciousness must deal with combine into a single coherent process. In fact, man himself has developed by means of the perpetual interaction between consciousness and reality, between his interior world and his exterior world."[55]

It would be impossible to enumerate all the changes that occurred to create the modern consciousness, but two that crucially affect the genre of the novel are the opening-up of nature, bringing knowledge that we dwell in an exploding, expanding universe, and the concomitant opening-up of art and philosophy, especially visible in the shift toward an existentialism that parallels an increasing indeterminacy in science. At the same time that scientists posited an exploding, relativistic universe, artists, though more because of a shared ambience than because of direct influence, began to recognize relativities in forms, genres, aesthetics. "The arts," writes Kahler, "in pursuing their own particular courses have arrived at the same disintegration and transcendental obliteration of the objective world of the senses as has physics—and at the very same time. The same evolution of consciousness and of the reality corresponding to that consciousness can be demonstrated in the most variegated kinds of human expression—and consequently in the transformation of art forms as well."[56] As absolutes about the world began to diminish, so did absolutes in art and literature. Now that we have the historical perspective, we see that in the novel this shift resulted in one important development: the novel lost its absolute, homogeneous, monolithic aesthetic, because it could no longer presume congruent epistemological and ontological bases. Thus, the novel did not *die* in the twentieth century; it was simply exploded, fragmented into those primary elements that had originally synthesized to create the genre. As I shall try to illustrate in an analysis of *The Sound and the Fury*, the traditional novel-as-genre has been replaced by a modernist variety of modes of the novel.

To say only that the mode of presentation in *The Sound and the Fury* is stream of consciousness is inadequate, if not misleading, in the light of decades of criticism of the novel. A generation of Faulkner readers has come to realize that there are probably more important differences in the methods of the novel's four sections than there are similarities, so the term *stream of consciousness* does more to limit than to expand our understanding of narrative method. Having served a worthwhile purpose, the approach to the novel through stream of consciousness ought now to be replaced by one that will more adequately account for the differences, instead of the resemblances, among the sections. If we may adapt an approach suggested by Cleanth Brooks, we might discuss each section not "under the rubric of poetry,"[57] but under the rubrics provided by the different presentational modes that come to fiction from other genres and arts. It has now become a critical commonplace to speak of "dramatic" novels, "lyrical" novels, "epic" novels, novels as "dramatic poems," and so on.[58] Far from being irresponsible impressionism, the critical approaches these labels suggest are well within the traditions established by Henry James, D. H. Lawrence, James Joyce, and others, but such approaches will offer valid insights into the presentational modes of modernist fiction only if the distinctions are made clearly enough and if we understand that, though combinations of elements from several genre-related modes are possible, often one pattern of elements will dominate all others in radically experimental works. The tremendous experimental vitality of *The Sound and the Fury*, however, is a result of Faulkner's counterpoising three separate generic modes against the traditional method of the novel-as-genre. Thus, not only do we find presentational analogies to drama, lyric poetry, and oral narrative in Benjy's, Quentin's, and Jason's "monologues," respectively, but we also find just plain "fiction" in the omniscient presentation of the fourth section. While it is possible to treat the four presentational modes of this novel in terms of the theories of Northrop Frye and the more recent structuralists, I shall try to deal with them in the conventional ways, out of the theories of the older generation of spokesmen as well as of the younger.

Benjy's section is widely praised for its concreteness, objectivity, and immediateness, presentational effects usually attributed to the idiot's stream of consciousness. But we actually praise in Benjy's section not the stream of consciousness, but its slanting of a lyrical technique to achieve purely dramatic effects. We do not know what an idiot's consciousness is like, but we do know the features of the dramatic form Faulkner has represented here. Percy Lubbock long ago outlined for us the characteristics of the dramatic novel. Lubbock's definition relies on two major distinctions: that the dramatic story "never deviates from a strictly scenic form"[59] and that there is "no admission of the reader into the private mind of any of the characters."[60] Both of these, besides two supporting distinctions under each, may be seen in the novel's opening section: Benjy's narration is totally scenic and, despite the first-person point of view, there is no admittance to Benjy's or any other's private mind. Further, because its form is scenic, Benjy's presentation is "limited to so much as the ear can hear and the eye can see"[61] and, therefore, "it is constituted by the aspect of the occasion and the talk and the conduct of the people."[62] And, finally, because it is objective, the "mind of the narrator becomes the stage," his *voice* is not really heard, and "the point of view becomes the reader's. . . ."[63]

It is precisely because Benjy's monologue is completely scenic that we have such difficulty getting through it the first time. As Lubbock tells us, in true drama there should be no sense that someone *"reports* the scene," so there can be "no interruption for any reflective summary of events."[64] Consequently, and this constitutes the major difficulty, Faulkner has linked each scene to the one preceding without any kind of discursive commentary, and he has justified the elimination of the seemingly necessary summary by his choice of narrators. Benjy Compson is a congenital idiot, and so he cannot possibly conjecture on the significance of events, nor, because he is oblivious entirely to time, can he summarize and foreshorten. What we get, then, is a series of scenes or, at times, fragments of scenes that are not synthesized but simply juxtaposed. Though similar to the succession of discrete scenes in the drama, Faulkner's arrangement of scenes here is also close to another form, the motion picture, that often turns to dramatic presentation. Because the shifts from scene to scene are so abrupt in Benjy's narration, Faulkner's technique is comparable to cinematic "cutting" devices. Benjy cannot give us narrative explanations for shifts in time, setting, or characters, but Faulkner "edits" the shifts so that some continuity can be established through similarities in actions, shapes, and sounds, much like cutting on form, movement, or sound in movies.

Benjy's first shift of scene, for example, is based upon the physical similarities of his being snagged on a nail as he crawls through a fence at two widely separated times:

"Wait a minute." Luster said. "You snagged on that nail again. Cant you never crawl through here without snagging on that nail."
Caddy uncaught me and we crawled through. . . .[65]

The scene with Luster takes place in present time, April 7, 1928, and the one with Caddy occurs at least a quarter-century before, but we are prepared for the shift by Luster's insisting twice in his brief speech on the repeatedness of Benjy's action. A second shift is also prepared for by the actions of Benjy's guardians, both of whom show concern for Benjy's getting too cold:

Keep your hands in your pockets, Caddy said. Or they'll get froze. You don't want your hands froze on Christmas, do you.
"It's too cold out there." Versh said. "You dont want to go out doors" [p. 3].

Here the concern with the idiot's getting cold and the pattern of the "you don't want" phrase provide the formal and auditory links between the scenes. Another kind of "editing" on similarities of form occurs a few pages later:

> We passed the carriage house, where the carriage was. It had a new wheel.
>
> "Git in, now, and set still until your maw come." Dilsey said. She shoved me into the carriage. T. P. held the reins. "'Clare I don't see how come Jason wont get a new surrey." Dilsey said. "This thing going to fall to pieces under you all some day. Look at them wheels" [pp. 8–9].

This change of scene is caused by the repeated image of the carriage and, more particularly, the wheel, the newness of which in the first scene is accounted for in the second. These examples of Faulkner's editing techniques suggest that what Olga Vickery calls a principle of "mechanical identification"[66] is actually a means for controlling and heightening the dramatic effects of Benjy's narration; the narration is indeed achieved by making Benjy's mind as retentive and "objective" as any mechanical device.

These techniques of cutting, based upon visual and auditory images, are also accounted for by the dramatic mode's being limited to what "the ear can hear and the eye can see,"[67] as Lubbock says. Aside from the olfactory images ("Caddy smells like trees"), there are few other ways that Faulkner might manipulate the scenic shifts in Benjy's narrative. This limitation—and it is seldom seen as that among the novel's critics—is also manifest in the details of the scenes themselves. The opening scene of the novel, for example, is entirely visual and auditory:

> Through the fence, between the curling flower spaces, I could see them hitting. They were coming toward where the flag was and I went along the fence. Luster was hunting in the grass by the flower tree. They took the flag out, and they were hitting. Then they put the flag back and they went to the table, and he hit and the other hit. Then they went on, and I went along the fence. Luster came away from the flower tree and we went along the fence and they stopped and we stopped and I looked through the fence while Luster was hunting in the grass.
>
> "Here, caddie." He hit. They went away across the pasture. I held to the fence and watched them going away.
>
> "Listen at you, now." Luster said. "Aint you something, thirty-three years old, going on that way. After I done went all the way to town to buy you that cake. Hush up that moaning. Aint you going to help me find that quarter so I can go to the show tonight" [p. 1].

But by restricting himself to what Benjy sees and hears, Faulkner achieves what Lubbock calls the "most finished form that fiction can take,"[68] for characters are depicted, as on the stage, only in terms of what they say or do—"their thoughts and motives are transmuted into action."[69] In the following scene, for example, although Faulkner adds an extra fillip by having Benjy view the actions in a mirror, both Caddy and her brother Jason are defined through their objective actions and expressed attitudes toward Benjy:

"He cut up all Benjy's dolls." Caddy said. "I'll slit his gizzle."
"Candace." Father said.
"I will." Caddy said. "I will." She fought. Father held her. She kicked at Jason. He rolled into the corner, out of the mirror. Father brought Caddy to the fire. They were all out of the mirror. Only the fire was in it. Like the fire was in a door. "Stop that." Father said. "Do you want to make Mother sick in her room."
Caddy stopped. "He cut up all the dolls Mau—Benjy and I made." Caddy said. "He did it just for meanness."
"I didn't." Jason said. He was sitting up, crying. "I didn't know they were his. I just thought they were some old papers."
"You couldn't help but know." Caddy said. "You did it just."
"Hush." Father said. "Jason." he said.
"I'll make you some more tomorrow." Caddy said. "We'll make a lot of them. Here, you can look at the cushion, too" [pp. 79–80].

Here, as throughout Benjy's section, all we are given for characterization is dialogue and conduct or actions, for Benjy nowhere verbalizes a preference for one person or another. He never says that he loathes Jason and loves Caddy and their father, that he is uncomfortable with Mrs. Compson and amply at ease with Dilsey. We learn Benjy's emotional attitudes from his actions and sounds, too, in the same way that we learn about the other characters. We might realize, for example, that he is devoted to Caddy by his moaning when he is reminded of her, but even the moaning is reported to us through the dialogue of others and is seldom reported directly to us by Benjy.

All of this—the scenic development, the auditory and visual emphases, and the presentation of characters only through dialogue and action—suggests two crucial points about Benjy's section. Because of Benjy's complete "objectivity," there is a strong impression, first, that the point-of-view character is concealed entirely from his audience and, second, that we are viewing events as directly as if they were enacted upon a stage rather than impinging upon a *mind*. In Lubbock's words, "the mind of the narrator becomes the stage" and "the point of view becomes the reader's."[70] Such effects are made possible, of course, because the idiot's mind is more a presenter of sensory impressions than an organ of thought; consequently, we seem to watch the other characters perform there, but we never get an impression of Benjy's personality through his commentary—since he gives no commentary. And as we watch the others perform, we become oblivious to Benjy and the point of view does, in a sense, become that of the reader. Thus, Benjy's section is an illustration of what Joyce's Stephen Dedalus in *A Portrait of the Artist as a Young Man* also calls the "dramatic," for not only is there a sense that Faulkner has withdrawn from the presentation, there is a corresponding sense that Benjy himself has withdrawn because he can never imaginatively or intellectually participate in it: with the other points of view in the novel, we look first into a mind or upon a character before we see the action, but with Benjy we look directly upon the scenes. Furthermore, in Benjy's section, as in drama, we are forced to supply our own meanings to the scenes, for, to use a figure familiar to Benjy's critics, Benjy is a mirror and not an interpreter of action and character. He can mechanically reflect, but he cannot meditatively reflect. Or, put in another way, Benjy simply performs the role of the camera and the recorder, and his section is a carefully edited series of discrete but clearly dramatized scenes. And that seems to be the section's weakness as well as its strength. Faulkner, aware that his meanings might not be accurately perceived by the novel's audience, felt it necessary to add to the story other sections that return us gradually to the more conventional presentational modes of the novel. But it is important to note, nevertheless, that in its original conception, *The Sound and the Fury* was to have been presented only through Benjy,[71] in what might have been the most purely dramatic episode in the American novel.

Although we might label Quentin's section a "dramatic poem" as F. R. Leavis has labeled such novels as *Hard Times, The Europeans*, and several of Lawrence's, more will be gained in a practical way if we concentrate on the specifically *lyrical* characteristics of the section. Since in this area we do not have a traditional theorist like Lubbock to work from, we shall adduce our own criteria.[72] The first factor in determining a lyrical mode of presentation is the set of relationships established or assumed among audience, narrative and characters, and author. Other factors expected in lyric poetry and, thus, in lyrical fiction might include a greater concern with theme, a greater introversion and a less continuous narrative movement, a strong reliance on associational patterns (in imagery, symbolism, and in language itself), and, perhaps, a closer affinity between the workings of the narrator's mind and the process of artistic creation than in the dramatic mode.

Both Benjy's and Quentin's narratives are forms of stream of consciousness, but there are probably as many differences as similarities between them. Benjy's section is essentially a dramatic presentation of a lyrical technique, because the mode of narration assumes that the reader simply sees through Benjy onto a stage where the other characters speak and act, with commentary from neither Benjy nor Faulkner, both of whom may as well be invisible to us. If the stream of consciousness were really a common denominator, we would get a similar impression from Quentin's section. Instead, simply because we can enter Quentin's private mind, we get very different impressions of the narrator's character and his relationship to us and the fictional material. First, there is an appearance that things are being filtered through an evaluating mind quite different from Benjy's *tabula rasa*; there is little objectivity in Quentin's narrative, for he constantly makes or implies moral and ethical judgments of events as well as of characters. Second, there is an impression that Quentin is speaking neither to us as an audience nor to another character, but is only talking to himself; in other words, Quentin's monologue is more accurately called a soliloquy, because it gives us access to the protagonist's innermost thoughts, while at the same time it denies that he is directing them *to* us.[73] As Stephen Dedalus says in *A Portrait*, "the lyrical form [is] the form wherein the artist presents his image in immediate relation to himself,"[74] and Quentin presents his "image" (narration) in relation to no one but himself. Thus, we see what Quentin sees, but we see it only over his shoulder since he has his back to us, whereas we see neither Benjy's back nor his front because, in more ways than one, he is not "there" at all. Finally, as in Benjy's section, Faulkner is also "absent" from Quentin's narration, appearing in neither "flesh" nor "spirit."

The need for the creation of different effects in Benjy's dramatic narration and Quentin's lyrical mode actually explains the formal differences in the stream-of-consciousness technique. There are the obvious stylistic differences necessitated by the two modes of presentation: for example, Benjy's style is concrete, immediate, and "sensational," while Quentin's is abstract, subjective, and "intellectual." But another difference caused by the modal presentations is in the narrative movements of the first two sections: Quentin's monologue moves at a snail's pace in comparison to Benjy's (or, for that matter, Jason's). The difference occurs because Benjy's passage is necessarily devoted to speech and action, but Quentin's is taken up with repeated verbal and symbolic associations. The echoes and reverberations of idea and imagery in Quentin's monologue continually throw us backward in narrative movement more often than forward; and, although devotion to his "death day" gives the section a definite narrative center, Quentin still has a hard time getting a story told because he has interest not in the telling but only in the meaning.[75] In the first pages, for example, no more than one sentence in five or six is devoted to narration; the others reveal Quentin's preoccupations with time, watches, shadows, death, sisters, and so on. The essential lack of narrative progression is shown, moreover, in the way paragraphs often begin with a key motif or word and then end on the same motif or word: the second paragraph, for example, ends, "And the good Saint Francis that said Little Sister Death, that never had a sister" (p. 94), and the end of the third paragraph picks up the motif: "That had no sister" (p. 94). The effect of such repetition is to contain and to invert; vertical rather than horizontal, it deepens thematic texture rather than broadening narrative perspectives.

A similar containment of narrative movement is the essentially musical ("lyrical") way words and phrases are often chanted: on the first few pages, for example, are the reiterations of "Roses, Roses," "Did you ever have a sister: Did you? Did you?" and "Dalton Ames. Dalton Ames. Dalton Ames," the three iterations of which are repeated three times on the same page.[76] A conventional lyric domination of visual imagery, moreover, also slows the narrative pace by tempting the reader to stop and study the "picture," to contemplate awhile before going on, as in such self-consciously "poetic" passages as the following:

Only she was running already when I heard it. In the mirror she was running before I knew what it was. That quick, her train caught up over her arm she ran out of the mirror like a cloud, her veil swirling in long glints her heels brittle and fast clutching her dress onto her shoulder with

62

the other hand, running out of the mirror the smells roses roses the voice that breathed o'er Eden. Then she was across the porch I couldn't hear her heels then in the moonlight like a cloud, the floating shadow of the veil running across the grass, into the bellowing. She ran out of her dress, clutching her bridal, running into the bellowing where T. P. in the dew Whooey Sassprillah Benjy under the box bellowing. Father had a V-shaped silver cuirass on his running chest [p. 100; Faulkner's italics eliminated].

Even when Quentin seems least preoccupied by his own problems and most concerned with immediate perceptions, he cannot refrain from the abstraction, the thematic generalization, the literary allusions that slow the narrative: recall, for instance, the passage relating Quentin's visit to the jeweler, or the one following in which he sits by a black on a streetcar:

When I first came East I kept thinking You've got to remember to think of them as coloured people not niggers, and if it hadn't happened that I wasn't thrown with many of them, I'd have wasted a lot of time and trouble before I learned that the best way to take all people, black or white, is to take them for what they think they are, then leave them alone [p. 106].

The introversion of the lyric form, moreover, is the major reason Faulkner uses different transitional devices in Benjy's and Quentin's sections. Where they are based upon sensation and "mechanical identification" in the former, they are based upon abstract and thematic associations in the latter. To illustrate the difference: where Benjy will bellow even at the sound of Caddy's name, his transitions between "scenes" are based upon yet more insistent physical parallels (as we pointed out, when he snags his trousers going through a fence, he "relives" another instance like it in which Caddy is present in place of Luster); Quentin, on the other hand, seems to recall past events because of related ideas, parallel *concepts*; for example, his first "flashback" is triggered by a concatenation of the month of June, "the month of brides," the idea of sister, the images of a window and a mirror, all leading to a memory of a scene during Caddy's wedding, then to a scene of "confession," and, immediately afterward, to a remembered comment suggesting guilt feelings toward Jason—all of which suggests psychological "montage" instead of dramatic "cutting," if we may use cinematic terms again:

She ran right out of the mirror, out of the banked scent. Roses. Roses. Mr and Mrs Jason Richmond Compson announce the marriage of.

Roses. Not virgins like dogwood, milkweed. I said I have committed incest, Father I said. Roses. Cunning and serene. If you attend Harvard one year, but dont see the boat-race, there should be a refund. Let Jason have it. Give Jason a year at Harvard [p. 95].

Throughout Quentin's section, memories are triggered by certain obsessively reiterated words, phrases, and ideas: *time, death, shadows, virginity, honor, honesty, sister, marriage,* and so on. Such conceptual associations, besides being out of Benjy's presumed mental range, give a different, hardly "dramatic," irony to Quentin's section, for where the significance of Benjy's narrative is totally lost upon him, Quentin, in the lyrical tradition, actually seems to play with manifold significances. Meanings are introduced, moreover, where none would be recognized in Benjy's monologue, as in the odd inversion of the "triangle" of Dalton Ames, Caddy, and Quentin in the triangle of Quentin, the little Italian girl, and Julio, the ironic significance of which Quentin himself draws attention to by his wild laughter when he is apprehended by the girl's brother.

The way Quentin virtually makes his own meanings, finally, is closely related to the affinity between the lyric and all creative activity, which appears to be an associative process that operates partly within the unconscious, through all kinds of sound, image, and meaning patterns, very much as the dream functions.[77] We see this creativity in Quentin's patterns of imagery, most of which involve himself, Caddy, her suitors, and his father, and his references to Eden, God, Christ, and St. Francis. We begin dimly to see that Quentin's narrative is to be accepted on an archetypal level, as a version of tragic romance: he is Adam, Caddy is Eve, Mr. Compson is God the Father, and the suitors are representatives of the underworld.[78] Still, all this remains on a high and ironic level of consciousness. As we move deeper into Quentin's section, however, we seem actually to move at times below irony and consciousness into the very dream itself. In the fight with Gerald Bland, about two-thirds through Quentin's section, all the dreamlike associative elements involving Quentin, Caddy, and Dalton Ames join together to break down the barriers between fact and memory, idea and symbol, and, for Quentin, the memory of the past and the actions of the present become completely interchangeable. Thus, where throughout most of Quentin's section there has been some tension between the past and the present, from here on the tension is greatly reduced, primarily because the dream (or nightmare) elements have begun to take over completely. Interestingly enough, therefore, the flashbacks themselves conclude with a discussion that is only imagined between Quentin and his father about an act of incest that never really occurred.[79] Consequently, there is a sense, in Quentin's section, of a withdrawal from objective reality and a retreat into a subjective reality, yet this withdrawal is wholly consistent with the lyrical mode of presentation. What Quentin seems to have done is to retreat from a real world that has little order and no meaning into a dream world that has infinite meaning, but still only infinitesimal order. Characteristically, therefore, this section, because of the lyrical presentation, is the most thematic and the least narrational in the novel, and it has become, as a result, probably the most critically controversial of the four sections.

Jason's section is identifiable as belonging to the mode of oral narrative, for Faulkner has created here an impression that Jason is telling his story, telling it directly to an auditor who stands for the reader. Aware that Jason has usurped the place of the author, who still remains invisible behind his work, we recognize that here "is the old, immemorial, unguarded, unsuspicious way of telling a story, where the author entertains the reader, the minstrel draws his audience round him, the listeners rely upon his word," as Percy Lubbock says.[80] Or, as Austin Warren writes, Jason, like an "epic poet," "tells a story as a professional story-teller, including his own comments within the poem, and giving the narration proper (as distinct from dialogue) in his own style."[81] All of which is to say that for the first time in the novel, Faulkner has represented a point of view which forces us to look at the narrator more than at his fictional material, his narrative. In the first section, we simply look through Benjy; in the second, we look over Quentin's shoulder or upon his mind; but in the third, we look full upon Jason Compson. And as a self-conscious narrator, Jason seems well aware of an audience, for he makes every effort to offer a narrative that is continuous, with episodes synthesized and burdened by neither thematic nor more than superficial character concerns; moreover, he makes sure that he shows the public persona rather than the private one, and he tries hard to entertain his audience through easily apprehended rhetorical devices and a simple, direct, colloquial prose style.[82]

In each of the first three sections of the novel, Faulkner has thrust "authority," the role of "author," upon a created character, but only Jason seems aware of that role. And he seemingly relishes it, perhaps because it offers him an opportunity to set his accounts straight with the world, to let the world know who is the real tower of strength in the Compson household. Consequently, as Faulkner justifies the mode of narration in the first two sections, he also justifies it here, for it naturally behooves Jason to appear open and honest and straightforward, while, at the same time, he is protecting his egoistic image of himself. Jason goes about this double task, first, by directing his colloquial speech toward us, his audience, and, second, by attacking those who threaten him through highly entertaining rhetoric. Both the method of direct address and the method of rhetorical attack may be seen in Jason's memorably characteristic opening words:

> Once a bitch always a bitch, what I say. I says you're lucky if her playing out of school is all that worries you. I says she ought to be down there in that kitchen right now, instead of up there in her room, gobbing paint on her face and waiting for six niggers that cant even stand up out of a chair unless they've got a pan full of bread and meat to balance them, to fix breakfast for her [p. 223].

Jason's colloquial informality of speech reveals itself in words like "bitch" and "gobbing," and in the irony of a phrase like "playing out of school," with its dual meanings, both scholastic and sexual. The entertaining but nonetheless vicious attack on his antagonists is shown in his references to Miss Quentin's truancy and cosmetic habits and to the "six niggers that cant even stand up out of a chair unless they've got a pan full of bread and meat to balance them." And the mode of direct address (at least to someone, if not to a genteel "dear reader") is reinforced by the repeated use of "I says," a form that is used in oral narrative.

Partly attributable to the mode of direct address is another element of Jason's oral narrative, his emphasis on narration at the expense of character and theme. Unlike Benjy's and Quentin's presentations, which are fragmented by innumerable changes of place, characters, and time, Jason's narrative moves smoothly and quickly from one event to another in time present, for, with one important exception, every scene Jason depicts occurs on April 6, 1928, the day on which Jason is narrating his tale. He begins in the morning at breakfast, and goes swiftly through his usual round of activities, at the store, the post office, and the telegraph office, as well as through some not-so-usual activities, including his futile attempts to chase down Miss Quentin and the man in the red tie, his bout with a gasoline-induced headache, and having the air let out of his auto tires, when he is five miles from town, by the objects of his quest. Jason's narrative ends, also naturally enough, at the end of the day, as he lies abed, after having earlier tormented Luster about the traveling show, listening to Benjy "snoring away like a planing mill" and thinking his usual thoughts:

> Like I say once a bitch always a bitch. And just let me have twenty-four hours without any damn New York jew to advise me what it's going to do. I dont want to make a killing; save that to suck in the smart gamblers with. I just want an even chance to get my money back. And once I've done that they can bring all Beale Street and all bedlam in here and two of them can sleep in my bed and another one can have my place at the table too [p. 329].

So not only does Jason stick rather closely to the order of events as they happen, he also rounds off the presentation nicely by a return to the opening motif of the section. And even where Jason violates the chronology, as he does when he flashes back to the events surrounding his father's death and Caddy's return to see her child, he does it carefully enough so that not even the most casual reader is likely to get as lost as we often do in the first two sections.

Because the interest in oral narrative is in the narration itself, there is usually a consequent shallowness of theme and character. In this mode, in fact, "theme" is usually identified with plot, so the real thematic elements get little attention. Such is the case in Jason's section, for his theme, self-justification, is not to be identified at all with that of the author, who remains invisible. Jason introduces a great mass of material—even more, perhaps, than Quentin—that looks thematic as he comments upon the actions and characters that make up his narration, but is actually only self-elevating moralizing and sententiousness that is usually introduced by "like I always say," or "I says," or "I'll say that." But self-aggrandizing as it may be, it still serves Jason's purpose (if not the author's), for often this commentary is the most interesting, the most entertaining, part of the section.

Finally, just as Jason's thematic interests are absorbed in a welter of personal clichés, his interest in other characters is also absorbed in a few stereotyping descriptions. In this kind of narration, all the characters but the narrator are likely to be flat and undeveloped.

Such superficial characterization happens partly because of the demands of the narrative and partly because of the formal need for easy stylistic embellishments. For whatever reasons, Jason uses many figures of speech that have little relevance except as entertainment and as a means for fixing other characters in a phrase. His narrow interest in characterization, for example, is illustrated in his opening depiction of the Compson servants ("six niggers that cant even stand up out of a chair unless they've got a pan full of bread and meat to balance them") and the sarcastic remark about Dilsey that is meant to define her relation to himself: "She was so old she couldn't do any more than move hardly. But that's all right: we need somebody in the kitchen to eat up the grub the young ones cant tote off" (p. 229). Jason delineates all women, including his mother, his sister, his niece, and his girlfriend, in a word—"bitches"—and he has a memorable epithet for Benjy, "the Great American Gelding," that suggests the limits of Jason's sympathy and the form he intends of our reaction to Benjy. The result of these efforts to stereotype other characters, who are defined solely in relation to the narrator, is simply that Jason becomes the only clearly realized character in his narrative, a result his ego would appreciate if it never became aware of the moral image actually created.[83]

Lawrence Bowling observed over two decades ago what every reader of Faulkner's novel must have recognized, that "the last section . . . is the most orthodox" in the book.[84] What he means is that Faulkner has set Dilsey's section well within the framework of the conventional novel-as-genre. Here, as in drama, actions, characters, and dialogue are presented directly to us; as in the oral narrative, there is a continuous narration; and, as in the lyrical mode, we are allowed occasional access to a character's private mind; but here, for the first time, the controlling medium is not the mind of a created character, rather the mind of an *author* whom we can identify as "Faulkner," if not as Faulkner, the historical person. Faulkner has said that he let the three Compson brothers try to tell the story, but when they failed he had to try to tell it himself. Consequently, not only do we have an authority who is analogous to the brothers and yet is outside the created narrative, we also have a moral judge who has no compunctions about setting values and valuations in a "truer" perspective, a balancing necessary, we feel, as Faulkner must have, because of the limitations of the other modes of presentation: the drama (Benjy) can present but cannot evaluate or comment; while the lyrical (Quentin) and the oral (Jason) may evaluate and comment, there is no guarantee that they will do so validly.

One way the valuation of character changes, for example, is in the disparity between Jason's conception of Dilsey and "Faulkner's" conception. Where Jason castigates her because he fears and distrusts her integrity, "Faulkner" praises her, however circuitously, in the pictorial presentation that opens the section. He does it through a combination of clinical description, elevated diction, somber tone, and slow, dignified prose rhythm:

> She had been a big woman once but now her skeleton rose, draped loosely in unpadded skin that tightened again upon a paunch almost dropsical, as though muscle and tissue had been courage or fortitude which the days or the years had consumed until only the indomitable skeleton was left rising like a ruin or a landmark above the somnolent and impervious guts, and above that the collapsed face that gave the impression of the bones themselves being outside the flesh, lifted into the driving day with an expression at once fatalistic and of a child's astonished disappointment, until she turned and entered the house again and closed the door [p. 331].

A passage such as this could be drawn right out of the nineteenth-century novel-as-genre, from James, or George Eliot, or, perhaps, Thackeray. Because he yokes realistic detail to the often highly literary diction, "Faulkner" avoids unwarranted sentimentality; he "invests Dilsey with an atmosphere of heroic dignity and at the same time mocks his own narrative technique."[85] But there is no doubt that Dilsey is the most admirable character in the novel. And while Dilsey is revaluated, Jason, too, is placed in a different light. When he reports Miss Quentin's crime to the sheriff, for example, qualities that were only implied in the third section are brought out explicitly: "Jason told him, his *sense of injury and impotence* feeding upon its own sound, so that after a time he forgot his haste in the violent cumulation of his *self justification* and his *outrage*" (p. 378, my italics).

"Faulkner" also alters the moral perspectives by placing different characters in significant literary or archetypal contexts. Jason, for example, sees himself as an avenging angel, a titanic hero:

> The air brightened, the running shadow patches were not the obverse, and it seemed to him that the fact that the day was clearing was another *cunning stroke* on the part of the *foe*, the *fresh battle* toward which he

was carrying *ancient wounds*. From time to time he passed churches, unpainted frame buildings with sheet iron steeples, surrounded by tethered teams and shabby motorcars, and it seemed to him that each of them was a *picket-post* where the *rear guards* of *Circumstance* peeped fleetingly back at him. "And damn You, too," he said, "See if You can stop me," thinking of himself, his *file of soldiers* with the manacled sheriff in the rear, *dragging Omnipotence down from His throne*, if necessary; of the *embattled legions* of both *hell* and *heaven* through which he *tore his way* and put his hands at last on his fleeing niece [p. 382, italics mine].

But the disparity between his imagined triumph and his actual defeat suggests that "Faulkner's" mode is mock-heroic and that Jason is deceiving no one but himself. Shortly after this passage, "Faulkner" shows Jason trying to decide whether to go on with the chase or home for some camphor since gasoline fumes from the auto are more than he can stand. In contrast, Dilsey sees herself in no particular light at all, yet "Faulkner" places her and Benjy, amidst the Easter sermon of the black preacher, in the context of Christ, the crucifixion, and the resurrection:

> Dilsey sat bolt upright, her hand on Ben's knee. Two tears slid down her fallen cheeks, in and out of the myriad coruscations of immolation and abnegation and time [pp. 367–68].
>
> In the midst of the voices and the hands Ben sat, rapt in his sweet blue gaze. Dilsey sat bolt upright beside, crying rigidly and quietly in the annealment and the blood of the remembered Lamb [pp. 370–71].

Such passages as these serve two major purposes of the novel: they help to carry the narrative along and, probably more important, they rearrange and realign characters and narrative in more significant terms because they are presented within the conventions of authority associated with the traditional novel. In other words, by entering Dilsey's section, "Faulkner" forces us to see the lives of Benjy, Jason, Quentin, Caddy, and the other Compsons in an expanded context. That context, eventually, involves not only the family, but also the South and, finally, all of mankind. The novel becomes, then, not just the story of the fall of a great house, or of the decline of southern aristocracy, but also the story of man's fall. And because of Faulkner's tone and authoritative style in Dilsey's section, we are left with the sense that for the Compsons, as for mankind, there are both a hope and a possibility of redemption. There is considerably more that one can say about the conventional pictorial mode of presentation of the novel-as-genre, but what we have seen suggests how retrospective, even atavistic, Faulkner's presentation is here.

The first three sections of *The Sound and the Fury* are only modes of presentation generated from *imitations* of the features of drama, lyric, and epic within the definite limitations of prose fiction,[86] a new critical orientation which makes several insights apparent. By seeing the first three sections this way, rather than only through the concept of stream of consciousness, the many differences among them will become more evident. To focus on stream of consciousness is to imply that it provides a common formal basis for each of them, though stream of consciousness is not a complete mode, but a limited technique; to focus on the modes of presentation, on the other hand, is to recognize quickly that the formal basis for each section is distinct from that of the others. Moreover, this approach allows us to see relationships, both inside and outside Faulkner's works, that we might otherwise miss. Within the Faulkner canon, for example, Benjy's section looks forward to the imitation of the dramatic form in *Requiem for a Nun*, and Quentin's anticipates the lyrical passages of *As I Lay Dying* and *Absalom, Absalom!* Outside Faulkner, the different sections also have their natural affinities: Benjy's to the dramatic and sensory immediacy of much of Hemingway, Quentin's to the lyrical presentation of Joyce's *Portrait* and some of the most recent American fiction, and Jason's to the more ironic first-person narratives in many writers, including even Henry James. The experiments with different presentational modes, in addition, provide further evidence of Faulkner's willingness to try different forms, techniques, and patterns, and casts yet another light on the relationships among, for example, *The Sound and the Fury, As I Lay Dying, Light in August, Absalom, Absalom!, The Wild Palms,* and *Go Down, Moses.*

Perhaps the greatest revelation of an approach through the modes of narration in *The Sound and the Fury,* however, is its correcting the fallacy of epistemological and ontological congruence we associate with the novel-as-genre. Faulkner explodes the assumption that differences in content somehow finally cause the differences in mode. Faulkner originally decided that the "short story" of Caddy and her brothers could be told as dramatically as possible, and he chose to tell it through Benjy's, the idiot's, point of view. But, as he says in his recorded comments, he became aware that the mode of Benjy's section was not adequate for his "dream," so he followed Benjy with the points of view of Quentin, Jason, and finally "Faulkner" himself. Significantly, however, each section, as it attempts to present the same story, moves closer to the conventions of the novel-as-genre, as Faulkner seemingly becomes aware that his story, his dream, requires elements that drama, lyric, and oral narrative do not offer, the primary one being a reliable commentary. Benjy can offer no commentary at all, and Quentin's commentary is invalidated by idealistic, as Jason's is by rationalistic, delusions. Only "Faulkner" knows enough and is unbiased enough to serve as a reliable arbiter. Yet, because Faulkner has exploded the novel-as-genre in *The Sound and the Fury*, he explodes his own role as author in a traditional fictional form. "Faulkner" ends by being only theoretically more authoritative than the Compson brothers. And the novel, congruent no longer in its ways of knowing and in its realities, is ultimately fragmented into its primary modes. In *The Sound and the Fury*, we see clearly how the novel-as-genre has become modes of the novel.

The fictions of William Faulkner suggest many of the principles of modernist art, but the main one for modern criticism in general is simply this: it is the autotelic literary form *as a model* itself that becomes the most important consideration of criticism, not the mimesis of a realistic content, an ontological orientation that had governed the criticism of the traditional, and especially the nineteenth-century, novel-as-genre. So, at the same time Faulkner exploded the form of the novel, he exploded—once and for all for modernist American authors—its presumption of the non-critical, naive realism that had so long seemed a part of the novel's very essence; what is more, he showed writers after him how to identify and exploit presentational modes and how to experiment with the elemental archetypes, themes, and *mythoi* available to American fiction. Since Faulkner, American novelists have been as free as Henry James in "The Art of Fiction" (1884) claimed they ought be, free indeed to do as they would with the traditions and conventions of the past.

Regardless of the profound impact of such writers as Anderson, Faulkner, Stein, Fitzgerald, Hemingway, and others on the traditional novel-as-genre, most were quite primitive in their critical consciousnesses. While, as E. D. Hirsch insists, it is unlikely that any writer is going to invent a totally new genre or form, it also seems true that these early modernist authors benefited by their naiveté, for, had they been more consciously critical, they might have reverted too hastily to traditional formulae. Their innocence—especially in the case of a radical innovator like Faulkner—made them open to "the same leap of imagination that flashed in Picasso when he turned a toy car into the head of a baboon."[87] They simply did what they felt they had to in order to do their tasks; if their epistemological and ontological tasks demanded techniques unknown or untried in the traditional novel, they simply tried them or discovered them through the imaginative combination or extension of known types or techniques. The examples of these writers suggest that they could communicate their discoveries to one another, but they seemed to do so best in a personal, almost communal setting—as in Gertrude Stein's salon—but not in the form of discursive critical writing. Fitzgerald and Faulkner seem to have eschewed the genre of theoretical criticism, and whenever Faulkner was asked why he tried a specific device—as he often was asked at the University of Virginia and Nagano, Japan—he ducked behind talk of "carpenters" and "lumber" and "chicken-houses."[88] Anderson and Hemingway both wrote about their techniques, but both are embarrassingly shallow in their comments, although we can be moved by the disparity between the simplicity of their expressions and the power of their fictional creations. These writers were *naive* in their awareness of what they had wrought upon the genre, but their lack of conscious critical discipline is precisely what freed them to do all they were capable of doing. When we get to sophisticated-phase modernist authors such as Kurt Vonnegut, Jr., and Richard Brautigan, we will see even more clearly the immense power that the mere appearance of a naive faith can give a writer.

Notes: Phase One

1. For a discussion of the concept of spiritual authority, see Northrop Frye, "The Problem of Spiritual Authority in the Nineteenth Century," in *The Stubborn Structure: Essays on Criticism and Society* (Ithaca, N.Y.: Cornell University Press, 1970), pp. 241–56; see also Charles F. Altieri, "Northrop Frye and the Problem of Spiritual Authority" *PMLA*, 87 (October 1972): 964–75, and see n. 20 to the Introduction herein.
2. Alfred North Whitehead, *Science and the Modern World* (New York: Macmillan, 1925), p. 109.
3. All previous quotations in this paragraph are from Wolfgang Iser, *The Implied Reader* (Baltimore: Johns Hopkins University Press, 1974), pp. 27–28.
4. For a supplemental discussion, going beyond J. Paul Hunter's *The Reluctant Pilgrim: Defoe's Emblematic Method and Quest for Form in Robinson Crusoe* (Baltimore: Johns Hopkins University Press, 1966), see Melvyn New, " 'The Grease of God': The Form of Eighteenth-Century English Fiction," *PMLA*, 91, no. 2 (March 1976): 235–44. New asks the question whether the early English novel depicted a providential universe; he answers by saying that the paradigmatic novels actually presented a world in transition, one moving from the earlier Puritan providential model to a less determinate one.
5. Iser, *The Implied Reader*, p. 28.
6. Whitehead, *Science in the Modern World*, p. 111.
7. R. G. Collingwood, *The Idea of Nature* (Oxford: Clarendon, 1945), p. 5.
8. *Ibid.*, pp. 6–7.
9. Whitehead, *Science in the Modern World*, pp. 106–7.
10. Thomas Carlyle used the term "natural supernaturalism" in *Sartor Resartus*, giving M. H. Abrams a title for the important book on romanticism cited in the following note.
11. M. H. Abrams, *Natural Supernaturalism: Tradition and Revolution in Romantic Literature* (New York: Norton, 1971), p. 91. For a treatment of the movement of literature "inward," one that is carried up to the end of the eighteenth century, see Erich Kahler, *The Inward Turn of Narrative*, trans. from the German by Richard and Clara Winston, Foreword by Joseph Frank, Bollingen Series 83 (Princeton, N.J.: Princeton University Press, 1973).
12. Abrams, *Natural Supernaturalism*, p. 91.
13. The quotations in this paragraph are from *Natural Supernaturalism*, pp. 77, 79; for additional discussion of the theme of artistic self-consciousness in poetry and fiction, see Abrams's analysis of the idea of *The Prelude*, pp. 74–80; see also his n. 6, p. 492, for further references, including Maurice Beebe's treatment of the theme in fiction: *Ivory Towers and Sacred Founts* (New York: New York University Press, 1964).
14. Collingwood, *The Idea of Nature*, p. 8.

15. *Ibid.*, p. 7.
16. Frye, *The Stubborn Structure*, p. 207.
17. *Ibid.*, p. 211. The standard discussion of the romantic strain of American fiction is Richard Chase, *The American Novel and Its Tradition* (Garden City, N.Y.: Doubleday, 1957).
18. J. Hillis Miller, *Poets of Reality: Six Twentieth-Century Writers* (New York: Atheneum, 1969), p. 2. Although Miller is mainly concerned with poets, he begins his discussion of changing conceptions of reality with Conrad.
19. *Ibid.*
20. Collingwood, *The Idea of Nature*, p. 11.
21. Charles Child Walcutt, *American Literary Naturalism: A Divided Stream* (Minneapolis: University of Minnesota Press, 1956), p. vii.
22. *Ibid.*
23. Collingwood, *The Idea of Nature*, p. 12.
24. *Ibid.*, pp. 152–53.
25. Henry Adams, *The Education of Henry Adams*, edited with an Introduction and notes by Ernest Samuels (Boston: Houghton Mifflin, 1974), p. 495. *The Education* was originally published in 1918 by the Massachusetts Historical Society.
26. Collingwood, *The Idea of Nature*, p. 154.
27. Adams, *The Education of Henry Adams*, p. 517.
28. One could put together an entire library full of volumes dealing with these subjects, but see the two volumes of Ronald Nash's *Ideas of History* (New York: E. P. Dutton, 1969), especially vol. II, *The Critical Philosophy of History*, and two books by Hayden White: *Metahistory: The Historical Imagination in Nineteenth-Century Europe* (Baltimore: Johns Hopkins University Press, 1973), and *Tropics of Discourse: Essays in Cultural Criticism* (Baltimore: Johns Hopkins University Press, 1978), in addition to Robert H. Canary and Henry Kozicki, eds., *The Writing of History: Literary Form and Historical Understanding* (Madison: University of Wisconsin Press, 1978), a volume that includes important essays by Lionel Gossman and Louis O. Mink concerning the literary or fictional or prefigurative aspects of history.
29. Iser, *The Implied Reader*, p. xiv.
30. *Ibid.*
31. *Ibid.*
32. *Ibid.*
33. *Ibid.*
34. See E. D. Hirsch, Jr., *Validity in Interpretation* (New Haven, Conn.: Yale University Press, 1967), pp. 262–63, for a concise statement of the relation between communication, in any form, and the conventions of genre, mode, and the like.
35. This is the second volume of the International Encyclopedia of Unified Science, originally published in 1962; a second edition, enlarged, was published in 1970, both editions by The University of Chicago Press.
36. I make this assertion because I employ a theory of Northrop Frye concerning what he calls "pre-generic modes" or narrative "mythoi": "There are," Frye says, "four main types of mythical movement: within romance, within experience, down, and up. The downward movement is the tragic movement, the wheel of fortune falling from innocence toward hamartia, and from hamartia to catastrophe. The upward

movement is the comic movement, from threatening complications to a happy ending and a general assumption of post-dated innocence in which everyone lives happily ever after" (*Anatomy of Criticism*, p. 162). Romance and irony-satire are the *mythoi* that move cyclically within the realms of innocence and experience, respectively. Regardless of whether one agrees with Frye's system, one must recognize the cogency of the argument, for, while one may create combinations of these movements, there seem no other ways to create narrative trajectories that will form meaningful patterns.

37. Harry Levin, in "What Is Realism?," discussing the philosophic base of the traditional novel, expresses the circularity plainly: "At the outset we can answer [the] question, positivistically and tautologically, by defining truth as the accurate correspondence between reality itself and a given account of reality" (*Aspects of Fiction: A Handbook*, ed. Howard E. Hugo [Boston: Little, Brown, 1962], p. 189).

38. Gerald Graff, "The Myth of the Postmodernist Breakthrough," *TriQuarterly*, 26 (Winter 1973): 383–417, 401–3.

39. Frank Kermode, "Novels: Recognition and Deception," *Critical Inquiry*, 1, no. 1 (September 1974): 106; Wolfgang Iser, "Indeterminacy and the Reader's Response in Prose Fiction," *Aspects of Narrative: Selected Papers from the English Institute*, ed. with a Foreword by J. Hillis Miller (New York: Columbia University Press, 1971), pp. 1–45. For my contentions in *The Exploded Form*, Iser's thesis is particularly important: "The reader of modern novels is deprived of the assistance which [for example] the eighteenth-century writer had given him in a variety of devices, ranging from exhortation to satire and irony. Instead, he is expected to strive for himself to unravel the mysteries of a sometimes strikingly obscure composition. This development reflects the transformation of the very idea of literature, which seems to have ceased to be a means of relaxation and even luxury, making demands now on the capacity of understanding because the world presented seems to have no bearing on what the reader is familiar with. This change did not happen suddenly. The stages of transition are clearly discernible in the nineteenth century, and one of them is virtually a halfway point in the development: the so-called realistic novel, of which Thackeray's *Vanity Fair* is an outstanding example. Here, the author-reader relationship is as different from the eighteenth-century 'dialogue' as it is from the twentieth-century demand that the reader find for himself the key to a many-sided puzzle" (p. 26). Iser focuses on the shift toward indeterminacy in British novels such as *Vanity Fair*, while Kermode and I focus on this development in James.

40. Kermode, "Novels: Recognition and Deception," p. 106.

41. For a more extended discussion of this novella, see my "Modal Counterpoint in James's *The Aspern Papers*," *Papers on Language and Literature*, 4 (Summer 1968): 199–207.

42. David Lodge, *The Modes of Modern Writing: Metaphor, Metonymy, and the Typology of Modern Literature* (London: Edward Arnold, 1977), p. 145. Lodge deals with many of the problems of the sophisticated phase of the modern, using Roman Jakobson's distinctions between the metaphoric and the metonymic; although it is sometimes difficult to follow the methodology as it is applied to specific works or authors, this is still a very valuable study.

43. *Ibid.*
44. *The Modern Tradition: Backgrounds of Modern Literature,* ed. Richard Ellmann and Charles Feidelson, Jr. (New York: Oxford University Press, 1965). On the modalities of narrative, see my "Narrative Forms in *Winesburg, Ohio,*" *PMLA,* 83 (October 1968): 1304–12.
45. I have discussed this aspect of Fitzgerald's novel in "Counterpoint as Technique in *The Great Gatsby,*" *English Journal,* 55 (October 1966): 853–59.
46. To extend the ramifications of the section on *The Sound and the Fury* I have been at work for some time on a detailed study of the four basic epistemological modes manifested by the sections of the novel. A long essay has been published from this work: "Faulkner's Jason and the Tradition of Oral Narrative," *Journal of Popular Culture,* 2, no. 2 (Fall 1968): 195–210. Other essays will show in detail how Benjy's section illustrates the mode of drama, how Quentin's section illustrates the mode of lyric, and how the Dilsey section illustrates the traditional (pictorial) mode of fiction. The analysis in part III, however, stays very close to the conventional terms and concepts of the standard spokesmen in order to suggest the most general dimensions of the dramatic, the lyric, the oral narrative, and the "pictorial" or fictional.
47. I have discussed some of the philosophical implications of this novel in "Faulkner's Philosophical Novel: Ontological Themes in *As I Lay Dying,*" *Personalist,* 48 (Autumn 1967): 509–23.
48. I have discussed the narrative archetypes of this work in "The Biblical Rhythm of *Go Down, Moses,*" *Mississippi Quarterly,* 20 (Summer 1967): 135–47.
49. *Anatomy of Criticism,* p. 73.
50. In "Indeterminacy and the Reader's Response in Prose Fiction," Iser writes: "This 'hermeneutic operation' of reading intensifies itself to the degree that the novel renounces definition of its intention. However, the fact that the novel does not set forth its own intention does not mean that no intention exists. Where is it to be found? The answer must be that the reciprocal correction of the positions opens up a dimension which only comes into being through the act of reading. It is only in reading that there occurs an uninterrupted modification of the various positions involved. The hero keeps sallying forth into the sordid world of reality, and thus continually provokes changing judgments on the part of the reader. But at the same time, the reader looks through the hero's eyes at the world, so that it, too, is subject to changing judgments. Out of these continually interacting elements, the reader's imagination can build up the pattern of the text—a pattern that varies according to the imagination that is forming it. So the reading becomes an act of generating meaning" (*Aspects of Narrative,* p. 25). Claudio Guillén comes at the problem of indeterminacy by focusing upon the author's role in relation to generic thinking: "The theoretical orders of poetics should be viewed, at any moment in their history, as essentially mental codes—with which the practicing writer . . . comes to terms through his writing. The structures of this order are no more alien to the poems [meaning any literary works] he produces than the linguistic code is to the actual utterances in his speech" (*Literature as System* [Princeton, N.J.: Princeton University Press, 1971], p. 390). Guillén is not necessarily speaking here of narrative *mythoi,* but the principle, I

believe, is the same whether one refers to, say, Guillén's "genre" of picaresque or the *mythos* of satire with which picaresque interfaces.

51. To augment the brief outline of Frye's system of *mythoi*, given in n. 36 above, I quote here Paul Hernadi's synopsis from *Beyond Genre* (Ithaca, N.Y.: Cornell University Press, 1972), p. 132: "Frye postulates the existence of four 'narrative categories of literature broader than, or logically prior to literary genres' (p. 162). In the course of impressively large-scale speculations concerning plot structure, he attempts to place every story that can be told on a gigantic conceptual map with the 'romantic,' the 'tragic,' the 'comic,' and the 'ironic' (or 'satiric') as points of compass. The four 'generic plots' or *mythoi* emerge as movements within a highly desirable world (romance), within a painfully defective world (irony and satire), downward from innocence through hamartia to catastrophe (tragedy), or upward from the world of experience through threatening complications to 'a general assumption of post-dated innocence in which everyone lives happily ever after' (comedy) (p. 162) [page numbers refer to *Anatomy of Criticism*]." All who have worked with Frye's schema have no doubt tried to construct diagrams to interpret the system; the one Hernadi provides on p. 133 and his simplification on p. 134 are among the most useful I have seen.

52. I have published the following essays that attempt to explain the ways in which different sections of *The Sound and the Fury* manifest different narrative *mythoi*: "Caliban as Prospero: Benjy and *The Sound and the Fury*," *Novel: A Forum on Fiction*, 3, no. 3 (Spring 1970): 233–48; "*The Sound and The Fury*: Quentin Compson and Faulkner's 'Tragedy of Passion,'" *Studies in the Novel*, 2, no. 1 (Spring 1970): 61–75; "Jason Compson: Humor, Hostility, and the Rhetoric of Aggression," *Southern Humanities Review*, 3, no. 3 (Summer 1969): 259–67; and "Type and Archetype: Jason Compson as 'Satirist,'" *Genre*, 4, no. 2 (June 1971): 173–88.

53. I have discussed this novel more thoroughly in "The Biblical Rhythm of *Go Down, Moses*," *Mississippi Quarterly*, 20 (Summer 1967): 135–47.

54. Lynn Gartrell Levins, "The Four Narrative Perspectives in *Absalom, Absalom!*," *PMLA*, 85, no. 1 (January 1970): 35–47, argues in some detail for different modes of presentation, but does not suggest their connection to Frye's historical or generic modes.

55. Kahler, *The Inward Turn of Narrative*, p. 4.

56. *Ibid.*, pp. 4–5.

57. Cleanth Brooks, *William Faulkner: The Yoknapatawpha Country* (New Haven, Conn.: Yale University Press, 1963), p. 326–27.

58. See F. R. Leavis, "The Novel as Dramatic Poem I: *Hard Times*," *Scrutiny*, 14(1946–47): 185–303. This is the first in a series of interpretations of English novels as "dramatic poems." Other novels discussed by Leavis are *The Europeans*, *St. Mawr*, *Women in Love*, and *The Rainbow*; G. D. Klingopulos so considers *Wuthering Heights*.

59. Percy Lubbock, *The Craft of Fiction* (New York: Viking, 1957; orig. pub. 1921), p. 253.

60. *Ibid.*, p. 254.

61. *Ibid.*

62. *Ibid.*, p. 262.

63. *Ibid.*, p. 256.

64. *Ibid.*, pp. 262, 253.

65. William Faulkner, *The Sound and the Fury* (New York: Vintage, n.d.), p. 3. All quotations from the novel are from this edition, which is reproduced photographically from a copy of the first printing in 1929. This edition also includes the Appendix Faulkner wrote for *The Portable Faulkner*, ed. Malcolm Cowley, 1946. For a thorough study of the texts, see James B. Meriwether, "Notes on the Textual History of *The Sound and the Fury*," *The Papers of the Bibliographical Society of America*, 56 (1962): 285–316. For useful collections of essays on Faulkner and this work, see *Twentieth-Century Interpretations of "The Sound and the Fury*," ed. Michael H. Cowan (Englewood Cliffs, N.J.: Prentice-Hall, 1968) and *Merrill Studies in "The Sound and the Fury*," comp. James B. Meriwether (Columbus, Ohio: Charles E. Merrill, 1970). For a book-length study of the novel, including an annotated bibliography of criticism, see André Bleikasten, *The Most Splendid Failure: Faulkner's "The Sound and the Fury"* (Bloomington: Indiana University Press, 1976).

66. *The Novels of William Faulkner* (Baton Rouge: Louisiana State University Press, 1959), p. 34. My analysis owes a large debt to Olga Vickery's seminal work, as well as to the work of Lawrence Bowling, H. H. Waggoner, Irving Howe, Lawrance Thompson, and Peter Swiggart, among others.

67. Lubbock, *The Craft of Fiction*, p. 254.

68. *Ibid.*

69. *Ibid.*

70. *Ibid.*, p. 256.

71. See Frederick L. Gwynn and Joseph L. Blotner, eds., *Faulkner in the University* (Charlottesville: University of Virginia Press, 1959), pp. 1–3, 73–74, 84.

72. I work from the useful set of distinguishing characteristics for the mode of lyric presentation offered by Northrop Frye in *Anatomy of Criticism*, pp. 249–50, 270–74. However, some of the characteristics of lyric art generally may be found in M. H. Abrams's discussion of "expressive" theories of criticism in *The Mirror and the Lamp*, pp. 21–26, 84–88. Each of the sections of *The Sound and the Fury* may be explained most readily through different critical orientations—Benjy's through an "objective," Quentin's through an "expressive," Jason's through a "pragmatic," and Dilsey's (which is the most "novelistic" of all) through a "mimetic" orientation. A basis for my approach is in Abrams's four "orientations": as Ian Watt and others argue, the foundation of the novel-as-genre is "mimetic," but I wish to suggest here that Faulkner has superimposed, in each section, a different "orientation" ("objective"-dramatic, "expressive"-lyrical, "pragmatic"-narrative) upon the "mimetic" base. Two other useful studies of lyric are Ralph Freedman, *The Lyrical Novel: Studies in Hermann Hesse, Andre Gide, and Virginia Woolf* (Princeton, N.J.: Princeton University Press, 1963) and Paul Hernadi, *Beyond Genre*, where a brief schema for the lyric and other presentational modes is offered (p. 166).

73. Abrams writes, for example, "The poet's audience is reduced to a single member, consisting of the poet himself" (*Mirror*, p. 25), and Frye says, "The poet, so to speak, turns his back on his listeners . . ." (*Anatomy*, p. 250).

74. James Joyce, *A Portrait of the Artist as a Young Man* (New York:

Viking, 1963), p. 213. The lyric mode often suggests to readers that there is nonetheless a close relation between a persona and the author; in this connection, Jackson J. Benson, in "Quentin Compson: Self-Portrait of a Young Artist's Emotions," *Twentieth-Century Literature*, 17, no. 3 (July 1971): 143–59, suggests a very close bond between Quentin and Faulkner himself. An excellent essay also related to this is Mark Spilka, "Quentin Compson's Universal Grief," *Contemporary Literature*, 11, no. 4 (Autumn 1970): 451–69.

75. Where an "expressive" norm is invoked, Abrams says that "plot becomes a kind of necessary evil" (*Mirror*, p. 24).

76. The repetition of only a few ideas and images has the effect of a "musical composition," in which all major themes are introduced in the novel's opening pages, according to Richard Chase, *The American Novel and Its Tradition* (Garden City, N.Y.: Doubleday, 1957), p. 228.

77. "The process that Freud calls the dream-work shows startling similarities with 'poetic work.' In both there is 'condensation' (the combining several images in one image), 'displacement' (the vesting in some apparently unimportant element the underlying significance of the whole), and 'overdetermination' (several quite different significances focused upon the same element so that it bears more than one meaning). In both poetry and dream, logical relationships are frequently evaded or transcended by the mere juxtaposition of images." William K. Wimsatt, Jr., and Cleanth Brooks, *Literary Criticism: A Short History* (New York: Knopf, 1964), p. 709. See also *Anatomy of Criticism* on lyric activity and creativity, pp. 271–72.

78. See my essay, "*The Sound and the Fury*: Quentin Compson's 'Tragedy of Passion,'" *Studies in the Novel*, 2, no. 1 (Spring 1970): 61–75, for a full discussion of this narrative *mythos*.

79. See *Faulkner in the University*, p. 262, where Faulkner says Quentin never did have those conversations with his father about committing incest with Caddy: ". . . they were imaginary."

80. Lubbock, *The Craft of Fiction*, p. 263.

81. Rene Wellek and Austin Warren, *Theory of Literature* (New York: Harcourt, Brace, 1956), p. 212.

82. Jason's two major concerns are precisely the concerns of the "pragmatic" critical orientation, as Abrams explains it: to "instruct" and to "entertain." See *The Mirror and the Lamp*, pp. 14–21. Hernadi, in *Beyond Genre*, calls narrative "envisioned action," lyric "enacted vision" (p. 166).

83. For a discussion of these elements within the context of *mythos*, see my essays, "Jason Compson: Humor, Hostility, and the Rhetoric of Aggression," *Southern Humanities Review*, 3, no. 3 (Summer 1969): 259–67, and "Type and Archetype: Jason Compson as 'Satirist,'" *Genre*, 4, no. 2 (June 1971): 173–88. For a full-scale discussion of the oral-narrative mode, see my "Faulkner's Jason and the Tradition of Oral Narrative," *Journal of Popular Culture*, 2, no. 2 (Fall 1968): 195–210.

84. "The Technique of *The Sound and the Fury*," in F. J. Hoffman and Olga Vickery, eds., *William Faulkner: Two Decades of Criticism* (East Lansing: Michigan State University Press, 1951), p. 176.

85. Peter Swiggart, *The Art of Faulkner's Novels* (Austin: University of Texas Press, 1964), p. 106.

86. I hope to avoid what Abrams calls the "endemic disease of analogical

thinking . . . hardening of the categories" (*Mirror*, p. 35). By its very definition, of course, an analogy must eventually "break down," but that does not obviate the analogy's usefulness.

87. *Validity in Interpretation*, p. 105.
88. The most thorough discussion I am aware of concerning Faulkner's own comments on the writing of fiction is in Joseph Reed, Jr., "One Single Urn or Shape," in *Faulkner's Narrative* (New Haven, Conn.: Yale University Press, 1973), pp. 1–11.

Phase Two   The Critical

I From Naive to Critical Modernism

> Having isolated a particular community of specialists . . .
> one may usefully ask: What do its members share that ac-
> counts for the relative fulness of their professional com-
> munication and the relative unanimity of their professional
> judgments? To that question my original text licenses the an-
> swer, a paradigm or set of paradigms.
>
> Thomas S. Kuhn
> "Postscript" to
> *The Structure of Scientific Revolutions* (1970)

> . . . the modern novel involved three factors. The first was
> what I called the breakdown of the implicit agreement be-
> tween author and readers about what was significant in
> human experience. . . . The second factor was the new con-
> cept of time and its relation to consciousness. . . . The third
> factor was the new concept of consciousness itself, which
> was now seen to exist simultaneously on different
> levels. . . .
>
> David Daiches
> "What Was the Modern Novel?" (1975)

Revolutions in literature follow a pattern like that of
scientific revolutions; these have been analyzed by Thomas S. Kuhn
in the influential book *The Structure of Scientific Revolutions*. In
science, according to Kuhn, revolutions begin with groups of adherents created around paradigms. Though given several working
definitions, paradigms include "accepted examples of actual scientific practice—examples which include law, theory, application, and
instrumentation together—[and] provide models from which spring
particular coherent traditions of scientific research."[1] In the history
of science, as in literary history, there are well-known exemplary
texts in which the revolutionary paradigms reside; Kuhn's instances
of such texts are Aristotle's *Physica*, Ptolemy's *Almagest*, Newton's
Principia and *Opticks*, Franklin's *Electricity*, Lavoisier's *Chemistry*,
and Lyell's *Geology*. Says Kuhn, "These and many other works
served for a time implicitly to define the legitimate problems and
methods of a research field for succeeding generations of practition-

ers." Two basic characteristics, which are applicable as well to literary texts, made it possible for these exemplars to achieve dominion: "Their achievement was sufficiently unprecedented to attract an enduring group of adherents away from competing modes of scientific activity. Simultaneously, it was sufficiently open-ended to leave all sorts of problems for the redefined group of practitioners to resolve."[2] In the history of modernist literature, these qualities—unprecedented achievement and open-endedness—are represented in exemplary, paradigmatic texts such as Joyce's *Ulysses*, Woolf's *The Waves*, and Faulkner's *The Sound and the Fury*. In these texts and others, modernist authors have since found what in science Kuhn calls "research traditions," traditions that have been systematically and critically extended in the middle phase of the modernist era.

As one might expect, paradigms in themselves have a "history," and it too—like epochs in my analysis—is dialectical. The three phases, which have been isolated by Margaret Masterman in her critique of Kuhn's work, include an early stage of conceptual constructive orientation in which "genius" seems to be at work in the naive discoverers; a secondary, essentially "sociological" stage in which the new or revolutionary modality gathers around it its group of proseltyes; and, finally, a stage of metaphysical extension in which the paradigmatic model (in some identifiable examples) is pushed to the point of subsuming an entire cosmology.[3] The first stage in the life of the paradigm is identified in the discovery, usually by what we call creative or intuitive genius, that a new model, analogy, or metaphor (in any case, a "picture") provides a new "way of seeing" something else so that distinct problems can be solved. In the history of modernist literature, paradigmatic fictions such as *Ulysses*, *The Waves*, and *The Sound and the Fury* solved specific problems located in the genre of the novel itself: the new definitions of reality that come from science and philosophy. An Einsteinian relativity model applied to fiction did in fact permit the locus of fiction's reality to move inside the observer's point of view, allowing the primal "ground" of reality to become human consciousness, thus completing the humanist project that began, says Martin Heidegger, with Plato.

The secondary, "sociological" phase of a paradigm's history is identified by the company it keeps. As paradigms, texts by Joyce, Woolf, and Faulkner have provided focal points for the modernist "students" who follow them, in much the same way that models, exemplars, paradigms have created scientific communities. According to Kuhn:

> The study of paradigms . . . is what mainly prepares the student for membership in the particular scientific community with which he will later practice. Because he there joins men who learned the bases of their field from the same concrete models, his subsequent practice will seldom evoke overt disagreement over fundamentals. Men whose research is based on shared paradigms are committed to the same rules and standards for . . . practice. That commitment and the apparent consensus it produces are prerequisites . . . for the genesis and continuation of a particular research tradition.[4]

Kuhn's commentary here suggests the notion that there can be no tradition or actual revolution until the paradigms have generated a second, critical stage in which the triumph of the new models or exemplars has been widely acknowledged. If there is no critical phase in which the implications of the new theories are extended by the practices of others, then the "revolution" is merely an aberration, an unproductive byway, a dead end. Were there no critical stage of modernism, *Ulysses*, *The Waves*, and *The Sound and the Fury* would be viewed—as, in its time, was Sterne's *Tristram Shandy*—as quaint, premature, untimely curiosities, rather than as the authoritative exemplary texts they have become for us today. But because the second stage has indeed occurred, these works, despite the fact that they have defined and predicted the major concerns of modernism, must nonetheless be regarded as naive in the perspective of secondary critique, as, in fact, Kuhn's own work has been regarded as naive by his later critics.

The exemplars of modernist paradigms are representative of a naive modernism in part because of their valuing the principles of irony and objectivity. The works of Eliot, Woolf, Joyce, and Faulkner converted everything—author, universe, text, reader—into objects, so that, except in some of Eliot's early criticism, there is no frame of commentary around these works, and adherents are left to work out "research programmes" from the evidence of the exemplars alone. The various, often apparently incompatible directions of the second stage of modernism have resulted from critiques of these texts. The extreme objectivity of the exemplars in their withdrawal of the traditional determining relationship among author, world, text, and reader, for instance, has had the suitably ironic effect of vastly increasing determinations from non-traditional sources. Now text and reader are able to supplant author and world as "authority."[5] Thus, one direction of the modern has been to aggrandize the reader's role in interpretation or hermeneusis and to elevate audience to an ontological status; another direction has been to increase the importance of the text-as-text, to make it, too, an ontological object as well as a way of knowing, an epistemological locus.

Naive modernism changes to critical modernism when the critiques of early paradigms begin to appear in the works of different authors. Critical results are shown in the ways that underlying, often unacknowledged or unknown presuppositions implied by the open-ended, exemplary works are disclosed or made visible in later generic works. The shift from modernism's early, naive phase to a later, critical phase can be observed, for instance, in such exemplary authors as Eliot and Joyce. In "The Love Song of J. Alfred Prufrock," Eliot exhibits modernist tendencies that are then synopsized in one of our most crucial exemplary texts, *The Waste Land.* But each of these is uncritically modernist in comparison to both "Ash Wednesday" and *Four Quartets:* these later poems exhibit needs created by the early works of Eliot, for instance, the need for an extrinsic, non-anthropomorphic authority, the possibility of which seemingly has been denied by the two earlier poems. *Four Quartets,* by hypostatizing the merely heuristic form of *The Waste Land,* stands in a critically redemptive relation to the early Eliot, so it is not only a meditation upon modes of transcendence, it is a virtual catalogue of the thematic concerns of modernism as it deals with time and history, language and art, and the reach of consciousness itself.

Joyce's major works show even more clearly the dialectical evolution. *A Portrait of the Artist as a Young Man,* exemplary in a straightforward way, within the confines of the fiction itself sets out a "programme" of formal discovery. The programme is exemplified in its conceptual phase by *A Portrait,* is undertaken critically in *Ulysses* and then with extreme metaphysical sophistication in *Finnegans Wake,* a work that, had it been given the central critical attention of the earlier novels, would simply have exploded modernism itself—as *Tristram Shandy* might have exploded prematurely the novel as a form had Sterne dominated fiction in the period between Richardson and Jane Austen. Certainly, at the same time the early works are models for modernist irony and objectification,

Joyce's late work pushes to an almost absolute limit the other major concerns—language, consciousness, myth, history, and the like—of those authors whom we designate "modern."

In modernist American fiction, this shift into the "sociological" second phase is readily observed in the ways younger novelists have joined forces with the earlier generation. But in doing so, their critique has led to changes, for they often have converted aspects of exemplary early works into dominant forms or have treated aspects as consciously articulated themes. In terms of form, for example, after Joyce, Woolf, and Faulkner—who share influence with James, Stein, Anderson, Hemingway, Fitzgerald, and others—had exploded the novel-as-genre into modes of the novel, many younger writers exhibited the formal modalities thrown up by the novel's whole history, but in most cases used the modes without the same philosophical or moral convictions that had lain behind the modal originators. Bellow, for instance, gives us a journal/diary/confession in *Dangling Man*, but he does so in such a way as to undercut the determinations upon which the confessional mode had once relied. Once it had been a way for Augustine, Rousseau, and others to achieve ethical or religious truth. But for the modernist "confessional" author, the indeterminacy of truth becomes fiction's "truth." Thus, Edith Kern suggests in *Existential Thought and Fictional Technique: Kierkegaard, Sartre, Beckett*, the use of diaries, letters, journals, and other modes of first-personal communication have become a large part of the project of modernist fiction. The reason is that this project is essentially the same as for existentialism itself, a philosophic mode that, Kern insists, has extremely close affinities to the modalities of fiction. Describing existentialism's origins in the early nineteenth-century Danish philosopher, Kern points out that "Kierkegaard's entire work is indicative of his search for new, more adequate forms to express his thought—for forms as expressive of his thought as thought itself: forms stressing subjectivity in its process of becoming and on its road toward inwardness, toward the eternal, essential truth, and thereby towards its Self."[6] But, for those modernist authors who cannot share the Christian philosopher's assurance of transcendent union between one's self and God's Self, the first-person projection now is essential because it can model a twentieth-century relativity. Thus, almost any use of a "confessional" form by a contemporary novelist—*Dangling Man* no more than Bellow's *Herzog* or *Hum-*

boldt's Gift—exhibits the mode in the same provisional way, as only one of many modes for achieving "truth" in a relative, indeterminate cosmos.[7]

Bellow, in fact, is perhaps our best representative of the sociological phase of the paradigm. He seems something of an "exemplary" critical-modernist author, for the development of his career appears almost a conscious working out of a "programme" determined by the early paradigms or the lessons derived from a critique of them. One modernist, Kierkegaardian truth is subjectivity, but a corollary truth is the impermeability of the "other." As fiction's history gives Bellow a model for *Dangling Man*'s subjectivity, so the history of fiction gives a form for dealing with the modality of otherness. In the form of Bellow's *The Victim*, a form straight out of Henry James, Bellow's central consciousness (Asa Leventhal) is engaged in sorting out problematical, ambiguous, ironic "truths" lying in a dramatic relationship between himself and an "other," though one who is also *Doppelgänger*. The double motif from myth and dream is especially important in this modernist dramatic modality in James and Bellow, for, ironically, it can still intimate a conjunction (as in the pictorial novel-as-genre) between *visibilia* and *invisibilia* in the universe, between concrete experience and ineffable spirit. Picking up on other modernist themes, Bellow takes *The Adventures of Augie March* and *Henderson the Rain King* back to familiar elements in fiction's history. *Augie March* is a modernist—which is to say, a consciously indeterminate—adaptation of the mode of the picaresque, whose natural inconclusiveness is made an overt theme in Bellow's recurrent imagery of Augie's endless "circling." The formal and thematic uses of myth, since *Ulysses* and Eliot's review of it, are almost requisite features of modernist literature, and Bellow's *Henderson* at once is formed upon myth and takes as a conscious theme the creation of myth, a reflexiveness which itself is also particularly modernist. And *Herzog, Mr. Sammler's Planet*, and *Humboldt's Gift*, each somewhat introverted or confessional in form, all treat themes—history, consciousness, man's existential situation in an exploding universe—that are, in one guise or another, the provinces of modernist fiction's early exemplars. Later discussions herein of such authors as Bernard Malamud and Joseph Heller will further suggest the sharing of modernism's paradigms, its "sociological" triumph.

The evolution from naive- to critical-modernist paradigms is also signaled by developments extrinsic to fiction itself. These developments are generally related to the metaphysical extensions of the paradigms of the modern. The thrust of modernist paradigms into aesthetics, for example, suggests the metaphysical drift. This thrust shows in the two most important advances in literary criticism since the advent of modernism. Emerging as results of modernist biases, these developments are, first, the "New Criticism" concerned with the hermetically sealed, objective text and its technical mechanisms and, second, the archetypal criticism concerned with the interface of consciousness and reality/text. The new critics—like existentialist man in a pluralistic, relativistic universe—attempted to come to terms with the discrete work as if it were a closed system embodying all its own determinations. The archetypal critics—vigorously seeking to combat such indeterminateness—have tried to get outside the work in order to locate stable referents in anthropocentric yet somehow comprehensive systems—in consciousness itself (including both the conscious and the unconscious aspects of mind) as it is viewed by Carl Jung, or in the archetypes of literature itself as Northrop Frye would argue. Whether placed in a verbal universe (Frye) or in a collective unconscious (Jung), the archetypes promise author and reader a potential authority that is inside man, thus permitting modernism its fundamental anthropocentrism, but nonetheless objective and extrinsic to the individual.

What these two types of criticism, in their contrasting emphases, have made their explicit concerns—though they had been mainly implicit, formal concerns of early modernist texts—is connected to a principle underlying the novel as a form. The genre began, Wolfgang Iser insists, as an attempt of man to use his experience as a means to discovery of salvation. Thus, Iser's comments on *Pilgrim's Progress* might just as well have been made of a critical modernist text such as *Henderson the Rain King:* "In a 'God-forsaken' world," says Iser, experience "offers the one chance of human self-understanding. Through it, the self and the world can be reconciled in a new way, but since there can be no paradigmatic, universally applicable reconciliation, literary fiction can only offer situational answers to each of the historical problems that need to be solved. The history of these problems and answers constitutes the history of the novel."[8] Iser would argue that his situation actually points to a universal principle in literature, for all literature, he says, seemingly "counterbalances the deficiencies produced by prevailing phil-osophies" within an epoch.[9] But, since the novel historically is a mimetic form, it exhibits more clearly than other genres the basic tensions within a cultural epoch. Thus, for example, speaking elsewhere of Fielding's *Tom Jones*, Iser writes that this novel shows the deficiencies in several systems, rational as well as latitudinarian. Fielding's novel, by showing the "gulf between the rigid confines of principles and the endless fluidity of human experience," thus sought to reestablish man's "confidence by providing a picture of human nature which offered a guarantee of self-preservation through self-correction."[10] This eternal tension within a culturally reflective form such as the novel (either as a genre or in any of its modes) is manifested very clearly in the two sides of the philosophy projected from modernist bases.

The projected philosophy of the modernist era represents one other extrinsic indication of the movement into a secondary, critical phase, at the same time that it further discloses the metaphysical drift of our modernist paradigms. The metaphysic that has dominated twentieth-century thought has been one form or another of existentialism. As Frye and Jameson, in different contexts, both suggest, existentialism is perhaps nothing but modernist anthropocentrism—or what Heidegger referred to as "the humanization of truth"—projected into the various aspects of philosophy, religion, and literature.[11] As with most other "environments," the intellectual environment created by existentialism—or the production of primary and critical texts of existentialist bias—has become most visible to us as we are now about to get outside it. Though today a spate of studies announce themselves as investigating "post-existential" literature, the use of the prefix *post* in these cases usually implies only that an existentialist metaphysic has triumphed over its rivals in this century. It thus remains appropriate to say, as critic Jean Kennard has said recently of the fiction of critical modernism: "Many of the commentators on contemporary fiction have found it necessary to discuss Existentialism in order to define the intellectual climate of the post-1945 world. Neither they nor I mean to suggest that every novelist is an attentive reader of *The Myth of Sisyphus* or of *Being and Nothingness* nor that all those who have read early Existentialist philosophy necessarily agree with its premises. But few would deny that the postwar atmosphere has been permeated with Existentialist concepts. . . ."[12] In a late modernist epoch, one that is now dominated by structuralism and the formistic metaphysics that travels with structuralism, it is inappropriate, however, to attach the condition such as Kennard does to the last statement: "But few would deny that the postwar atmosphere has been permeated with Existentialist concepts *since the notion of the absurd seems to define the contemporary situation so well.*"[13] If the "notion of the absurd"—that is, the indeterminacies of modernism in general and of existentialism in particular—has taught us anything it is this: that the world is what our constructive, conceptual metaphors make of it. The "world," for the modernist, is not a *datum*, but a human artifact, an object of his own creation.

One of the finer ironies of existentialist projections is the irony directed—as Kierkegaard would have had it more than a century ago—at the modality of existentialism itself. There is, nonetheless, a very important conclusion to be gathered from Kennard's *since* clause: many fine critics of modernist fiction have conceded "reality," the "world," the "cosmos," to existentialist models. Consequently, taking this triumph as my *donnée*, I wish to consider next the "crisis" within the existentialist metaphor as applied to modernist fiction of the middle period, a crisis that shows itself in a reversal of values—negative to positive—and the beginnings of a shift from the literal back toward the metaphorical aspects of the model, the paradigm. This dynamic of epochal growth, implicit in the evolution of a metaphor through its dialectical "life" and no doubt related to the principle of counterbalancing that Wolfgang Iser describes in *The Implied Reader*,[14] is exhibited in the work of two critics of widely divergent approaches: Ihab Hassan and Nathan A. Scott, Jr.

II Existentialism and Consciousness

> If the broad existential view of this study amounts to anything, it amounts to an admission that a critique of the novel must ultimately seek the elusive boundaries between art and action, imagination and fact, order and disorder, the boundaries, that is, at which one form of human awareness blends into another. A critique of fiction is a criticism of dreams that have taken form, yearnings and denials that have taken shape.
>
> Ihab Hassan
> *Radical Innocence* (1961)

> Nor can we forget the role that has been played in this development by the deep fears generated by the continual expansion of the universe being mapped out by modern science and modern cosmology. . . . Of course, even far more frightening than the universes of modern physics have been the perils of modern historical existence itself. . . .
>
> Nathan A. Scott, Jr.
> *The Broken Center* (1966)

In *Radical Innocence: The Contemporary American Novel* (1961) Ihab Hassan offers a comprehensive study of many of the writers of the 1940s and 1950s who have moved into what I have identified as a second phase of the modern. For Hassan, nearly two decades ago, the writers considered at substantial length included William Styron, Harvey Swados, and Norman Mailer; Frederick Buechner, Bernard Malamud, and Ralph Ellison; Herbert Gold, John Cheever, and J. P. Donleavy; Carson McCullers, Truman Capote, J. D. Salinger, and Saul Bellow. We would now drop many of these writers as of minor consequence, keeping perhaps only Styron, Mailer, Malamud, Ellison, and Bellow. But, no matter; Hassan's discussions of various works remain of utmost importance to my argument, for they insist that the most impressive feature of "contemporary"—I would say critical-modernist—fiction is its having become "existential." But he would not use the term in a restrictive historical way:

Our hypothesis is that the pattern of experience in contemporary fiction is largely existential. There are those, no doubt, who still believe Existentialism to be a foreign and new-fangled philosophy, irrelevant to the concerns of American letters. This is not a point we wish to dispute. . . . The term *existential*, however, carries broader connotations. It is less exclusive. . . . Serious writers, such as Ralph Ellison, Norman Mailer, William Styron, Paul Bowles, and perhaps Saul Bellow, have often placed the existential pattern of experience at the center of their work.[15]

In this essay, Hassan looks back to the early modernist authors and tries to suggest briefly their relationship to the contemporary: "The most compelling authors of thirty years ago—Faulkner, Hemingway, Dos Passos, Farrell—do not continue to sustain themselves in an ever-changing tracery of new forms. These men, like European writers of their time, dramatized the shocking difference between their own values and those which their society still upheld by a violent breakup of accepted literary forms. But the revolt of one generation may be the orthodoxy of the next" (p. 100). While Hassan's comment here about two later naturalists and two exemplars of modernism is meant to suggest that the "contemporary" novelists have transcended them, the real point, I would argue, is that they have critically framed the objectives of the earlier authors. My thesis is as easily supported as Hassan's by a comment he quotes from Ralph Ellison: "*Ours is a task which . . . was defined for us* to a large extent by that which the novels of the twenties failed to confront, and implicit in their triumphs and follies were our complexity and travail."[16] So when Hassan, taking his cue from Wright Morris's *The Territory Ahead,* says that "the contemporary novelist, despite the atomism, the discontinuities, of his world, no longer needs to fear the rawness of American experience; he no longer lacks the resources of technique" (p. 101), he would ignore the fact that the now-accepted vision of the world and the resources of technique available to novelists for conveying it have actually been bequests of the early exemplars of modernism. So, too, I would insist, are the varied ironic forms operating in the "contemporary" authors Hassan discusses.

The distinctive pattern Hassan associates with human experience in the modern world is assimilated to a philosophic conception that seeks to frame a universe of exploded space, time, and value. Experience in this world, Hassan insists, rests on five basic premises, and each premise relates to corresponding formal elements in "contemporary" fiction. Hassan's first premise is that "Chance and absurdity rule human actions" (p. 116), the second, that "There are no accepted norms of feeling or conduct to which the hero may appeal" (p. 116). The first is converted, in fiction, into patterns that recognize "disorder—gratuitous actions, demonic intrusions, obsessive motives," a form that "reflects the inward darkness of things," with fiction's traditional causality transformed into causelessness. The result of the second is a "pattern of fiction . . . contained and self-reflexive," subsistent upon parody, violence, "autonomous dream," "arbitrary and personal truth." These two conditions suggest the extent to which the old Newtonian world, with its causes and effects, and the former world of the novel-as-genre, dependent upon social or other external environments, have given way to relativity and subjectivity.

The contrast between the modes of the contemporary and the novel of realism and naturalism is further elucidated by the differences in the types of "heroes," explained in Hassan's third premise: "Rebel or victim, the hero is at odds with his environment. He is at odds with himself. His energy is the energy of opposition, and his aggressions are either directed against himself (the victim) or against the world (the rebel). In either case, he remains an alien to society, a misfit." Such a hero, Hassan recognizes, might have been consistent with a more pessimistic type of naturalism, one in which "time itself is destructive; it serves to eventuate only defeat" (p. 117). But there is a significant difference, the result of a merging of the "legacies of Dreiser and Hemingway," for "unlike the fiction of Naturalism," this fiction involves no external necessity. "Necessity is an inner compulsion, purposeless and self-destructive. It is spiteful of itself." This situation meshes with Hassan's fourth premise, that "human motives are forever mixed; irony and contradiction prevail," giving us in the fiction a form whose function is, first, "to develop distance, and, second, to create conflicting levels of meaning, a complex interplay of points of view" (pp. 117–18). This distance is an ironic distance that sets off the role of the hero in such fiction, delineated in Hassan's fifth point: "In a world dominated by error, even heroes do not possess the gift of complete knowledge. The hero acts or is acted upon, but his perception of the situation remains both limited and relative" (p. 118). All these points, taken together, regardless of their accuracy as a description of the world, result in a type of fiction that Hassan finally summarizes: "The pattern of fiction is therefore neither tragic nor comic. It shows the hero to be a child of ironies, a mediator of polar claims. The pattern diffuses insight and fractures the whole truth. It is a parody of man's quest for fulfillment. The form provides the hero with more freedom of action than tragedy strictly allows, and less freedom than comedy permits. Form becomes, as it were, an ironic mask, weeping and leering in one concerted grimace at the proud fallibility of man. The grimace itself is the measure of man's dignity" (p. 118).

"The contemporary hero demanded," says Hassan, concluding this essay, "a new language of experience, a different mold of expression. This mold we labeled, with some qualms, the existential pattern, and we perceived it to be a variant of an established ironic mode" (p. 123). The distinctive pattern of contemporary fiction is projected into three variable forms, each discussed at chapter length in three subsequent essays. One is what he calls a "closed" mode of extreme irony, wherein the hero is victim or scapegoat; it is illustrated in its plasticity through discussions of three novels: Styron's *Lie Down in Darkness* (1951), Swados's *Out Went the Candle* (1955), and Mailer's *The Naked and the Dead* (1948). A second is a "suspended" form, wavering between comedy and tragedy and edging toward romance; it is represented by Buechner's *A Long Day's Dying* (1949), Malamud's *The Assistant* (1957), and Ellison's *Invisible Man* (1952). A third and final form is "open," one in which a comic, alazonic hero permits man at least the illusion of escape; Hassan illustrates its variability in discussions of Gold's *The Optimist* (1959), Cheever's *The Wapshot Chronicle* (1957), and Donleavy's *The Ginger Man* (1958). None of Hassan's three forms of fiction's contemporary pattern, not even the open one, suggests that the hero or fictive world ever really transcends "the atomism, the discontinuities" of an exploding, ironic universe as formally presented in early modernist paradigms.

But, what is more important to my purpose, they do suggest that the melding of fiction with a correlative philosophic structure has assured the literary triumph of the modern. The chaos, the absurdity, the discontinuity of fiction's modes, by having become accepted by the "intelligentsia" as true reflections of the world beyond fiction, have once again allowed the novel—or its constituent modes—to internalize and capitalize upon a *mythos* of life that, like romantic idealism, might easily have destroyed the genre itself. Even more germane to my purpose is Hassan's reiterated recognition that the *mythos*—whether applied to "life" or to fiction—is embraced by a conception of irony such as is explained in *Anatomy of Criticism*. It is not merely that the specific forms of the novels of the contemporary are recognized as manifestations of irony; it is also—and more significant—that the ironic forms belong as well to an ironic historical epoch, the epochal force of these paradigmatic fictions coming as results of the convergence of the synchronic ironic form with the diachronic historical ironic mode. Hassan writes:

> The ironic hero emerges as the father of existential man; the ironic mode crystallizes the ambiguities we have already discovered in the existential pattern. For irony isolates from the tragic situation the element of arbitrariness, the sense of isolation, the demonic vision; from comedy, it takes the unlawful or quixotic motive of the *picaro*, say, the savagery which is the other face of play, as in the saturnalia, and the grotesque scapegoat rituals of comic expiation; and from romance it adopts the quest motif, turning it into a study of self-deception, and the dream of wish-fulfillment, transforming it into nightmare. Indeed, Frye's penetrating study shows irony to be the form to which all other forms tend when disintegration overtakes them [p. 121].

In short, what Hassan allows us to conclude is that the fiction of modernism belongs to the historical epoch of irony, that the mode of irony is the frame for a world conceived as chaos, that an aesthetic of irony can account for the dispersion of the constituent modes of the novel-as-genre, and that the *mythos* of irony embraces the most appropriate metaphysics for an exploding universe.

The triumphant domination of literature by the mode of thought called "existential" during the period in which modernism became "critical" is easy to demonstrate from another direction. One has only to turn to those literary critics whose approaches are philosophical, theological, and, more crucially, Christian. It would appear, for instance, that Christian theology would have the most to lose in conceding the philosophical turf to existentialist thought, but we know that the century's most influential Christian theologians—Tillich, Barth, Teilhard, Niebuhr, Bultmann—broadly considered, have been "existential." But the Christian theology is important for another reason: it has set in relief the more affirmative elements of the philosophy that Sartre insisted were there from the beginning, even though almost the only aspect widely acknowledged was the first premise, the nihilism of the absurd universe. If the paradigms of modernism are to leave the dead center of nihilism, then, and to begin to move back toward the affirmations of myth—as Frye explains in *Anatomy*—some new authoritative vision must be enunciated. Nathan A. Scott, Jr., has propounded both the triumph of existentialism and the affirmations possible within its literary and philosophical idioms.

One of Scott's more recent books, *Three American Moralists: Mailer, Bellow, Trilling,* is indicative of existentialism's dominance in literature not only in his simply assuming that an existential view is congruent with the reality literature and theology must face, but also in the argument for a more affirmative cast to that view. The concluding essay in Scott's book is very revealing in both respects, for in it Scott proves considerably more hostile to Lionel Trilling than to either Saul Bellow or Norman Mailer. Scott is not bothered by Trilling's secularity nor by his Judaic background, but by something else in his response to literature and reality. That something is a nineteenth-century, even enlightenment, humanism that has resisted vitalization by the existential eschatologies of modernism's emerging metaphysics.

Scott begins a serious, systematic look at Trilling's work—which includes one novel (*The Middle of the Journey,* 1947)—by asserting that the essays "now constitute one of the great and beautiful achievements of the American literary intelligence in our time."[17] The major contribution of Trilling's work, Scott says, lies in its bringing "into focus the nub of that central perplexity which is felt by the people whose placement in history has permitted them to be deeply affected by the legacy of Rousseau and Marx and Freud. And thus he makes a kind of *exemplum* which, in some small degree perhaps, we fail to contemplate at our peril" (p. 154). But Trilling falls short, in Scott's estimation, because "on no occasion . . . has he consented to confront any of the great religious geniuses of the tradition [of Western humanism]: for all his wide-ranging culture, Augustine and Pascal, Kierkegaard and Barth, Tillich and Niebuhr are quite as if they had never been: so confirmed is he in the prejudices of the Enlightenment that not even, as a Jew, does he pay attention, say, to a Moses Hess or a Franz Rosenzweig, to a Martin Buber or an Abraham Heschel" (p. 210).

This, Scott insists, is the tradition to which Trilling really addresses his work, but that work, unlike the predominantly existential thought of those theologians who provide the basis for the "central modern traditions of secular thought," provides no positive alternatives to the essentially negative vision Trilling conveys, or, I would say, that Hassan also conveys. Scott calls Trilling's method one of "aposiopesis" because it creates a gap it does not attempt effectively to fill: "And the gingerliness with which he had skirted this final aspect of his enterprise makes for the special sort of disappointment which his work calls forth" (p. 211). Thus, the essential reason for Scott's disappointment lies in Trilling's departure from the existentialist "orthodoxy" of the "modern" (a word that appears in nine of Scott's book titles). Scott works the same territory Trilling had, and probably no one in contemporary letters now is more familiar with the literature, the criticism, the philosophy, and the theology than Scott. And it is Scott—rather than Trilling and his enlightened humanism—who speaks the new orthodox word—an existentialism turned to transcendent account, and, with it, a fiction turned to a more traditionally mythic account.

Important in another way, then, are Scott's discussions of the two novelists, Bellow and Mailer, who, with Trilling, "may be said— without reference to the momentary fluctuations of the cultural stock market—to be at the absolute center of what is most deeply animating in American literature of the present and recent past" (p. 11). They are central because they express complex visions that explain a radical apocalypticism—a sense of the exploding world— and a corresponding need to find what Tillich calls "the courage to be." Scott's sympathy lies with Bellow and Mailer, with the existential accommodation, the capitalization upon modernism's demonic myth. "Indeed," writes Scott, "the bewitching glamor of Apocalypse today suggests that recovering the courage-to-be may present the most fundamental of all the various hard imperatives confronting the spirituality of our period" (p. 9). Scott is drawn to these two "exemplary" writers because, "though they propose different forms of courage as normative for the human venture, neither permits his vision of the extremest boundaries of the world to overrule his sense of man's being unable to get anywhere except by way of a path that leads *through* the concrete materialities of his condition" (pp. 10– 11). It is out of this sense of these writers' attempts to come to grips with historical contingency that Scott identifies them as "moralists," and the term intimates just how socially oriented existential presuppositions have now become. For Scott, each of these writers suggests, each through a different idiom, a "large confidence . . . in the strength of the human thing [that] gives them the status of public moralists in a period when . . . so many harbor the gravest doubts about the capacity of man to survive the stringencies of historical time" (p. 11).

Mailer and Bellow illustrate a critical phase of modernism in the eschatological "idioms" they speak. Their major fictions represent specific alternatives modernists have chosen for facing the exploding universe, the existential void. One alternative, dramatized in the forms of such early-modernist works as *Ulysses, The Waste Land, The Sound and the Fury,* and *Four Quartets* (which also has begun to articulate it as a theme), is, simply, language. This alternative is the one Scott sees emphasized in Mailer.[18] Considering Mailer as *our* "Whitman" (p. 23) because he has taken on the role as "spokesman for the American conscience" (p. 97), Scott emphasizes the transcendent elements of Mailer's philosophy. He admits that Mailer's metaphors of "psychopathy and orgy and violence and death . . . were shockingly nihilistic" (p. 50), but prefers to examine the ways in which Mailer tried to show that "the psychic outlaw, the 'existential hero'" (p. 50) could reveal human potentialities "not by fleeing from the abyss but by confronting it" (p. 50). Rojack, of *An American Dream,* is Scott's exemplary hero in Mailer's myth, because he looks into the abyss and finds a means of grappling with its demons, a means particularly characteristic of modernism and Mailer himself: "in the wonderfully uninhibited vivaciousness of the language of Rojack's narrative . . . the moral drama of the novel lies. It is not . . . his deeds—which are a tall story he playfully fabricates—but his rhetoric that establishes Rojack as a psychic outlaw, that proves him indeed to have moved out into a world beyond that of the *New York Times*" (pp. 68–69). For Rojack, as for Mailer, language becomes the one weapon capable of mastering a demonic world, and, of Mailer, Scott can say: "Thus it is that this unmanageable chameleon would present, through the agency of the word, a redeeming model of freedom. And, as impresario of a language appropriate to freemen, his never-ending surprise at the marvelous feats of which he proves himself capable so fills him with delight that his voice is witty and exultant, even when the facts it is reporting are dark and ominous" (p. 83).

Mailer's characters may stretch the resources of language in order to transcend their worlds, but in Bellow the main concern is to make language simply meet the world in some kind of philosophic equation. In Bellow there is more of the speculative use of language and less of the instrumental, and his characters are engaged more frequently in lives we ourselves might lead. Bellow is thus a more conventional novelist, who, though "modern," has not gone to any extreme from the novel-as-genre. As Scott says, "It deserves to be stressed that the inquiry into the meaning of human existence carried forward by Mr. Bellow's protagonists is not, experientially, a bootless thing of abstract dialectic. It is, instead, a search into which they are plunged by the pressure of concrete circumstance, by the wreckage of hope and the bitter taste in their own lives of inauthenticity" (p. 108). The paradigmatic hero in Bellow's work is Herzog. Herzog may be, as Scott points out, a failure in most of the normal dimensions of his life—as scholar, lover, husband, father—but he does not plan to get out of history (p. 132); Herzog—himself a professional historian—recognizes the moral imperative Scott insists these writers follow in their different ways: "Our job . . . is not to get outside of life but to find within the human situation itself a redemptive center and a healing grace" (p. 132). And Herzog—perhaps speaking for Bellow—finds that redemptive center in history itself.

I have developed my discussion of the middle, critical stage of the modern American novel by drawing upon Hassan and Scott because I would take as a given the triumph, in American literature, of an existential conception of human life. One can turn to *Radical Innocence* or to any number of Scott's works—*Rehearsals of Discomposure* (1952), *The Broken Center* (1966), *Craters of the Spirit* (1968), and *Negative Capability* (1969)—for arguments providing further support for my assumption. My own argument is concerned primarily with what Scott calls the "idioms" by which modernist novelists have confronted "discomposure," "broken centers," "craters of the spirit"—the crisis of exploding ethical, religious, and metaphysical worlds. The idioms are those means by which writers are enabled to replace "redemptive centers" of validation, sanctification, or "healing grace" once the old worlds have been dispersed. Christianity, romanticism, and even Newtonian mechanics provided an extrinsic "authority" by positing for man's experience some central, unmoved or unmoving idea, but modernism's relativity, at least in the beginning, made such a center almost unimaginable. But as Scott insists, new centers will always identify themselves, though what these new centers must become to man in the existential void is vividly imaged by Scott, in a comment upon Bellow's *Mr. Sammler's Planet.* They are "what men have together around the campfire that staves off the dark wilderness beyond" (p. 146). What *men have together*, as Vico, Marx, Nietzsche, Joyce, Faulkner, and others have shown, is precisely what of necessity have become the new centers: language, history, consciousness, and art, each apotheosized in some way by almost every important modernist writer.

In American fiction, the modernist revolution is climaxed by and given paradigmatic forms in the work of Faulkner. The entire revolution can be localized in the texts that have since become most exemplary: *The Sound and the Fury, As I Lay Dying, Absalom, Absalom!*, and *Go Down, Moses.* These novels, together, manifested early all the major "idioms," accommodations, or new centers of authority for the American modernist, but each was also primarily an objective demonstration through form of what would become conscious themes in the middle stage of the modern American novel, or what will become parodied or abstracted—whose "as" will be transformed into a fabulous "as if"—by the later, sophisticated modernists. Although other alternatives are available in these texts, I want to discuss here only one of the modernist centers of authority—consciousness—and its presentation in one "contemporary," critical-modernist author (Joseph Heller) as his work— mainly *Catch-22*—is contrasted to works of a naive modernist (William Faulkner).

In Heller's *Catch-22* and *Something Happened*, certain features related to the authority of consciousness and seen clearly in Faulkner begin to be modified, not because Heller denies Faulkner's premises, but because he has become more fully aware of them. In *The Sound and the Fury, As I Lay Dying,* and *Absalom, Absalom!* Faulkner had created forms that authenticate the power of consciousness, but neither the forms nor Faulkner himself in extrinsic comments yet reveal the positive, unifying, creative potential of the human psyche. And for decades the critics of Faulkner, not unreasonably, had supported the negative, disjunctive, deconstructive aspect of Faulkner's psychological forms. Instead of what Frye calls "the constructive power of the mind, where reality is brought into being by experience,"[19] in Faulkner, for example, it has been the dispersive aspect of indeterminacy, in the novels we consider most "Faulknerian," that seems to operate almost from the opening pages.[20] The work of the reader, consequently, is made especially difficult, to the point that unprepared readers of the first section of *The Sound and the Fury,* for example, may simply quit.

But for those who persevere with naive texts in the process of creating new conventions, positive results can develop. As Wolfgang Iser argues, readers first confronted with almost intolerable levels of indeterminacy of form could raise the question "as to what insights into the workings of the human mind literature can open up" and, at the same time, "conceive the relation between text and reader as the starting point for a more thoroughgoing investigation of the connection between literature and consciousness."[21] In fact, the direction of Faulkner criticism after about 1939—the year of publication of George Marion O'Donnell's essay on Faulkner's mythology—has gone toward just such explanations as Iser proposes. Now we indeed see Faulkner as an advocate of the "constructive power," the ability of the mind to bring "reality . . . into being by experience," but our view has been conditioned by the effects of critique by critics and novelists alike, who have recognized the ontological and epistemological loci of Faulkner's reality in subjects rather than objects, especially recognizing that a major locus lies in themselves.

As Joseph Heller belongs to the critical phase of the modern, his novels *Catch-22* and *Something Happened* display the effects of modernist critiques of Faulknerian presuppositions and practices. Heller's novels identify, as in Faulkner, the creative and ordering potency of consciousness, but Heller begins to modify naive, objectivist emphases. In the phenomenon of *déjà vu* in either novel, Heller accounts for both a content—the ontological status of *Catch-22* and *Something Happened* must be regarded as the human consciousness—and an epistemological technique. But—especially in *Catch-22*—he leaves open the answers to questions concerning where the phenomenon is to be assigned most prominently. It seems sometimes to operate traditionally, within the mind of an invisible narrator, but at other times it seems inside created characters, and, eventually, perforce, in the mind of a reader, in much the same well-known way that Joycean techniques of epiphany and narrative disjunction work. Heller's texts are quite insistent, in any case, upon their need for the reader's response, proclaiming, as Robbe-Grillet says of France's "new novels," the writer's "absolute need of the reader's cooperation, an active, conscious, *creative* assistance."[22] In *Catch-22*, for example, readers frequently find themselves in the psychological quandary of Heller's protagonist, Yossarian, in his journey through Rome, or in the hospital talking to the chaplain, or of the chaplain himself, who, "for a few precarious seconds, . . . tingled with a weird occult sensation of having experienced the same situation before in some prior time or existence. He endeavored to trap and nourish the impression in order to predict, and perhaps even control, what incident would occur next, but the afflatus melted away unproductively, as he had known beforehand it would. *Déjà vu.*"[23]

Heller's manipulation of *déjà vu* as technique and content is an affirmative modification of the presuppositions of the modernist, presuppositions that have been returned to us by our own critical sense of historical *déjà vu*. We have already seen—and now have been enabled to assimilate—the conventions originated by naive modernists such as Faulkner, whose early novels, particularly, rely upon language and events from previous experiences returning to us again and again as they return to his characters. Similarly, just about everything in *Catch-22* is introduced as if one had seen it before, so one suitably conditioned tries to trap and nourish impressions as they occur: the images, for example, of the dead man in Yossarian's tent, of Snowden dying in back, the naked man sitting in the tree, of the soldier in white, of Clevinger's plane disappearing into a cloud, of Orr working on the tiny valve or paddling a big yellow life raft with a small blue oar. Like the chaplain's, a reader's afflatuses may melt away, too, but they leave behind questions and, of course, the images themselves. Because it raises questions that must be answered (given Iser's ideal of a persevering reader), Heller's essentially lyrical method forces the recurring images to accumulate meanings until their full significance, their essence, is finally perceived. Hence, as Northrop Frye comments about the phenomenon Kierkegaard calls "repetition," *déjà vu* in Heller "means, not the simple repeating of an experience, but the recreating of it which redeems or awakens it to life."[24]

It is not so much that Joseph Heller is simply more considerate of his readers than is Faulkner, but only that he is critical of the creative power of mind as it works upon experience through archetypal or mythic modules such as operate, apparently, at the core of consciousness. Critical awareness of archetypal form, heightened as well as informed by modern psychology, anthropology, linguistics, and the literary exemplars of the modern, has enabled writers and readers to synthesize frames around different narrative formulae. It is this critical perspective that Faulkner, at least in the early exemplary works, *The Sound and the Fury*, *As I Lay Dying*, and *Absalom, Absalom!*, fails to provide, probably was unable to provide before he had himself reached the critical-modernist plateau exhibited in *A Fable* (1954) and *The Reivers* (1962). Because early critics often viewed Faulkner's first great novels as failures, in a large sense our criticism of naive-modernist paradigms has in fact redeemed them from failure. Now we know how to read a "Faulknerian" novel. *Absalom, Absalom!* (1936), for instance, presents Thomas Sutpen's life through multiple narrative frames. Our modernist critique suggests that the frames created by different subjects or consciousnesses, each embodying radically different literary modes, are each congruent with entirely different archetypal patterns. These formal modules, in addition, if aligned critically in a particular order, can be shown to display the purported development of historical modes in literature, described in Frye's *Anatomy of Criticism* as the gradual shifting of literature's "center of gravity" downward from romance, to high mimesis, low mimesis, and on to irony, a sequence represented easily in the narratives, respectively, of Rosa Coldfield, Father, Sutpen, and Shreve. But Faulkner's novel's form leaves these distinct modules unsynthesized, so that what a reader is left with is a burning mansion danced about by an idiot, with, thus, an exploded, relativistic world of possible meanings, but no final determinate meaning, not even one to be identified with consciousness itself. The pluralism here in Faulkner seems to insinuate itself as an insurmountable reality, so that only lately have we been led to ask of *Absalom, Absalom!* what more might be done with the different modalities or with consciousness itself.

Heller, in contrast to Faulkner, has now identified a stable base in the archetypes of consciousness. Both manifest in and identified by literary constructs, these archetypes permit Heller (and others) now to project a more determinate fictional form than a naive existentialism would permit. The archetypal pattern of romance, which becomes the projected frame for Heller, offers his novel a construct within which he—projecting through the consciousnesses of his characters—can determine form and meanings. Discrete, disjunctive details of imagery and events begin to draw together around the archetypes at the core of consciousness—author's, character's, and reader's. So that despite the large gaps locally in Heller's novel, the overall form has revealed itself as rather more insistently determined than one might otherwise expect. This is a point made well by David Richter, in an analysis of completeness and closure in this and other novels. "It is not clear," Richter says, "just what sort of ending would have satisfied Heller's captious critics," but for him no possible ending could be more effective for the novel as it was constructed than the one Heller provided.[25] And if the critics are captious because the novel's determined ending is not bleakly existential enough, the critics need only recognize that Heller has benefited from the emergent critique of naive existentialism, having begun, as Richter suggests, to move beyond Sartre and Camus to a vantage point from which "the absurd" is "less a metaphysical commitment than a literary technique."[26]

III Heller's *Catch-22*

> *Catch-22* is not to my mind a far-out novel; it is not to my
> mind a formless novel. If anything, it was constructed almost
> meticulously, and with a meticulous concern to give the ap-
> pearance of a formless novel. Now that's much different, in
> much the same way as with Joyce's *Ulysses*, which is possi-
> bly one of the most confusing novels when you first approach
> it, and yet there's a structure and tension in virtually every
> word.
>
> Joseph Heller
> "An Impolite Interview with Joseph Heller" (1962)

Some of the dimensions of the second phase of modernism are well illustrated by Joseph Heller's *Catch-22*, a work that,
curiously, is both more "experimental" and less ironic in its hero's
achieved end than the more recent second novel, *Something Happened* (1974). Overlooked in the enthusiastic furor over *Catch-22* is
Heller's reuse of a method of modern lyrical fiction. The method, to
use Heller's own label, is *déjà vu*—a term that suggests something
of the delusive experience, hallucinatory quality, and disjunctive
expression of reality in *Catch-22*. The term, familiar in medicine
and to philosophers such as Bergson, appears several times in the
novel. In chapter XXV, for example, the chaplain asks Yossarian,
"Have you ever . . . been in a situation which you felt you had been
in before, even though you knew you were experiencing it for the
first time?"[27] Yossarian nods yes, but when asked if he has that
feeling now, "Yossarian shook his head and explained that *déjà vu*
was just a momentary infinitesimal lag in the operation of two
coactive sensory nerve centers that commonly functioned simultaneously." Yossarian, not then ready to understand the full significance of that "lag," defines it in purely physiological terms, but
to the chaplain it has enormous philosophical significance, for it is
concerned both with physical perception and metaphysical understanding, with what the chaplain feels is "the effort to rip away at
last the voluminous black folds shrouding the eternal mysteries of

existence." And the "lag" has yet another significance for the reader, for in the unfolding of the story it creates a discontinuity between a character, a symbol, a narrative event, and its meaning. Hence, like the character called "The Soldier who saw Everything Twice" (XVIII), whose plight Yossarian emulates, one "sees" twice, at least, everything that has importance, but for a reader, as for the chaplain and, eventually, for Yossarian, the "lag" is between the *seeing* and the *understanding*. A reader is thus also like the character, caught in one of Yossarian's circular arguments, who says in desperation, "Yes, now I see. But I still don't think I understand" (VII).

A method that seems to lead only to needless repetition and redundancy, *déjà vu* is actually neither simply repetitive nor redundant but is rather complexly incremental and progressive, for the examples of *déjà vu* of character, thematic motifs, and events that Heller offers move inevitably toward completion and resolution. Consider the way the method, somewhat in the manner of Proust's or Joyce's use of what Joseph Frank calls "spatial form," affects the meaning of characters of whom one sees a sequence of "pictures" or images spaced over a long period of time. Even on a relatively low level of thematic seriousness, characters such as Chief White Halfoat and Captain Flume generally expand in significance. In chapter V, for example, one learns of Halfoat's threats to murder Captain Flume in his sleep and of his prophecy that he himself will die of pneumonia; in the next chapter, one learns of Flume's great fear of Halfoat and his hermit-like retreat into the woods to live, where, in chapter XII, he is discovered to be living, unkempt and in ill health; in chapter XXV, one learns of the chaplain's encounter with Flume, now the "mad hermit," in the woods, and his taking Flume's words, that he will return before winter, as the words of a prophet; then, finally, in chapter XXXII, one finds that Halfoat "felt cold and was already making plans to move up into the hospital to die of pneumonia. Instinct told Chief White Halfoat it was almost time. His chest ached and he coughed chronically. Whiskey no longer warmed him. Most damning of all, Captain Flume had moved back into his trailer. Here was an omen of unmistakable meaning." All this seems comically absurd—and it is—but at the end of the sequence one has the overwhelming sensation that Halfoat *will* die, for behind the comic absurdity of these two characters is the discovery of a strange world of tragic consequences. No better illustration of this discovery may be found than in the recurring references to Hungry Joe, to his self-defeating lusts for women and for making photographs of nudes, his chronic nightmares (III), his dreams of a cat sleeping on his face (VI), or his comic fight with Huple's cat, after which "he went to bed victorious and dreamed again that Huple's cat was sleeping on his face, suffocating him" (XII). Such idiosyncrasy seems humorous enough until one learns in chapter XLI that Hungry Joe "died in his sleep while having a dream. They found a cat on his face." As a consequence of the method of *déjà vu*, then, many characters like these, including Major Major, Dunbar, Doc Daneeka, and Major —— de Coverly, who look at first only like insignificant figures of comic idiosyncrasy, become at last meaningful figures of ironic obsession or compulsion.

A thematically more important aspect of Heller's technique may be seen in the treatment of characters like the soldier in white, the dead man in Yossarian's tent, and Kraft, all of whom are handled in a rhythmical way parallel to E. M. Forster's use of "expanding symbols" (E. K. Brown's term). One hears very early (I) about the soldier in white, but he is not fully depicted until many chapters later: "The soldier in white was constructed entirely of gauze, plaster and a thermometer, and the thermometer was merely an adornment left balanced in the empty dark hole in the bandages over his mouth early each morning and late each afternoon by Nurse Cramer and Nurse Duckett right up to the afternoon Nurse Cramer read the thermometer and discovered he was dead" (XVII). The dead man in Yossarian's tent is mentioned first in chapter II, early in Chapter III and late in the same chapter, and again late in chapter IX, but it is only in chapter X that one learns his name is Mudd, and in chapter XXIV that he was actually killed in a flight over the bridge at Orvieto, and that it is not he but his gear that Yossarian refers to as the dead man in his tent. Kraft, on the other hand, is associated with the run over the bridge at Ferrara during which Yossarian, flying lead bombardier, took his squadron of six planes over the target not once, but twice, destroying the bridge and winning a medal and promotion, but losing Kraft and his crew.

Kraft, the dead man in Yossarian's tent, and the soldier in white, like the more concrete characters of Halfoat, Flume, and Hungry Joe, take on added meanings as mention of them recurs, but the meanings (with apologies to Cassirer) are more symbolic than actual, for they come to represent forms of death and responsibility—two of the most important subjects in *Catch-22*. Moreover, a recognition of the meaning of these symbolic characters contributes to the development of Yossarian, the novel's central character and consciousness. Kraft, for example, makes Yossarian aware of death, violent death, just as the dead man in his tent is a constant reminder of its presence, but Kraft also makes Yossarian aware of his moral responsibility in the war. Thus, although Kraft is introduced quite early (VI), the most meaningful details of his death do not appear until chapter XIII, where it is revealed that Yossarian "killed Kraft and his crew," but was uncertain how he was supposed to feel about him and the others, "for they had all died in the distance of a mute and secluded agony at a moment when he was up to his own ass in the same vile, excruciating dilemma of duty and damnation." The medal and the promotion given to Yossarian are emblematic of the official attitude toward Kraft's death, but Yossarian himself begins to feel both a responsibility and a guilt that prepare him for his criticism of Milo Minderbinder, who denies *any* responsibility for his role in the death of the man in the tent, this despite his having masterminded the bombing run over the bridge at Orvieto. Hence, for Yossarian, Mudd becomes a tangible symbol for Milo's generalized irresponsibility. The soldier in white, on the other hand, epitomizes for Yossarian the "neater," more delicate and tasteful death he can expect in the hospital, one for which even the responsibility is difficult to determine, though "now that Yossarian looked back, it seemed that Nurse Cramer, rather than the talkative Texan, had murdered the soldier in white; if she had not read the thermometer and reported what she had found, the soldier in white might still be lying there alive" (XVII). Although he, along with Kraft and Mudd, represents a form of the responsibility that must accompany any potential "decision to terminate," the "excruciating dilemma of duty and damnation" that faces every soldier, perhaps every man, the soldier in white nonetheless represents a death that seems less personal, less threatening than those more violent forms, until, rhythmically, he reappears for the last time (in chapter XXXIV) and terrifies the hospital's inmates even more than death outside. For besides being unsure that the man in the bandages even exists, they cannot be certain that his death is *not* the responsibility of some official act, like Nurse Cramer's, some official "decision to terminate," a "disappearance" like Dunbar's and Major Major's and Major ——— de Coverly's, or a bureaucratic "death" like that of Doc Daneeka, who is physically alive but technically dead because he was supposed to be on a plane that crashed, killing all the crew. Ultimately, therefore, this kind of death, for which even the living such as Cathcart, Korn, Black, Dreedle, Peckem, and Scheisskopf are discovered to be representatives, is even more to be feared than death by violence.

Like the characters, both real and symbolic, who gradually gain in significance, a thematic concept such as "Catch-22" also changes in meaning as it recurs. Presented in the first chapter as if one had seen it before ("Catch-22 required that each censored letter bear the censoring officer's name"), it is somewhat more fully defined in chapter V, where Doc Daneeka explains to Yossarian why he cannot ground men like Orr, who is thought to be cracking up: "There was only one catch and that was Catch-22, which specified that a concern for one's own safety in the face of dangers that were real and immediate was the process of a rational mind. Orr was crazy and could be grounded. All he had to do was ask; and as soon as he did, he would no longer be crazy and would have to fly more missions. Orr would be crazy to fly more missions and sane if he didn't, but if he was sane he had to fly them. If he flew them he was crazy and didn't have to; but if he didn't want to he was sane and had to." The absurd law that, according to Northrop Frye, must often be overcome in a comic plot, Catch-22 is itself as delusive, as hallucinatory, as *déjà vu,* for while at one moment Yossarian can see "it clearly in all its spinning reasonableness," its "elliptical precision," "its perfect pairs of parts" that are "graceful and shocking, like good modern art," at other times Yossarian "wasn't quite sure that he saw it all, just the way he was never quite sure about good modern art."

There are other, infrequent references to Catch-22 and its manifold clauses. The most important view of Catch-22 comes near the end of the novel, however, when Yossarian, making his way through the nightmare world of "The Eternal City" (XXXIX) in search of Nately's whore's kid sister, encounters an old woman who tells him that "all the poor young girls" with whom they had once cavorted are gone—driven into the streets by American M.P.s and Italian *carabinieri:*

"What right did they have?"
"Catch-22."
"*What?*" Yossarian froze in his tracks with fear and alarm and felt his whole body begin to tingle. "*What* did you say?"
"Catch-22," the old woman repeated, rocking her head up and down.

"Catch-22. Catch-22 says they have a right to do anything we can't stop them from doing."

Yossarian questions the old woman further but learns only that Nately's whore and the kid sister are also gone, "chased away with the rest." Yossarian, however, reaches a significant conclusion about the absurd law: "Catch-22 did not exist, he was positive of that, but it made no difference. What did matter was that everyone thought it existed, and that was much worse, for there was no object or text to ridicule or refute, to accuse, criticize, attack, amend, hate, revile, spit at, rip to shreds, trample upon or burn up." As a consequence of his understanding, Yossarian has begun to prepare himself for the final confrontation with the "law." In the chapter (XL) entitled "Catch-22," Yossarian is offered a "little deal" by Colonel Cathcart and Colonel Korn if he will desist from his one-man rebellion against flying more missions. The catch this time, Korn tells him, is that Yossarian has to like them: "Like us. Join us. Be our pal. Say nice things about us here and back in the States. Become one of the boys." If he will like them, he can be sent home, after another promotion and medal, to make speeches "for morale and public-relations purposes." But Yossarian, finally realizing that the "catch" means a moral if not a physical death, rejects the "little deal," though sorely tempted, and makes his only viable choice among flying more missions, a court-martial, and desertion: he makes a decisive leap beyond the realm of the circular—and encircling— principle and heads for Sweden to join his friend Orr.

It is the very close relationship between the kind of story being told and the method of *déjà vu* that actually justifies the method in *Catch-22*. John Wain, the English novelist-critic, has said that Heller's method is relevant because things are held back until readers are ready for them and because it fits the facts of a flyer's life: "To these bomber-pilots, life does not flow in a regular, unfolding ribbon, experience falling on from experience, as it does in even the most tumultuous life in peace-time."[28] However, a better explanation for the disjunction of narrative, the seeming chaos, lies neither in its fidelity to the external facts of a flyer's life nor to the needs of a reader. Rather, it is the protagonist's moral life, his inner life, his psychological needs that account for the novel's delaying tactics. The protagonist of *Catch-22* is John Yossarian, a bombardier in the 258th Bomber Squadron, and the narrative center of the novel is

Yossarian's painful recognition of his own mortality and personal involvement, his acceptance of individual guilt and a need for a new set of values. He takes a long time to discover these things, for with himself he plays "censor games" like those he plays with the letters of the enlisted men while he is in the hospital and engages in what one of his doctors calls the "business of illusion." It is, therefore, Heller's identification with Yossarian's mind, his ego-consciousness, that explains and realizes the method. Because the ego is caught, as it were, between the superego, or society, on one side, and the id, the individual's repressed desires, needs, or memories, on the other, Heller's novel can be felt to move in three directions: outward toward the social expressions of authority found in the satire of figures like Dreedle, Cathcart, Korn, and Black; still outward, but toward the symbolic expression of universal archetypes; and inward, or downward, toward the structure of the personal unconscious and the meaning of repressed individual experience. In Yossarian's narrative, the two figures who centralize these varied movements are Milo Minderbinder and a "strangely familiar kid" named Snowden.

One critic has said that "Heller could have used Milo Minderbinder, the soldier businessman who profits so heavily from the non-sense of the war, to crystallize a direction and purpose for the book," but argues that Milo is "far too outlandish a character, far too preposterous and overdrawn to contribute to any sort of social criticism."[29] Viewed outside the context of the novel as it progresses, such criticism might be valid. But as one reads about Milo in the course of the novel itself, one must recognize that he does crystallize at least one of the directions and purposes of the book. Through Heller's technique, the delayed revelation, the incremental repetition, of *déjà vu,* one is led, even tricked, into accepting the reality of Milo and of exploits that show both the possibilities for and the failure of an important aspect of American culture. It is his recognition of what Milo stands for that forces Yossarian to reject untrammeled private enterprise, a utilitarian business ethic, and the entire moral superstructure of American capitalism itself.

One first hears of Milo, the pilot/mess officer, at the end of chapter II, where Yossarian learns that he is away "in Smyrna for the fig harvest," but forty pages pass before one learns *why* Milo has gone there for the fig harvest: he has used Yossarian's letter from Doc Daneeka that orders the mess officer to give Yossarian all the dried fruit and fruit juices he wants. Seeing the letter a splendid way to get extra goods for reselling, Milo thus uses Yossarian to begin his fantastic career. There are many hints about the stages of that career, hints about his buying up the entire Egyptian cotton crop and his bombing the squadron, but the full details of even the early stages are not given until midway through the novel, in a chapter describing Yossarian's and Orr's harried journey with Milo through his kingdoms. To their astonishment, they discover that Milo has parlayed Yossarian's letter into a vast empire called M & M Enterprises, of which "everyone has a share." Milo has become Mayor of Palermo and most of the other towns in Sicily, which he has made the world's third largest exporter of Scotch, become Major Sir Milo Minderbinder in Malta, Vice-Shah in Oran, the Caliph of Baghdad, the Imam of Damascus, and the Sheik of Araby: "Milo was the corn god, the rain god and the rice god in backward regions where such crude gods were still worshipped by ignorant and superstitious people. . . . Everywhere they touched he was acclaimed with honor . . ." (XXII).

But like a tragic hero, Milo reaches too far, and on the return journey through Cairo, he "cornered the market on cotton that no one else in the world wanted and brought himself promptly to the brink of ruin" (XXII). In order to extricate himself from the cotton crisis, Milo, who now has his own airforce of planes plying the world for goods for the mess halls of the American armies in Europe, contracts with the Americans to bomb the German-held bridge at Orvieto and with the Germans to defend the bridge with antiaircraft fire against his own attack—both on a cost-plus-six percent agreement and, from the Germans, a thousand-dollar bonus for each American plane shot down. And, sharp trader that he is, Milo manages to get both governments to do the jobs contracted for—after all, they did have the men and materials on hand. So "in the end Milo realized a fantastic profit from both halves of his project for doing nothing more than signing his name twice" (XXIV). Heartened by this coup and still pressed by the Egyptian cotton, Milo contracts next with the Germans to bomb the American squadron, for which he was still mess officer. But this time he went too far, and there was an intensive investigation: "Not one voice was raised in his defense. Decent people everywhere were affronted, and Milo was all washed up until he opened his books to the public and disclosed the tremendous profit he had made. He could reimburse the government for all the people and property he had destroyed and still have enough money left over to continue buying Egyptian cotton" (XXIV). With that kind of profit on the books and the fact that everybody has a share of M & M Enterprises, of course Milo is exonerated completely.

Milo is exonerated, that is, by everyone except Yossarian. And it is the scene in which Yossarian rejects Milo that becomes the center of gravity of the novel, for in that scene occur the keys to Heller's method, the pivotal point in Yossarian's development, and the images of the death and birth that give the narrative its shape and significance. The scene is presented from two separate points of view, Yossarian's and the chaplain's, the one giving the personal meaning of the encounter and the other suggesting its archetypal significance. When Heller focuses on Yossarian, who is sitting peacefully and nakedly in a tree, one sees clearly enough that the bombardier has finally rejected Milo's arguments justifying the casualties that occur as a result of his business schemes. To Yossarian, Milo's crimes against humanity, like those of governments, armies, and corporations, are really too huge for comprehension, but his crime against one individual, Mudd, the dead man in Yossarian's tent, is enough to particularize Yossarian's disillusionment with his friend, whom he has more or less unwittingly launched on his career. Despite the fact that everyone has a share of Milo's syndicate (including Mudd), Yossarian has begun to feel that neither this nor his protests that he wasn't even there can obviate Milo's responsibility for the man's death, and his remarks to Milo switch from a tone of awed admiration to one of disillusioned sarcasm as he "advises" him to bribe the government to buy his cotton and to tell everyone that "the security of the country requires a strong domestic Egyptian-cotton speculating industry" (XXIV). In the end, therefore, Yossarian refuses Milo's invitation to "come with" him in his business and to sanction his offering of chocolate-covered cotton to the world.

When Heller focuses on the chaplain, who had been conducting Snowden's funeral during the same time, the archetypal form of the encounter is fully revealed. The chaplain's view of the scene, presented in flashback, is interwoven with his concern for memory and perception, vision and hallucination, the various seeings—*presque jamais*, and, particularly, *déjà vu*—and his curious "feeling that he had met Yossarian somewhere before the first time he *had* met

Yossarian lying in bed in the hospital" (XXV). Though the chaplain never identifies Yossarian as the naked man in the tree, he at least suspects that their first "meeting" was on some occasion "far more momentous and occult" than that in the hospital, was "a significant encounter . . . in some remote, submerged and perhaps even entirely spiritual epoch in which he had made the identical, foredooming admission that there was nothing, absolutely nothing, he could do to help him" (XXV). And it is in connection with the "enigmatic vision" of the naked man in the tree, "the most extraordinary event that had ever befallen him" (XXV), that the chaplain brings up with Yossarian the phenomenon of *déjà vu*, though the chaplain fears that not even *déjà vu* is flexible enough to include his "vision." As the chaplain wonders about it—"was it a ghost, then? The dead man's soul? An angel from heaven or a minion from hell?"—some of the archetypal symbolic potential begins to emerge, a potential that is more clearly suggested when Heller writes that "The possibility that there really had been a naked man in the tree—two men, actually, since the first had been joined shortly by a second man clad in a brown mustache and sinister dark garments from head to toe who bent forward ritualistically along the limb of the tree to offer the first man something to drink from a brown goblet—never crossed the chaplain's mind" (XXV).

Putting these details in their place with Yossarian's ironic reference to the tree as the "tree of life" and the "tree of the knowledge of good and evil," one must finally recognize the dual purposes of the scene, taking place as it does on the third day after Snowden's death and the third day of Yossarian's nakedness. On the one hand, it certainly represents Yossarian's "temptation" by Milo, the Jungian "shadow" in his "sinister dark garments" and the Christian Satan, identified with the serpent, who "inches" up the tree, "hisses" at Yossarian, and breathes fire, albeit a "virtuous fire." For Yossarian, this confrontation is the first real step in his moral regeneration. As C. G. Jung writes in "Aion: Contributions to the Symbolism of the Self": "The shadow is a moral problem that challenges the whole ego personality, for no one can become conscious of the shadow without considerable moral effort. To become conscious of it involves recognizing the dark aspects of the personality as present and real. This act is an essential condition for any kind of self-knowledge, and it therefore, as a rule, meets with considerable resistance. Indeed, self-knowledge as a psychotherapeutic measure frequently requires much painstaking work extending over a long period."[30] Jung's comment here is almost a description of Yossarian's development; it is therefore hardly surprising that, after Milo, near the end of the novel, has been absorbed by the socio-authoritarian structure (he joins forces with Wintergreen, Cathcart, Korn, and others), he should be replaced, in Yossarian's delusive vision in the hospital for the last time, by another shadowy figure saying, "We've got your pal, buddy." For Yossarian to have gone with Milo (or with Cathcart and Korn, when they make him their offer of a "little deal") would be to suggest that the *shadow* had gotten him too, just as it had Dunbar and Major Major. To know and yet to deny the shadow is to know and affirm one's moral being.

If the rejection of Milo represents the birth of moral consciousness, the death of Snowden and the simultaneous regression of Yossarian to nakedness represent for the latter a death and a rebirth of self. Of particular concern here, then, is the way the method of *déjà vu* forces both reader and character beyond meanings they might see only half through the novel to the final meanings in Snowden's death, meanings that are implicit in Yossarian's experiences from the start but that, like those around Milo, are able to push only slowly and tortuously out of memory into consciousness. The recognition of Snowden's full meaning parallels both the moral and archetypal patterns of death and birth; for, through Snowden, Yossarian comes to an awareness not only of the fact of death but also of the possibility for life—for himself and for others.

That Snowden has particular significance for Yossarian is suggested in the first appearance of the name in a question Yossarian asks at an indoctrination session: "Where are the Snowdens of yesteryear?" he asks an instructor, parodying Villon's question in French, *"Où sont les neiges d'antan?"* and "ready to pursue him through all the words in the world to wring the knowledge from him if he could . . ." (IV). But he gets no answer this time, although the reader gets the information that Snowden had been killed over Avignon, and one suspects that the pursuit of that knowledge of Snowden will be for Yossarian a long and tortuous rite of passage. Later, in the midst of an explanation for Yossarian's great skill at directing the plane's evasive action, we are told that Yossarian has not yet "resigned" himself to the idea that he was going to die; and for a moment, there is an abrupt descent into the memory of "the pitiful time of the mess on the mission to Avignon when Dobbs went crazy in midair and began weeping pathetically for help" for the bombardier. But Yossarian is the bombardier, so he yells he is all right, and Dobbs begs, "then help him, help him." And the chapter concludes with the oft-recurring line: "And Snowden lay dying in back" (V). The next time the name recurs, Yossarian is in the hospital because "being in the hospital was better than being over Bologna or flying over Avignon with Huple or Dobbs at the controls and Snowden dying in back." To Yossarian, "there was none of that crude, ugly ostentation about dying that was so common outside the hospital. They did not blow up in mid-air like Kraft or the dead man in Yossarian's tent, or freeze to death in the blazing summertime the way Snowden had frozen to death after spilling his secret to Yossarian in the back of the plane" (XVII). At this time one learns that Snowden had whimpered "I'm cold. . . . I'm cold," and Yossarian had tried to comfort him with, "There, there. . . . There, there." And shortly after this one learns part of what Snowden's secret is, the part that causes Yossarian to spend so much time in the hospital, to become so proficient at directing the plane's evasive actions, and, eventually, to refuse altogether to fly combat missions and, instead, to walk around backwards with a forty-five in hand so that no one can slip up on him from behind; the secret "Snowden had spilled to him on the mission to Avignon" was that "they were out to get him; and Snowden had spilled it all over the back of the plane" (XVII).

There are other remembrances of Snowden's death, both by Yossarian and other characters on whom the incident also has a tremendous effect. Through Doc Daneeka's point of view, one sees the state of shock Yossarian is in when he gets off the plane, stark naked, after the mission. Through the chaplain's point of view, one sees the rather frozen, pictorially depicted scene around Snowden's grave, when Milo slithers up the tree to sit with the still-naked Yossarian. And from Yossarian himself one gets a gradually accumulating series of details concerning his passage out of the nose section, through the labyrinthine crawlway, "up over the bomb bay and down into the rear section of the plane where Snowden lay on the floor wounded and freezing to death in a yellow splash of sunlight . . ." (XXII). But it is not until the penultimate chapter that one learns the full details of Snowden's death and the entire secret that he spilled, and it comes only after Yossarian's nightmare journey into the "Eternal City," after Milo had caused his friend Nately's death, a love-death struggle with a "terrible mother" in Nately's whore, the offer of the "little deal" by Cathcart and Korn if he will desist from his rebellion and be shipped quietly home, a nearly fatal stabbing by Nately's whore, and after visits by the shadowy dream-figure saying, "We've got your pal, buddy" (XLI). In this chapter, entitled "Snowden," the novel comes full circle, with Yossarian again talking to the chaplain as he had been in chapter I, and one finally learns the full text of Snowden's message: "Man was matter, that was Snowden's secret. Drop him out a window and he'll fall. Set fire to him and he'll burn. Bury him and he'll rot. . . . The Spirit gone, man is garbage. That was Snowden's secret. Ripeness was all."

As a result of Snowden's *full* message, Yossarian goes beyond the belief in mere existence to find a life in a belief in "The Spirit," the essence, of man. But, obviously, existence does precede essence, and to fulfill the latter one must insure the former. Thus, caught, as one has seen, between the Scylla of court-martial and the Charybdis of Catch-22, Yossarian makes his "leap" of faith and lights out for Sweden, behind Orr, his mentor, but, like Huck Finn, ahead of the rest.

It is the strategy of Yossarian's retreat to Sweden that creates the most vexing problems for most readers of the novel, bringing under scrutiny as it does both the values of American society and culture and of Yossarian. Read in one way, conservatively, shall we say, the retreat is an egocentric denial of social responsibility, but read in another way, radically perhaps, it is an existential act of individual affirmation. To date there has not been much of a middle, liberal, position; for how can Yossarian's leaving for Sweden be both an individual affirmation and an affirmation of American culture? According to Joseph Campbell, one can reconcile such contradictions simply by seeing the rejection of society as a birth *from* rather than a denial of it; society therefore becomes "a fostering organ," a kind of exterior "second womb," "wherein the postnatal stages of man's long gestation . . . are supported and defended," and the individual simply becomes himself and, thus, fully human.[31] Hence, Yossarian's rite of initiation—his experiences with Kraft and Mudd and the soldier in white, Nately and the whore and her kid sister, and Milo and Snowden—is, as one has seen, a "second birth," and Yossarian, following in the footsteps of just about every major hero of American literature, becomes "truly the 'twice born,'" freed from the pedagogical devices of society, the lures and threats of myth, the local *mores*, the usual hopes of benefits and rewards."[32] Having proved himself and, in a sense, his society by fulfilling yet another form of the American dream, Yossarian achieves his freedom and his maturity, ready now to become, like Nately and the chaplain, a "father" in his own right as he sets out to find the "kid sister" who reminds him of a lot of other "kids"—Snowden, Huple, the boy in the streets of Rome, Sampson, Dobbs, Kraft, Mudd—in order "to try to break the lousy chain of inherited habit that was imperiling them all" (XXXIX). Consequently, *déjà vu* in *Catch-22* applies not only to the images of the external world of social consciousness, the eternal world of the archetype, and the internal world of the personal consciousness; the narrative these images create also applies to a universal myth, the myth of the journey into the underworld, the labyrinth, the heart of darkness. In the novel, therefore, *déjà vu* involves both form and content, for not only is it the material that creates but also it becomes the method that penetrates this labyrinth of memory.

Notes: Phase Two

1. Thomas S. Kuhn, *The Structure of Scientific Revolutions,* 2nd ed. enlarged, *Foundations of the Unity of Science,* vol. 2, no. 2 (Chicago: University of Chicago Press, 1970), p. 10.
2. *Ibid.*
3. Margaret Masterman, "The Nature of a Paradigm," in *Criticism and the Growth of Knowledge: Proceedings of the International Colloquium in the Philosophy of Science, London, 1965,* vol. 4, eds. Imre Lakatos and Alan Musgrave (Cambridge: Cambridge University Press, 1970), pp. 59–89. Also see Kuhn's Postscript added to the second edition of *The Structure of Scientific Revolutions,* for it takes into account the critiques made of the first edition, Kuhn becoming "critical" in relation to his earlier "naive" position. See, as well, Kuhn's two separate contributions to the Lakatos/Musgrave volume, and the essay by Michael McCanles, "The Literal and the Metaphorical: Dialectic or Interchange," *PMLA,* 91, no. 2 (March 1976): 279–90, which treats the way a metaphor describing reality may eventually be taken as a literal description of the world. Such a notion lies in the background of my dialectical sequence, as the literal-metaphorical of the naive phase becomes the literal of the critical phase, which then returns to the merely metaphorical of the sophisticated phase.
4. Kuhn, *The Structure of Scientific Revolutions,* pp. 10–11.
5. See the essays by Wolfgang Iser, "Indeterminacy and the Reader's Response in Prose Fiction," and Edward W. Said, "Molestation and Authority in Narrative Fiction," in *Aspects of Narrative,* ed. J. Hillis Miller (New York: Columbia University Press, 1971), pp. 1–68, for related discussions of the problem of hermeneutic centers.
6. Edith Kern, *Existential Thought and Fictional Technique: Kierkegaard, Sartre, Beckett* (New Haven, Conn.: Yale University Press, 1970), p. 5.
7. Besides the several recent studies of the confessional novel, one ought to see also two works that treat the "fable" as a mode of modern fiction: Robert Scholes, *The Fabulators* (New York: Oxford University Press, 1967) and David H. Richter, *Fable's End: Completeness and Closure in Rhetorical Fiction* (Chicago: University of Chicago Press, 1974).
8. Wolfgang Iser, *The Implied Reader* (Baltimore: Johns Hopkins University Press, 1974), p. 28.
9. *Ibid.*
10. Wolfgang Iser, "The Reality of Fiction: A Functionalist Approach to Literature," *New Literary History: A Journal of Theory and Interpretation,* 7, no. 1 (Autumn 1975): 28; see also the discussion in Iser's n. 47, p. 37, for added perspective to the problem of "reality" and "philosophy."
11. See Frye's *Anatomy of Criticism,* p. 65, and Fredric Jameson, *The Prison-House of Language: A Critical Account of Structuralism and Russian Formalism* (Princeton, N.J.: Princeton University Press, 1972),

p. 14, for the remarks on irony and the existential projection. For my reference to the Heidegger phrase, see Nathan A. Scott, Jr., "The Literary Imagination in a Time of Dearth," in *Existentialism 2: A Casebook*, ed. William V. Spanos (New York: Crowell, 1976), p. 234.

12. Jean E. Kennard, *Number and Nightmare: Forms of Fantasy in Contemporary Fiction* (Hamden, Conn.: Archon, 1975), p. 9.
13. *Ibid.*
14. I would call attention again to the works by Kuhn, Masterman, and McCanles cited in n. 3 above.
15. Ihab Hassan, *Radical Innocence: The Contemporary American Novel* (New York: Harper Colophon, 1966; orig. pub. Princeton University Press, 1961), p. 115. Further quotations from this source will be given by page numbers within parentheses in the text whenever practicable.
16. Quoted by Hassan from *The Living Novel*, ed. Granville Hicks (New York: Macmillan, 1957), p. 75.
17. Nathan A. Scott, Jr., *Three American Moralists: Mailer, Bellow, Trilling* (Notre Dame, Ind.: University of Notre Dame Press, 1973), p. 153. Further quotations from this source will be given by page numbers within parentheses in the text whenever practicable.
18. Like Scott, Joyce Carol Oates has observed the authoritative power Mailer invests in language. In an essay on Mailer in *New Heaven, New Earth: The Visionary Experience in Literature* (New York: Vanguard, 1974), Oates writes that for Mailer, as for most post-Whorfian intellectuals, "Reality exists; death exists; injustice exists; I exist; and yet, without language, such forms of existence are totally inaccessible. . . . Through the systematic control of language, the tyrannical powers at the center of the modern anonymous state seek to enclose the individual, to make him (in Marcuse's eerie metaphor) one-dimensional, like a playing card seen from one side. . . . To assert himself against the oppressive language-system, then, the individual must be a kind of artist; he must attempt the creation of his own special language. To create a mythology in order to escape being enslaved by someone else's has been, perhaps, the dynamic urge behind much art, at least art created in a time of social confusion" (pp. 184–85).
19. Northrop Frye, *The Stubborn Structure: Essays on Criticism and Society* (Ithaca, N.Y.: Cornell University Press, 1970), p. 207.
20. An entire book has been devoted to the treatment of unresolved tensions and ambiguities in Faulkner's works; see Walter J. Slatoff, *Quest for Failure* (Ithaca, N.Y.: Cornell University Press, 1960).
21. "Indeterminacy and the Reader's Response in Prose Fiction," p. 6.
22. Alain Robbe-Grillet, *For a New Novel: Essays on Fiction*, trans. Richard Howard (New York: Grove, 1965), p. 156.
23. Joseph Heller, *Catch-22* (New York: Simon and Schuster, 1961), chap. XXV.
24. *Anatomy of Criticism*, p. 345. Wittgenstein's sense of man's experience as a kind of "picture album" he browses through upon occasion, each time getting a new perspective upon any single picture, is similar to the phenomenon discussed here as *déjà vu*, which is also a kind of Proustian *temps retrouvé*.
25. David H. Richter, *Fable's End: Completeness and Closure in Rhetorical Fiction*, p. 163.
26. *Ibid.*, p. 165.

27. Joseph Heller, *Catch-22*. Throughout this essay the Roman numerals in parentheses refer to chapters in *Catch-22*.

28. "A New Novel about Old Troubles," *Critical Quarterly*, 5 (1963): 169.

29. Joseph J. Waldmeir, "Two Novelists of the Absurd: Heller and Kesey," *Wisconsin Studies in Contemporary Literature*, 5 (Autumn 1964): 195.

30. Quoted from *Psyche & Symbol: A Selection from the Writings of C. G. Jung*, ed. Violet S. de Laszlo (New York: Doubleday, 1958), p. 7.

31. "Bios and Mythos: Prolegomena to a Science of Mythology," in *Myth and Literature*, ed. John B. Vickery (Lincoln: University of Nebraska Press, 1966), p. 20.

32. *Ibid.*, p. 21.

PHASE TWO

Phase Three The Sophisticated

I Modernist versus Post-Modernist

> One could say, of course, that the complicated plot in which
> everything works out and resolves itself in the end belongs
> historically to centuries where not necessarily the writer but
> the writer's audience more or less believed in some kind of
> destiny or fate that saw things worked out. . . . You could
> say that the age of the plotted novel belongs to the age when
> people took that more seriously than they *can* take it in the
> twentieth century.
>
> John Barth
> Interview

> . . . my whole idea about fiction is that it's a normal, if I may
> use the word, epistemological procedure; that is, it is at the
> very center of everybody all the time at any period, and you
> don't have to search for psychological reasons, although they
> may be there too. But I think the epistemological ones are far
> more important and anterior. It's a way of making up the
> world and making sense of it.
>
> Ronald Sukenick
> Interview

> The history of fiction is in part a record of the efforts of its au-
> thors to create for fiction its own forms.
>
> William H. Gass
> Interview

The most obfuscated of the three phases of modernist
fiction—as of any diachronic spectrum—is the late or *sophisticated.*
The reason is that we are simply too close to the phenomena to see
anything but the dimmest outlines; and in any final phase of a
movement, the heterogeneity achieved by what Alastair Fowler
calls "conscious innovation"[1] or Frye "the pure variable," the "deliberate attempt at novelty or unfamiliarity," the "disguising or
complicating of archetypes,"[2] results in a very real confusion. In
terms of epochal metaphors or paradigms, the results are of
phenomena Thomas S. Kuhn would call "crisis," the period of transition between an old, largely discredited paradigm and a new, not-
yet-defined paradigm. We are in such a phase of transition, according

to both Nathan A. Scott, Jr., and Ihab Hassan. Using the later work of the philosopher Martin Heidegger, rather than the early *Being and Time* (1927), which provides the foundation for the more ironic modes of existentialism, Scott suggests: "The situation of man, at the end of the modern age, is, in Heidegger's reading of it, something open, in the sense of its being located in a great intervenient space, in a great *Between*. As he says, in the clumsy stiltedness of manner so typical of his strange rhetoric, ours 'is the time of the gods that have fled *and* of the god that is coming. It is the time of *need*, because it lies under a double lack and a double Not: the No-more of the gods that have fled and the Not-yet of the god that is coming.' "[3] Hassan, like Scott, would argue that we are between epochs, between critical stances, though to the questions raised by the criticism itself, Hassan says: "I have no answer. Yet I believe that an answer must go beyond our current shibboleths: disconfirmation, decreation, demystification, deconstruction, decentering, depropriation, difference, etc. Perhaps we need to go beyond Irony (as Nietzsche sometimes did), beyond the current aversion to Wholeness and Meaning, to some working faith in . . . What?"[4]

Such a period of crisis has prompted critics of recent American fiction to react in various ways, but the constant in their responses is to insist that we have now entered a post-modernist age. They so insist even when the crux of their argument rests at the point of intersection of existentialism and the fiction itself, as in Jean Kennard's *Number and Nightmare: Forms of Fantasy in Contemporary Fiction* (1975). Others insist upon an epochal shift, as does Raymond M. Olderman, even when they suggest that the forms of fiction are now the results of man's imaginative response to the blurring of fact and fiction, "the explosion of the ordinary by the fabulous," even when the controlling metaphor is quintessentially modernist, the "*image of the waste land* . . . meant to stand for the overall configuration of myth and metaphor which can assist us as a critical tool in understanding the dominant pattern of vision in the contemporary novel."[5] And a critic such as Jerome Klinkowitz similarly insists even when the "disruptive" values of a presumed postmodernist fiction include nothing more than "formal experimentation, a thematic interest in the imaginative transformation of reality, and a sometimes painful but often hilarious self-conscious artistry."[6] But it would seem to me that what is involved in these studies—each valuable in its own way—is the clearer identification of a phase of the modernist paradigms represented in *Winesburg, Ohio, Ulysses, In Our Time, The Sound and the Fury, Absalom, Absalom!*, the poetry of Stevens, Eliot, cummings, Williams, and others. We *are* at an end, as the pessimists say, but we also are at a beginning.

One of the critics to argue for the turn toward an authentically *new* fiction has been Philip Stevick. Stevick has established his critical authority by editing a widely used anthology of essays, *The Theory of the Novel* (1967), and an anthology of contemporary "anti-fictions" (*Anti-story*, 1971), but his most important statement so far is an essay, "Scheherazade runs out of plots, goes on talking; the king, puzzled, listens: *an essay on new fiction*," which appeared in the excellent series of issues of *TriQuarterly* devoted to "On-going American Fiction." According to Stevick, "What recent fiction tells us on every page is that it is of another age than the modernist masters."[7] Discussing three recent authors—Brautigan, Barthelme, and Coover—Stevick suggests that representative quotations from their works point to the definitive features of the "new fiction":

> an extraordinary innocence, either genuine or feigned, even a kind of common prose rhythm deriving from the unwillingness to subordinate and complicate that is an attribute of that innocence, a readiness to confront certain extremities of life, in these cases pain, accident, death, and mourning, but an investing of these extremities with an odd and terribly distant artifice, a playing off of a method of wit, tough, flip, and facile, that is reminiscent of the stand-up comic . . . against a personal fragility and vulnerability that is very different from the classic toughness, knowingness, and irony of the dominant modernists [p. 334].

And there are other aspects, not necessarily features of the brief excerpts from the novelists, that Stevick identifies with "new fiction." These include the disruption of conventional epiphanic narrative structures, the fiction's disengagement from physical space, the a-temporalizing of fictive time, and the abandoning of traditional fiction's usual epistemological bases (p. 342). Seeing such features in Barthelme, Brautigan, and Coover prompts Stevick to argue that the fiction of such writers as these three is no longer modernist. Despite his comment that the label "post-modernist" is an "annoying and unhelpful" epithet, Stevick persists nonetheless in claiming "that recent fiction no longer orients itself according to its own relations to the modernist masters and that this sense of discontinuity with the dominant figures of modernism is one of the few qualities that unites new fiction" (p. 338).

But one must seriously question Stevick's thesis. Not one of the featured aspects Stevick identifies in the excerpts from Barthelme, Coover, and Brautigan can be limited only to "recent fiction." In fact, if we are to continue to consider legitimate such critical works as *Love and Death in the American Novel, The American Adam, The Reign of Wonder, The Machine in the Garden,* and *Radical Innocence,* we simply cannot accept Stevick's view. All these critical works suggest in one way or another that American literature in general and, often, American fiction in particular are characterized by "innocence," "voice," "readiness," "artifice," and a counterpointed "toughness" and "vulnerability." We can go farther down Stevick's list, seeing also in modernist forms a pervasive structural disjunction that, with its abandonment of traditional spatiotemporal epistemologies, also abandons realism's traditional ontologies, the mimetic "worlds" of fiction. These aspects, which Stevick would relegate to the new, post-modernist fiction, are very much the aspects many critics—Maurice Beebe for instance—have tried to suggest are at the heart of modernism itself. I have suggested throughout the narrative interludes herein that the conventions of the novel-as-genre have incorporated basic elements of American literature—its traditional, naive, often pastoral, innocence, simplicity, and concreteness, and that even after the explosion of the novel into multiple, competing, autonomous modes, the various modes have tended to embrace nonetheless these particularly American aspects, so that even the most radically experimental mode might still appear radically American as well. Consequently, when Stevick says, "One thing that we can say about new fiction is that the range of fictional options has increased enormously in the last decade" (p. 352), I would suggest, instead, that what he observes is merely the result of a phenomenon that first occurred somewhere just after the turn of the century, the phenomenon that resulted in the exploded form, as I have called it. We do see more of it in the mid-1970s, but that would be because the process has accelerated, as it were, in ratio to its distance from its point of origin.

But Stevick's essay is perceptive in many of its insights describing recent fiction, and I would not dismiss it out of hand for its inadequate historical perspective. Stevick himself may well realize the inadequacy, for, after having devoted about twenty pages to proposing various historical explanations for a new aesthetic for fiction, he says, "What we do not need is criticism of new fiction as pure technique, disengaged from its cultural ambiance, 'read,' explicated, exhausted, like a metaphysical lyric. What we also do not need is more criticism which uses fiction as an exhibit in a historical design, new fiction being the end of something, or the beginning of something else, or an element in a cyclic movement, or evidence for the triumph of one historical principle or the defeat of another. What we do need is an aesthetic of new fiction" (pp. 354–55). And Stevick proceeds to give us seven "axioms" of a new aesthetic, concluding with one that I shall consider as both the sign of modernism and the omen of its end. Spread over several pages and followed by discussion and examples, the seven axioms (italics eliminated here) include:

1. New fiction, although aggressively non-traditional, shows less involvement with the tradition of prose fiction than any fiction since the beginning of the novel [p. 355].

2. New fiction is the first substantial body of fiction that self-consciously seeks an audience that is less than universal, attempting to establish a community of sensibility that is willfully limited [p. 355].

3. New fiction contains and often intensifies the tendency in most fiction of any period to assimilate and transform the bad art of its own time [p. 356].

4. New fiction consolidates an attempt rare in fiction before the modern period to present elements of its texture as devoid of value; yet new fiction, in contrast to certain areas of modern fiction, seeks this value-less quality not as an act of subtraction, or de-humanization, or metaphysical mystification, not as a gesture of despair or nihilism, but as a positive act in which the joy of the observer is allowed to prevail as the primary quality of the experience [pp. 356–57].

5. New fiction presents its texture as devoid as possible of aesthetic and philosophical depth [pp. 358–59].

6. New fiction permits itself a degree of latitude from the illusionist tradition greater than in any body of fiction since the beginning of the novel [p. 360].

7. New fiction, finally, in common with only a few scattered instances before it, seeks to represent, explicitly or implicitly, the act of writing as an act of play [p. 361].

I do not wish to take up at length the argument here, but I must point out that these "axioms" can generally be applied to certain earlier modernist fiction as easily as to recent, or—as in axiom two—can be applied in any period to any fiction that emerges into dominance, or—as in axiom one—can be demonstrated as totally inapplicable: new-fiction writers can hardly be uninvolved with the various traditions of fiction when so many are parodists, so many are academics: in Stevick's own words, "involvement with the teaching of literature . . . has made a difference with writers of new fiction, particularly in enlarging their sense of formal options" (p. 354). I could extend the argument and give examples that would suggest the limitations of Stevick's view as a historical phenomenon of the last decade, but again let me say only that what he identifies as axioms of "new fiction" can really be—where they are valid at all—axioms of modernist fiction in general. The difference between early modernism and the late modernism Stevick actually describes is a difference of degree, not of kind. As I have indicated before, I prefer Gerald Graff's explanation in another essay appearing with Stevick's in the same issue of *TriQuarterly*: "To characterize post-modernism as a 'breakthrough,'" says Graff, "is to place a greater distance between current writers and their predecessors earlier in the century than is, I think, justified" (p. 385).

Stevick's seven axioms toward an aesthetic of "new fiction" are not without their usefulness, however. To begin with, they do articulate the feelings of any "avant-garde" practitioners toward their own work and the work of their predecessors, as most of the axioms may be associated with aspects of avant-garde movements assessed by Renato Poggioli.[8] But for my purposes, Stevick's most important axiom is the seventh, for it does offer a useful way to show how rather disparate writers like Updike, Styron, Vonnegut, and Brautigan may all be included in a single movement or phase of a movement. Many recent critics, including Stevick, Olderman, and Klinkowitz, have tended to exclude Updike and Styron (along with Heller, Oates, and others) from any group that might include Vonnegut and Brautigan (as well as Barthelme, Kosinski, Sukenick, and Sorrentino), intimating or arguing explicitly that the sorts of consciousness exhibited by the former in works like *The Centaur* or *The Confessions of Nat Turner* could no longer claim a central place in our value systems. The concept of "play" that Stevick's axiom describes, however, can be expanded in a direction that may legitimately include all these authors, for it can show that their particular orientations, even when they diverge, have grown out of the aesthetics of modernism, thus representing offshoots rather than the entirely new growths that took root, according to Klinkowitz, in the year 1967.

Some recent fiction—like modernist fiction in general—does seek to some degree, "explicitly or implicitly," to represent "the act of writing as an act of play." Other writers are much less interested in the performative orientation of fiction, so if playfulness enters into their art it does so in the art object itself, rather than in the act of the artist. Consequently, it is imperative we recognize the corollary term *game:* one then can see a meaningful relationship between the performative term *play* and the artifactive term *game.*

The game-oriented writers are those who, like Nabokov, Barth, and Hawkes, take an essentially objective stance toward universe, audience, self, and work. Their fictions tend to be self-contained and, like *Pale Fire,* self-reflexive, a house of mirrors such as Barth adverts to in *Lost in the Funhouse.* They also tend to be more heavily textured and, occasionally, like *The Blood Oranges,* more traditionally pictorial than Stevick would admit in axioms four, five, and six. In these works, the source of authority, of sanctification—of grace, if you will—exists in the work, whereas in the traditional novel-as-genre it has existed in the universe depicted. It is not, for the game-oriented writer, in the writer writing, nor in the act of writing, nor in the universe, but in the object produced—the iconic art object itself.

Play-oriented writers, such as Brautigan, Vonnegut, Barthelme, and Sukenick, are much more pragmatic: they emphasize the old values of storytelling, the entertainer's values, the necessity to keep the audience attentive, to move it from moment to moment, to play on its conditioned responses to various formulae—of "reality," of artists and audiences, of literature itself. They play outrageously with the straightfaced conventions of traditional fiction in works like *The Hawkline Monster, Breakfast of Champions, Snow White,* and *Up,* but their main effort seems to be to keep the good times rolling. And certainly, these books are a lot more *fun* to read than, for example, Hawkes's *The Blood Oranges.* Few of us would suggest, however, that the more playful authors have produced a finer piece of literature than Hawkes's novel, and several critics—Nathan Scott and Warner Berthoff, for example—lay upon the performative writers the charge of "a weakness of intellectual substance and structure."[9] But intellectual substance seems not to be the objective of these authors; they simply like to play and they do seem to care whether the audiences they have created (or discovered) enjoy themselves, too. Value, grace, and sanctification exist for these writers in the reciprocity of the activity, in the performance itself, rather than in work or world, author or audience alone.

The contrast between the impulse to construct a game and the impulse simply to play seems to go back to the contrast between the classic notion of a stable, mechanically structured universe whose secrets can be mastered in formula and diagram, and the romantic notion of a phenomenal, dynamic, emerging universe whose secrets cannot be known in anything other than the relationship of knower and known, self and object. But there is a clear sense in which both *play* and *game*, as metaphors for an aesthetic orientation, may go back to the romantic origins of the entire modernist aesthetic, which splits in the directions of Plato and Aristotle. This aesthetic has been given cogent summary by Charles Altieri in an essay devoted to a post-modern American poetics. According to Altieri, the basis for the primary dichotomy in modernism's symbolism versus its imagism lies in the split between a Wordsworthian and a Coleridgean view of art: "The argument can be summarized by distinguishing between Coleridge's recreation of the object through the subject and early Wordsworth's sense that the subject is created by means of its participation in the object."[10] While Altieri is mainly concerned with American poetry, he nonetheless makes the connection of the two aesthetic poles to the modernist novel: "Perhaps a final and almost absurd manifestation of the dangerous extremes at each pole can be found in contemporary American fiction with one exemplified by reporter novelists and the other by elaborate explorations of the theme of fiction, and of the fantasies of the fictive mind."[11]

The traditional novel-as-genre was based on the former realist, Aristotelian premise, the major premise also of traditional science; the modernist drift toward adopting modes of the novel rests upon the more idealist, Platonic notion, the lyrical or dramatistic sense of the world-as-flux drawn into a realm of ideas or an essentialist Self. But even within modernism there has remained a strong feeling for the more traditional, classic sense of objective order, and one of the major themes of the modern has been the tension that results when the recidivistic nostalgia for one confronts the necessity to face the other in an expanding, relativistic, exploding universe. It would be a decided oversimplification to eliminate either impulse from modernist fiction, and to me that is precisely what Stevick has done, for the fiction he identifies as "post-modernist" really is only one of the two continuously interwoven strands that have made the whole modernist tradition. Although Stevick sees the *play* fictionists as an independent movement, they really are only carrying on the popular, Wordsworthian (in Altieri's distinction), imagist experiments of Stein, Anderson, and Hemingway, experiments which have been capable of becoming lyrically expressive just as easily as dramatistically objective. But it is possible to retrace the route from *naive* modern to *sophisticated* modern and thereby to show how the performative sophisticated writers now stand closest to the threshold of a truly new epoch.

Gerald Graff has argued, in "The Myth of the Postmodernist Breakthrough," that the old master, Henry James himself, is largely responsible for the aesthetic formulations that eventually exploded the novel.[12] The tenets of point of view, the main doctrine of Jamesian aesthetics, focus upon the primacy of a center of consciousness as the medium of exchange between the author, his audience, and the world; there is no distinguishing yet between *real* world and *fictive* world, for the conscious intention of James, expressed in the 1884 essay "The Art of Fiction," is to suggest that the two remain congruent, though James is not so naive as to believe that no problems begin to arise at the juncture of the two. For as soon as we suggest that the world depends upon a view of the world, the abyss of solipsism yawns before us. Reality becomes pluralistic worlds, not a single, knowable, communicable world. And the questions that preoccupy James, in the beginning only questions of technique, become, eventually, epistemological questions. "Really, universally," says James, "relations stop nowhere," and a work such as *The Golden Bowl* suggests how both the genre and the world open out on James in the late phase, as the world had for his brother William, whose *A Pluralistic Universe* (1909) offers an important statement of the presuppositions of "the modern" in the twentieth century: "Everything you can think of, however vast or inclusive," William writes, "has on the pluralistic view a genuinely 'external' environment of some sort or amount. Things are 'with' one another in many ways, but nothing includes everything, or dominates over everything. The word 'and' trails along after every sentence. Something always escapes."[13]

The situation for literature, where indeterminacy of form and world begins to reign in the place of determinacy, becomes the same as that for science. Writers became increasingly aware that "something always escapes" our knowledge, our theories. "I would hardly be exaggerating if I claimed that the very existence of our sciences and arts in their present shape is predicated on the problem of knowledge having become a problem," writes Louis Kampf in *On Modernism*. "Reflections of an epistemological sort become an integral part of the sciences," adds Kampf, "just as the meditations on the possibility of artistic form become part of—no, create—[for example] Proust's great work."[14] For both science and the arts, the modernist questions asked now are about the object of study or representation, the mode of analysis or presentation, and even the ability of man himself—as agent or recipient—to come at the object of knowledge. The issues and the possible resolutions are expressed succinctly by Werner Heisenberg. In *The Physicist's Conception of Nature*, Heisenberg makes the point that a materialistic physics had permitted the nineteenth century's essentially monistic view of the world to retain its grip on metaphysics well into the twentieth, but eventually atomic physics forced abandonment of that tidy, simplistic materialism. Now, he says, all we modernists can know is the *knowledge* of objective nature. "Science," says Heisenberg,

> is now focused on the network of relationships between man and nature, on the framework which makes us as living beings dependent parts of nature, and which we as human beings have simultaneously made the object of our thoughts and actions. Science no longer confronts nature as an objective observer, but sees itself as an actor in this interplay between man and nature. The scientific method of analysing, explaining and classifying has become conscious of its limitations, which arise out of the fact that by its intervention science alters and refashions the object of investigation. In other words, method and object can no longer be separated.[15]

But even after we recognize that modernist science and aesthetics have exploded the naive monistic materialism of nineteenth-century science and literature, there remain central issues about which questions will revolve, especially in a critically self-conscious age such as the modern. If "reality" is a function of "relationships," what are the determining relations? What are the aspects of the "field," the irreducible elements no literary work can avoid exhibiting, in greater or less proportion? In literature and literary criticism, any such questions, according to M. H. Abrams, must focus on the "four elements in the total situation of a work of art" which can enter into relationships. Abrams identifies these elements in the "Introduction" to *The Mirror and the Lamp.* "First, there is the *work*, the artistic product itself. And since this is a human product, artifact, the second common element is the artificer, the *artist*. Third, the work is taken to have a subject which, directly or deviously, is derived from existing things—to be about, or signify, or reflect something which either is, or bears some relation to, an objective state of affairs. This third element, whether held to consist of people and actions, ideas and feelings, material things and events, or super-sensible essences, has frequently been denoted by that word-of-all-work, 'nature'; but let us use the more neutral and comprehensive term, *universe*, instead. For the final element we have the *audience*; the listeners, spectators, or readers to whom the work is addressed, or to whose attention, at any rate, it becomes available."[16] Orientations toward these elements result in *objective* critical theories, *expressive* theories, *mimetic* and *pragmatic* theories, and in the history of fiction, as I have suggested previously, these theoretical orientations have resulted in various types or modes of the novel—the dramatic, the poetic or lyrical, the realistic and the "popular."

The novel-as-genre is predicated on and exists because of a presumed possible congruence between world and work, so the orientation of the traditional realistic novel and its criticism, like that of traditional science, is toward the universe imitated, mirrored, pictured. Any reorientation of fiction toward the other elements— work, artist, audience—makes it look innovative, experimental. Experimentation with form has become one of the defining features of the modern. "Indeed," writes Maurice Beebe, in "What Modernism Was," "the attempt to escape the limitations of individual forms has been a dominant feature of the entire Modernist movement."[17] The easiest ways fiction writers find to experiment are to skew the traditional form of the novel-as-genre toward the poles Abrams identifies as objective (work), expressive (artist), and pragmatic (audience). When these shifts in theoretical orientation result from metaphysical convictions, they redefine a novelist's centers for determination, validation, and sanctification—define, in short, his presumed grounds for authority. This often means, then, that novelists give us novels that have taken over the major authoritative bases of other genres. We get dramatistic (objective) novels, "poetic"/lyric (expressive) novels, and popular (pragmatic) novels that return very closely to traditional or "primitive" *mythoi* and formulae, because such experimental forms represent modernist attempts to exploit other centers of authority than that provided by the old naive realistic relationship posited between man and universe in the mimetic orientation. So, not only did modernism "cross national boundaries," writes Beebe, "but it also saw a breakdown of genres as writers, painters, and composers sought to borrow techniques and achieve effects like those in the other arts."[18]

Experiments in fiction will always remain tentative, merely exploratory. Unless a writer decides to abandon "the novel" altogether, he seldom will launch assaults on the deepest authority of the traditional genre that lies in mimesis. Modernist writers, regardless of their experiments, remained committed to the idea that in their fictions no merely arbitrary something could be imitated; if the novel is to remain the novel, it must remain grounded in something imitable outside itself. If modernist thought takes away the external objective world, novelists will turn to the still instrumentally objective internal one opened to them by modern psychology and mythology. If an objective social world of human actions seems meaningless to imitate, novelists might turn to mythic or archetypal or verbal worlds whose authority exists outside the individual, either in a "tradition," in a collective unconscious, or in language itself. Or in the event that myth, archetype, and language are subverted—as they have been by sophisticated modernists—the novelist may then turn for subject and authority or validation to the act of writing itself.

These shifts in orientation are exhibited in important novels of naive modernism early in the century. Novelists turned to the subjective center of consciousness not merely for a form (as Henry James preferred it), but for content and authorization. The "lyrical" novels that result fuse self and world, identity and the imagery of space/time—a process observed in such stream-of-consciousness novels as Woolf's *To the Lighthouse* and *The Waves* and Faulkner's *As I Lay Dying*. Joyce's works—just as "lyrical," but pointing in another direction—seem concerned with discovering a basis for determination beyond consciousness: in isolated archetypal patterns of character, as in *A Portrait of the Artist as a Young Man*; in structuring myth, as in *Ulysses*; or in the matrix of language itself, as in *Finnegans Wake*. Still other naive-phase works reduced the action imitated in fiction to the act of writing a fiction; these are the "contents" of Proust's *Remembrance of Things Past*, Gide's *The Counterfeiters*, and Huxley's *Point Counter Point*, novels which make it possible for late modernists to thematize such performance as an ultimate authority beyond the Self.

In the critical phase of modernist fiction, the underlying—often unacknowledged—assumptions of paradigms by Proust, Joyce, Woolf, Faulkner, and others have been disclosed to our awareness. They have become predominant themes, where often they were purely formal manifestations in the naive models. Thus, myth, history, language, and consciousness (including the "Un" side) have become primary concerns—explicitly articulated—in writers such as Bellow, Ellison, Malamud, Knowles, Heller, and many others— Baldwin, Mailer, Percy, Styron, and Warren. But the fact remains that for the novel, as a genre, these thematic concerns simply point to a grounding for what must remain a mimetic orientation. These themes, as centers of authority, have only replaced what Abrams calls "the universe," for they end up serving the same purpose as the figural or symbolist world once had. They serve as a common ground for communication—perhaps communion and, even, transcendence—between author and audiences. In the critical phase, myth, history, language, and consciousness provided, as the "world" once had for novelists, a possible resolution of the Cartesian dualism of self (subject) and other (object). To understand this situation has taken much of this century, but it now seems clear that "belief" in any of these constitutive, constructive fields—one of which (language) provides a basis for contemporary structuralism—permitted an existential or absurdist writer to avoid a merely subjective validation, determination, or authority for the fictional enterprise.

In the sophisticated phase of modernist fiction, however, even these bases of authority have begun to lose their "objectivity" and, thus, their validating power. We can see certain works—if not the *oeuvre* of any single author—beginning to undercut various ones of these modernist authorities. Barth, in *End of the Road*, debunks myth as merely "mytho-therapy," and then in *Giles Goat-Boy* he demolishes myth as a serious authority. Updike's *The Centaur* appears at first to be mythocentric, but, like Stevens's "Sunday Morning," in the end it, too, proves to validate neither any specific myth nor myth in general if that means relying totally upon the myths imagined by other men. Vonnegut does in the claims of consciousness—particularly, *self*-consciousness—in his later novels, and Styron, in *The Confessions of Nat Turner*, ends (though I don't think he intended to) by subsuming the authority of history in that of God, a reversion to a center of literary authority presumably dead since Nietzsche, but one apparently resurrected by the later T. S. Eliot. In *Trout Fishing in America*, Brautigan sends up history (among other things), and in various works Mailer, Burroughs, Baraka (Jones), Kelley, Ishmael Reed, and others have exploited the claims of language, but only in order to get at something more authoritative beyond language, anterior to language. Consequently, the situation of the late-phase modernist author has come to this: not only can he not believe in the world "out there," physical or historical, a belief available to be given up by the early modernists; neither can he believe any longer in most of those modernist authorities posited for the world "in here," the interior worlds of man's intellect or imagination.

But no author (as the word suggests) can continue to write without authority, even if it's only the authority of "the void" upon which to project mental edifices, and what the critics of late-modernist authors have begun to consider as their authority is the artistic performance itself. Critics such as Richard Poirier, in *The Performing Self* (1971), and Philip Stevick have begun to raise questions and, especially in Poirier's book, to suggest answers concerning the values of performance. However meaningfully this center is regarded, it must not be regarded as irreducible, for, as the structuralists suggest, it cannot evade the dichotomy of the signifier and the signified. Thus, the concept of performance can be construed in two antithetical ways: as the process or as the product, as—in our earlier terms—*play* or as *game, act* or *artifact, event* or *icon, context* or *text*. Each construction of performance is identifiable with a powerful strain of modernist literature's early paradigms, strains, using Marshall McLuhan's vocabulary, we might describe as *hot* and *cool, visual* and *audial,* eye-oriented and ear-oriented. Perhaps as a result of the theism of previous generations, the dominant strain of the generation of early modernists has appeared to need the authority provided by one pole of the antithesis, by—that is—the text, the symbolic, the signified (as structuralists such as Lacan and Derrida refer to it). The recessive strain of modernism starts from the other end, for, oriented toward performance, it solves for modernists the problem of authority—aesthetic and metaphysical—by reducing the work/performance to a *voice*, one like the emanations heard from Emerson's "Merlin,"

> Blameless master of the games,
> King of sport that never shames. . . .

II The Performative Mode

> Efforts to institutionalize the study of literature, to find order
> and design within particular works and to expand these into
> the larger designs of literary tradition, or literary con-
> tinuities, or of literature as a field of knowledge, have all had
> the result of suppressing the kind of energy I try to locate in
> the word "performance." It is an energy in motion, and it sel-
> dom fits the explanatory efforts either of most readers or even
> of most writers.
>
> Richard Poirier
> *The Performing Self* (1971)

> . . . while American writers have established an authenti-
> cally realistic . . . literary tradition, there has also been from
> the start in American literature an intermittent sense of the
> futility of pretending that the putative exactitude of words
> can ever measure up to the actual mystery of things. Along
> with this has gone a suspicion that there can be something
> damaging in confusing names and their referents. So while
> there is often an almost sportive sense of how easily language
> can float free from a given environment, there is sometimes a
> feeling that it is dangerous to get too involved in the unreal
> world of words.
>
> Tony Tanner
> *City of Words* (1971)

The exploding of the worlds of thought, space/time,
and traditional fiction made increasingly important the performative act of artistic creation. Toward the close of the nineteenth
century, *art pour l'art* had already invested the art object with
serious meaning, and art became, in the first half of the modern
century, more significant than ever, for, once traditional religious
sanctioning had been exploded along with everything else, art's
stakes became nothing less than man's salvation. But as Robert
Onopa reminds us, "Although a connection between art and religion
has been asserted in a variety of ways since the beginnings of
Romanticism, the institutionalization of art into a formal religion
has never taken hold. What has taken hold, however, at least in the
premises of modernism, is the notion that the uses of art are very

much like the uses of religion, that art can serve, in its own way, even the highest function which traditional religion purportedly serves, the function of transcendence."[19] But with the modernist, the faith in art was no *fin de siècle* "art-for-art's sake." It was art for the sake of the artist, yet the operative value for many was not the artifact, but the creative making. For such modernists as Stevens, who more and more, in his "metaphysics of imagination," seems our paradigm from early modernism appropriate for late, everyone must perform as an artist, must discover, bestow, and create order in a real, however bare, however elaborated, world. Art was for the sake of mankind itself, then, another thing entirely, though it has to have begun in the objectivist doctrines of a Pater or a Wilde and to have gone through the stage (Proust, Gide, early Joyce) of art as self-discovery rather than transcendence.

For early-modernist American writers, formed by a New-World pragmatism, the aesthetics of Emerson, Whitman, and Twain, and the politics of democracy, the most important question, however, became this: how to fuse the uniquely American vision with the modernist's experimental forms and their new metaphysical authorities. In the scramble for new systems of sanctioning during the first two or three decades of the modern century, European writers generally worked from iconic, aristocratic bases, and one strain of American modernists did turn in the directions suggested by Proust, Gide, Woolf, and Joyce. But aside from Faulkner, few naive-modernist American writers were ever as effective exhibiting the realms of archetype, myth, or language as were the British and French authors, who have provided our most powerful paradigms for those authorities. American writers work as a rule from a naive Wordsworthian realist base rather than from a Coleridgean idealist one; they work, that is to say, from a primitivist, oral, demotic base, as most of our compelling historical theories (*The American Adam, The American Novel and Its Tradition, Love and Death in the American Novel, The Reign of Wonder,* for example) have suggested. Tony Tanner makes the point clearly, suggesting that "wonder and the naive vision," though not absent in European writers, were "put to much more far-ranging uses in American writing than in any other literature" and, together as a stance, they have "*remained* a preferred way of dealing with experience and confronting existence among American writers."[20]

For American writers, American history offers a powerful reason for modernists' using this mode, the historical prevalence of which Tanner calls "the reign of wonder" in American literature. But it also has the authority of a more inclusive history, one quite properly identified with an aspect of the traditional performative mode in any literature, the mode also associated with the aesthetic orientation Abrams calls "pragmatic." The three most distinct features of American literature, therefore, that Tanner notes—which are "the interest in the naive eye with its unselective wonder; the interest in the vernacular with its immediacy and concrete directness; and the effort to slough off the Past and concentrate exclusively on the present moment"[21]—are aspects also of any actual or simulated popular, formulaic, naive "literature," one exemplified by performances ranging from *The Odyssey* to *The Hawkline Monster*. Tanner is right in his theory concerning "naivety and reality in American literature," then, but the more authoritative category for the phenomenon is "the tradition." American writers have found—often unwittingly, no doubt—their sources of validation in what we know now is a recognizable mode in the world's literature.[22]

But there is a double sense of "tradition" in modernism. Writers as diverse as Gertrude Stein, Wallace Stevens, Ezra Pound, T. S. Eliot, Sherwood Anderson, Ernest Hemingway, Scott Fitzgerald, and William Faulkner have resolved their problems of "making it new" (Pound's cry) through a return—in varying degrees—to the primitive, the archaic, the pre-literary oral tradition, but the more visualist among these have also regarded as models and sources "the great works" (Brautigan's epithet) from the literary tradition. The modernist perspective transforms either tradition, but the transformations have taken the routes of the performative and the artifactive. The artifactive operation has been the habit of the "classic" modernist poets—Pound and Eliot; the performative has been the habit of the early phase of modernist fiction writers, including Stein, Anderson, Hemingway, and Fitzgerald. The former, represented by Eliot's "Tradition and the Individual Talent," has construed the "tradition" as iconic artifacts to be displayed in poems—like Eliot's—as if they were verbal museums; the latter—though, Stevens aside, without a powerful spokesman like Eliot—has construed the "tradition" as a method, a manner, a style, that is, as a dynamic process. The visualists have turned to myth—as an artifactive construct—as their authority, their court of last resort. The audialists have turned to *mythos*, the sense of myth as an informing principle of story, as their authority; it suggests less the gatherings of myth by anthropologists, adverted to by Eliot, than the actual performance of myth-making by the shaman or singer of tales, an attitude expressed clearly in both the poems and the essays of Stevens, whose *The Necessary Angel* suggests imagination is a value, not just an activity. Among American writers, William Faulkner—if anyone really has—has bridged the gap between the two groups, whose biases are exhibited in *The Sound and the Fury*, though absorbed in the contrast between Benjy's and Jason's versus Quentin's and Dilsey's modes of presentation.

One of these "traditions" has been more privileged in modernism than the other. Charles Altieri makes very clear in his essay that "classic" modernist literature, including both naive and critical phases, has exaggerated the claims of the iconic and, thus, has been canted in the objective direction toward the artifactism honored by our New Criticism; until their resurgence in late modernism, the cooler, performative exhibits have been left very much in the wings. Given this dominant orientation, modernist literature and criticism have emphasized the text as "well-wrought urn"—the densely textured, complex, verbally ironic work that begs for a religious devotion expressed in rituals of explication. But since there are in fact two different major strains of modernism, this orientation has led to peculiar critical *faux pas*. American criticism has given a particularly favored status, for example, to the two largely iconic sections in *The Sound and the Fury*, especially ignoring the pleasures of Jason's "performance." Hemingway's *The Sun Also Rises* and, later, *The Old Man and the Sea* in themselves not only lack, but reveal an author actively avoiding, a dense verbal texture, yet they have been subjected to the minute operations of a New Critical methodology. They have had a "texture" created from whole cloth by criticism itself, as an almost sacramental enthusiasm for icons has engendered a variety of explications for Hemingway from the extrinsic materials of biography, psychology, and the cultural mythology of "the lost generation."

Even so, in much of Hemingway our interpretations are either too little or too much; he resists our attempts at explication because his works are self-sufficient in ways a more traditional written fiction could no longer be. Now, aware of his interest in performance—as expressed in his language of craft, skill, expertise—we realize that Hemingway (as opposed to James's devoted Aspernian critic) was preoccupied less with the product, the verbal icon, than with the authority of the process, the act of writing. Thus, he could be an artist creating works of art which at the same time were also "anti-art," or simply beyond art. Consequently, if we now reassess the "performances" of certain authors—poets like Frost, Stevens, and Williams, and novelists like Anderson, Hemingway, and Fitzgerald—we see that they can be construed in ways compatible with the peculiarities of works by very recent authors like Barth, Barthelme, Brautigan, Coover, DeLillo, Kosinski, and Vonnegut. The reason is plain: many of the naive modernists were already involved in "minimal" or even anti-art, and these late modernists, in taking them up, have taken up a particular strain of naive-modernist fiction. And as critical modernism converted into themes some of the implied bases of the early modernists, so these sophisticated modernists have transformed into themes and authority the assumptions of their predecessors, turning the very act of writing into a devotional—however playful—to the vitality of the human imagination, discovering in the process that they have linked themselves, as well, to a vastly more authoritative power in the ancient mode of narrative art. They thus tap two sources of power equally, either of which is probably sufficient to explain for us Emerson's notion of the "kingly bard" who is every bit as muscular and athletic as Hemingway or Fitzgerald would have him, and who in the smithy of his soul is pounding out

> Artful thunder, which conveys
> Secrets of the solar track,
> Sparks of the supersolar blaze. . . .

One of these sources, as structuralist psychologist Guy Rosolato suggests, seems to be located in the psyche of the author, in that region of the unconscious from which emanates the "voice" of the Father, the voice of the primal life source. The other source, as Jacques Derrida would argue, is one residing also in the audience, and that is the authority of cultural History, the "center" now mandated anew by structuralist ethnographers such as Lévi-Strauss.[23] These may appear mighty big clubs for relatively small works to wield, but there may be a rule in the game these late modernists play that calls for such potent authority when the performances themselves are deliberately understated.

Among the late-modernist writers, Richard Brautigan illustrates best this performative strain. Brautigan's works seem to model the general shift of modernist fiction from the "tradition" of the intensely introverted self-reflexive work as artifact or game to the "tradition" of the extraverted performance, the work as act, ritual, play. *Trout Fishing in America* seems, finally, in the face of an increasingly corrupted environment, to fall back to the authority of the autonomous art object, though the activity of imagination remains important in the book. The later works, by becoming less dense and more obviously performative, undercut the autonomy of the art object and increase the theme of the value of the creative activity of the artist or performer behind it. The tensions between expressive lyrical art object and pragmatic imagination caught between world and audience energize *In Watermelon Sugar* (1968) and suggest that Brautigan has become critical of his own implied themes in *Trout Fishing*. The later book insistently calls attention to the author's role as storyteller in the opening invitation to the reader to come into the world of watermelon sugar, the world—one surmises—of the creative imagination, here a world largely pastoral, idyllic, and benign. It again calls attention to the authorial-storyteller role at the end, amidst the preparations for a ritual dance that concludes the performance, Brautigan's last words being, "It would only be a few seconds now, *I wrote*."[24] And in between we get the most beguiling fantasies of a gentle storyteller who tries his best to escape the limitations of both the world beyond imagination and the demands of storytelling. Both these realms are characterized by conflict, however, and while the watermelon-sugared imagination may prefer to eschew violence and death, the narrative-artist/storyteller, no more than the world, can exist without them. Thus, philosophically, the gentle reader, like the author, may prefer iDEATH to inBOIL, but the world and storytelling-as-art demand that the latter appear, to conquer or be conquered. *In Watermelon Sugar* may not be oriented toward the world, may, indeed, seem so solipsistic as almost to deny the world, yet it nonetheless appears to be a work that manifests Brautigan's uneasiness with the purely solipsistic or purely aesthetic.

The other recent works seem to reveal the necessity of living, and living imaginatively, in the world. The world and the artist's imaginative responses are both acknowledged in the parodic "romance," *The Abortion* (1971). This novel, which makes a plot of a journey to the underworld (Tijuana, Mexico) to achieve abortion rather than conception or birth, treats a problematic subject that has evoked ambivalent interpretations not thought consistent with Brautigan's playfulness. The playfulness is more obvious in *The Hawkline Monster* (1974), but, while again in a parodic form (setting the formulae of the western against those of the gothic), there is also an underlying problematic tension in the book, this one between the machismo methods of the western-American gunfighter and the Faustian—and Western—methods of the scientist, mad or otherwise. It is a fun—and funny—book, but it retains a serious base to it, as a pastoral novel does always. The same playfulness is evident in *Willard and His Bowling Trophies* (1975). It gently parodies the conventions of the pornographic novel, as it refers explicitly to *The Story of O* and reveals one of its two sets of married couples trying halfheartedly and ineptly to follow its sexual programs; it also parodies the sort of film, often in western or gangster-desperado genres, that documents the fall into crime of a group, often relatives, often—as here—brothers. It, too, has at its center two very serious themes—sex and violence in American life, but its lesson most characteristic of Brautigan's fiction is the saving grace provided by imagination. Imagination and playfulness are what doom the first couple and the three desperate Logan brothers, for they have neither, and save the second married couple, for they have both. Imagination, then, Brautigan tells us in one crucial section of this novel, is what moves and animates us and the world.

The position that Brautigan's fiction expresses is not really far from the various related positions expressed in modernist fiction of five decades ago. But it does not require a profound twist for his themes to be shaped toward what may well be the central preoccupations of a post-modernist literature. I cannot say precisely what those will be, but I suspect they will involve a reevaluation of both the physical world and man in it. Brautigan's—and others'—emphasis upon play and the imaginative exchange between knower and known begins to restore a meaningful value to both, where the tenets (never reduced to a creed) of modernism tended to deny the value of one or the other. Though the whole popular tradition, through it all, did maintain much of the dignity and value of artist and audience, if not of art and world, even the writers most in tune with this tradition—Stein, Anderson, and Hemingway—have been interpreted as harbingers and purveyors of modernist absurdity, nihilism, emptiness. Brautigan, for one, has distilled the essentially affirmative assumptions of value from the tradition within which he works, and by doing so he may easily appear—in a few decades—as the post-modernist Philip Stevick and others have labeled him.

Brautigan's *Trout Fishing in America* (1967) artfully gathers together elements of a wide-ranging tradition of pastoral/performative American fiction.[25] The tradition goes back, in one line or the other, to Irving and Hawthorne, Melville and Twain, Anderson and Hemingway, Fitzgerald and Faulkner, Steinbeck and Malamud and Kerouac. Brautigan's connection to this tradition fits primarily into the performative line of modernist and American literature, but the combination in *Trout Fishing* can help us account for his simplicity and his complexity, his essential modernism. In the modernist avatars of the tradition we may see the colloquial style familiar in our literature, but at the same time we may see a sophisticated lyricism and perhaps a metafictional playfulness. On the one hand, we may perceive Brautigan as the heir of Stein, Anderson, and Hemingway; on the other, however, we may see him as the heir of Joyce, Kafka, and Borges. In one place he may be regarded as of the "school" of the Nabokov of *Pale Fire*, the Barth of *Lost in the Funhouse*, the Coover of *The Universal Baseball Association*; in another place he may be regarded as a brother-in-arms of the Hawkes of *Second Skin* and *The Lime-Twig*, the Heller of *Catch-22*, and the McGuane of *The Sporting Club* and *Ninety-two in the Shade*. In short, Brautigan, like Kurt Vonnegut, Jr., writes cool, lightly textured works that permit themselves to be thrown into whichever stream of American fiction one happens to be fishing in at a given moment.

The tradition of American pastoral/performative fiction to which Brautigan belongs seems infinitely expansive, as a look at this tradition since Sherwood Anderson will show. At the beginning of modernism, Eliot made clear how valuable a sense of tradition could be. The main reason any writer turns to a "tradition"—pastoral/performative or literary/historical—is to solve his problem of authority, his problem of legitimacy and validation. For a naive-modernist writer such as Sherwood Anderson, the authoritative element in the popular tradition lay in the performance, in its posited relationship between the audience and the voice of the story*teller*, a term privileged by pastoral writers, who discredited the intellectualist term *author*. In his letters and elsewhere, Anderson insists that he "spoke" for and to the common man. In the story told in the oral-formulaic tradition, upon which, as Jarvis Thurston clarifies for us, Anderson's art securely rests, the relationship, not the produced artifact, is deemed sacramental, for in this tradition the *vates*, the bard, the singer does not put his auditors in touch with himself; instead, through his voice, he puts them in touch with the tradition that embraces both teller and audience, but that exists outside both and is yet independent of either.[26] It is, of course, also a pastoral role the voice enacts as it creates a community of its respondents. In *Winesburg, Ohio* this sense is reinforced in a subtle way, in a doubling of this vatic nexus. One form exists in George Willard's relationship to the "grotesques" of Winesburg, just as another exists in Sherwood Anderson's relationship to his readers. But the sense of communal authority is reinforced in yet another way, in Anderson's also formularizing his tales in the book so that they may express a conventional folk "wisdom." It is less the characterological, mythological, symbolic, or thematic structures of the different tales, however, than the voice's style and a point of view that interest Anderson in the tradition within which he works. As Milman Parry, A. B. Lord, and other academicians since the 1930s have shown, the assumption of the vatic voice—with its accompaniments of characters, plots, symbols, and lore—is enough to permit Anderson to tap into a powerful source of authority, and it is authority, not just a content alone, that Anderson the would-be-novelist needed to help establish a pastoral/performative strain of modernist fiction.

Another naive modernist, Ernest Hemingway, learned much from Sherwood Anderson, but the younger writer found an overtly vatic burden onerous and withdrew instead into an oracular objectivity. But the same American tradition happens also to provide that potentiality. Hemingway could parody Anderson mercilessly in *The Torrents of Spring*, then, but the modes of the two writers became recognizably the same once Hemingway discovered what he really wanted to do. And what he wanted to do, it appears, had less of the purely dramatic in it than of the purely oral-formulaic: this is evident in the best pieces of *In Our Time*, *The Sun Also Rises*, *Green Hills of Africa*, *For Whom the Bell Tolls*, and, especially, *The Old Man and the Sea*. The Hemingway style, founded upon a classical sense of a natural language, is really only the naively transparent, formulaic, timeless prose of the oral tradition; so between author and audience, the sacramental act, for Hemingway as for Anderson, was the performative act of "telling" a story cast into writing, a story stripped to the essences of language, character, event, and form. Just as Anderson found his center of validation in the sounds of communion, so Hemingway found his in the ritual performance of an action. Consequently, behind the work of either author resonates an absolute in the voice of the primal authority—the voice of the Father or of the culture or of both together.[27]

In what most would consider not only his best but also one of the best novels of early modernism, *The Great Gatsby*, Scott Fitzgerald also turns toward a popular tradition of the told-story in his use of Nick Carraway as the first-person narrator. But Fitzgerald goes to neither extreme exhibited by Anderson and Hemingway. Where Anderson's critical axis is drawn between vatic artist and communal audience and Hemingway's between the objective, ritual structure of the traditional *mythos* and the audience, Fitzgerald's is still between the knowing self and the external universe. Thus, Fitzgerald retains the orientation of the novel-as-genre, but at its center—just as in those centers of consciousness in James—we see Carraway, a dual protagonist/artist, trying to come to terms with his experience in the world and seeing his own struggle mirrored in Gatsby's struggle to maintain the "colossal vitality" of his illusions. The shape that Carraway discovers/confers, in that experience of which Gatsby and his illusions are the center, is conveyed to us in a narrative voice and through archetypal forms. In the end, displayed in that perorational final paragraph, Fitzgerald's center of narration, though more "literary," possesses as much a sacramental—and American—voice as Anderson's or Hemingway's "voices." The popular, oral, performative tradition, as it ranged from the extremely personal of Anderson, through the moderately personal of Fitzgerald, to the extremely impersonal of Hemingway, has been very adaptable, and it is no surprise at all that a variety of later novelists have taken up this aspect of modernism instead of the iconic or symbolist one.

Anderson, Hemingway, and Fitzgerald, in addition, are all in some crucial way to be associated with a literary and formal pastoral element in the tradition. The style of each returns us to pastoral ideals of simplicity, directness, and concreteness, aspects which have been analyzed in Tony Tanner's *The Reign of Wonder*, but their styles are also related to a particular conception of character and theme. As William Empson says in *Some Versions of Pastoral*, "The essential trick of the old pastoral, which was felt to imply a beautiful relation between rich and poor, was to make simple people express strong feelings (felt as the most universal subject, something fundamentally true about everybody) in learned and fashionable language (so that you wrote about the best subject in the best way)."[28] The disparity between the subtle, universal themes and the simple styles and characters will work, Empson says, only so long as an author continues to pretend he is unconscious of the relation.

Naive-modernist fiction, rooted in Twain, has found that the best way to keep up this pretense is to turn over the narration to a naive character: a rustic or rogue, child or fool—any naif, Tony Tanner suggests in *The Reign of Wonder*. In Anderson, the child and the rustic are fused in major characters such as George Willard and the old writer, who introduces *Winesburg, Ohio* in "The Book of the Grotesque." But others of Anderson's characters also fit Empson's description: many, like Dr. Reefy, are simple men who seem fools, but any one of them "yet has better 'sense' than his betters and can say things more fundamentally true."[29] In Hemingway, the pose of the narrator in the early works maintains elements of both the "truth-telling" and the "stoicism." Empson does not concede that Hemingway (of whom he speaks directly) is largely pastoral in this technique, but he does suggest that "the purpose behind a Hemingway character is to carry to the highest degree the methods of direct reporting—his stoical simple man is the type who gets most directly the sensations any one would get from the events. This is a very general method for stories of action and has a touch of pastoral so far as it implies 'the fool sees true.' "[30] In Fitzgerald, the pose of the narrator is pastoral, in Empson's sense especially. Fitzgerald sets an innocent "Western" against sophisticates (Eastern), who are rich, as well. Fitzgerald's Nick remains far more literary than either Anderson's or Hemingway's various personae, but a consequence of Nick's literary value is that we are given a clearer structural sense of the contrast between West and East, naif and sophisticate, poor and rich, idealist and pragmatist, and thus we see the ultimately tragic consequences of that corrupted American Dream so eloquently apostrophized by Nick at the novel's end.

Of authors who might have been treated in this study, the work of Bernard Malamud seems very much to exhibit this strain of naive-modernist fiction, though, like Bellow's, it is largely a work of critical consolidation. If Bellow is in the "hotter" tradition of James, Malamud takes the "cooler" modes of an early modern like Anderson, assimilates them, and makes them his own, though he does not really (nor does he need to) transform them. But Malamud's best work is no simple art. He uses as effectively as any critical modernist the basic epistemological mode of the lyric novelist in order to treat themes of alienation and suffering, at the same time that he uses the modes—which he begins to parody—of comedy and tragedy, the ironic and the romantic. In *The Natural* he draws upon the tradition—largely popular—of sports fiction in America, one seen or felt vividly in Anderson, Ring Lardner, Hemingway, Fitzgerald, and even Faulkner. In *The Assistant*, as Malamud creates an urban landscape as vital but threatening as any from the naive tradition of American naturalism, he also creates a hero who is as powerless, as psychically indeterminate, and as bent upon self-definition as one of Bellow's "dangling men." In *A New Life* Malamud writes yet another of those "academic novels" with which American fiction abounds; in *The Fixer* he turns to the treatment of an actual historical crime and punishment, similar in some ways to *An American Tragedy* and *Native Son*; *Pictures of Fidelman*, like *Winesburg, Ohio* and several works in Faulkner, is a cycle of stories focusing upon the development of one character. *The Tenants* seems to owe less to other fictions than to the allusively poetic world of Shakespeare's *The Tempest*, yet it, too, depends upon the sort of intellectual, physical, even erotic conflict between Black American and White that we see in Faulkner, Warren, Baldwin, Styron, and Updike.

The tradition in Malamud, as it had been for the naive modernists, becomes epistemological and ontological, the performative and pastoral elements providing both a way of knowing and a content to be known. The mode of perception that the performative voice gives Malamud allows him to exploit fully the resources of the pastoral as a content. Through it Malamud can employ very simple people as his protagonists, antagonists, and supporting characters; these people can accept their own most foolish, as well as their own most heroic, actions in the most matter-of-fact ways; and they can talk about themselves, their world, and its values in the most uncritical vocabularies available to the popular mind. Moreover, the pastoral mode permits him to structure his plots as if they belonged to the *mythoi* of tragedy and comedy. But, while Malamud's voice seems to validate the ways in which his characters see the world, in his best novels—*The Natural, The Assistant, The Fixer*—there is always a note of parody that comes out of his use of popular "myths" such as the tragedy of the ball player Shoeless Joe Jackson, the ecstatic romance of St. Francis of Assisi, and the nightmare terrors of Russian Bolshevism. That undercurrent of parody, as one expects in a modernist work, leaves forms and meanings subtly indeterminate. Like Faulkner, Malamud is disposed—as the Russian formalists say—toward "baring his devices," as he forces us to study his fictive worlds at the same time that we regard his epistemological and ontological modes, but less like early Faulkner than like the critical modernists, he opts for formal openness rather than for formal pluralism. Malamud's exploiting the possibilities of pastoral and the naive popular consciousness, however, pushes him slightly closer than, for example, Saul Bellow to the late modernism of Vonnegut and Brautigan; still, one would not wish to overstate their differences. One must agree with Max Schulz's views of Malamud and the modern Jewish novelists in general: ". . . willingness to accept the world on its own terms—disorderly, incoherent, absurd—'without any irritable reaching after fact and reason,' and yet without losing faith in the moral significance of human actions, underlies the confrontation of experience in the best of the contemporary Jewish-American novels."[31]

III Brautigan's *Trout Fishing in America*

> . . . for all of the astonishment he expresses at the wilder-
> ness of their own contriving in which Americans dwell, Mr.
> Brautigan's principal concern, one feels, is, in the midst of
> hell, to *play*. . . .
>
> Nathan A. Scott, Jr.
> "History, Hope, and Literature" (1973)

The pastoral/performative tradition to which Brautigan belongs has been extremely elastic, adaptable, and fluid. One can see in his work at some points strains of the lyrical novel, that sub-genre focusing upon the contents and shifting forms of consciousness and represented in works of Bellow, Coover, Hawkes, Heller, Exley, and others, and in Brautigan's *In Watermelon Sugar*. At other points one can see the strain of authorially self-conscious metafictions—those fictions about the writing of fiction, represented currently in Nabokov's *Pale Fire*, Barth's *Lost in the Funhouse*, and, again, in Brautigan's *In Watermelon Sugar*. At yet other points one can see aspects of those fictions that convert the artistic process into a literary or metaphysical game of some sort, as in *Ada* and several other works of Nabokov, Coover's *The Universal Baseball Association, J. Henry Waugh, Prop.*, Don DeLillo's *End Zone*, Roth's *The Great American Novel*, and Updike's *The Centaur*. Brautigan touches this strain in *Trout Fishing in America* and in all his works that have their primary impulse in the parody or mimicking of popular, formulaic types: *The Abortion* and its parody of a "romance" such as *A Farewell to Arms; The Hawkline Monster*, a parody of the gothic and the western; and *Willard and His Bowling Trophies*, which parodies both pornography and the gangster genre of films such as *Bonnie and Clyde* and *Dillinger*. *A Confederate General from Big Sur* fits here, too, for it seems a parody of such bohemian or Beat works as Henry Miller's *Tropic* novels and Kerouac's *On the Road*, this latter especially. Brautigan does seem located at the very center of late modernist fiction, and he seems so not despite but because of his roots in the tradition of American naive or pastoral fiction that runs back through Malamud, Kerouac, Steinbeck, Faulkner, Hemingway, Fitzgerald, Anderson, Stein, Crane, Twain, and, according to Tanner, even beyond. Like his older but temperamentally contemporary colleague Kurt Vonnegut, Jr., Brautigan does what the best pastoral writers have always done: he treats topical themes (which, in the tradition, are always universal) in the language of simple people so that the extremes, the best and worst, of our culture become more clearly visible.

In Brautigan every study must begin with *Trout Fishing in America* (1967). All those naive quirks and pastoral preoccupations that make his work significant and reveal his indebtedness to the tradition appear here. Perhaps the first traditional aspect of *Trout Fishing* that strikes one is point of view, the *pose* of the author. Because, as Walt Whitman had before him, Brautigan actually includes a photograph of himself with his work, the term pose applies literally as well as figuratively; the old-fashioned openness, directness, and rusticity of the author in the photograph seem clearly embodied in the prose. When Brautigan's first chapter "explains" the cover, unless we notice that he makes no mention of himself and the woman who shares the picture's space, he would not seem to be anything but direct in his style:

> The cover for *Trout Fishing in America* is a photograph taken late in the afternoon, a photograph of the Benjamin Franklin Statue in San Francisco's Washington Square.
>
> Born 1706—Died 1790, Benjamin Franklin stands on a pedestal that looks like a house containing stone furniture. He holds some papers in one hand and his hat in the other.[32]

It seems a transparent prose, apparently interested only in the representation of the scene before us: at first glance here or in the next longish paragraph, wherein Brautigan explains the word "Welcome" appearing on the four sides of the statue and describes three almost leafless poplars and wet February grass, all the attention of the language appears to be directed toward the universe outside man, outside language, outside consciousness. All the interest seems horizontally directed toward depiction and narration.

But there is one disjunction in those two short paragraphs quoted above—the simile "like a house containing stone furniture." The simile here—and throughout Brautigan, as also in the whole tradition of colloquial/vernacular American literary style—introduces a movement away from the picture or the action and toward some vertex—a theme, idea, meaning. It raises all sorts of questions that we feel obliged to answer, but at this point there is virtually nothing upon which to base our answers, so we read on, having slowed down the pace and prepared to pause again if similar vertical disjunctions recur. They do. We must pause again at "a tall cypress tree, almost dark like a room," and again at the church's "vast door that looks like a huge mousehole, perhaps from a Tom and Jerry cartoon." If Brautigan's prose remained horizontal and continued to point at the universe outside the book or outside language and man's consciousness, *Trout Fishing* would be one of the fastest reads in the history of the novel (perhaps only *The Old Man and the Sea* might match it outside Brautigan's canon). The novel reads slow and long, however, and the reason lies in these vertical dispersals of style. They create disjunctive, reflexive, micro-rhythms that generate more interest than do the meta-rhythms of plot continuity and that development of character seen as "an unbroken series of successful gestures"—as Scott Fitzgerald defines personality in *The Great Gatsby*.

Trout Fishing in America is not *naively* naive, not a simple pastoral fiction; it is a subtle poetic novel by a lyrical poet, built upon the popular conventions of a widely shared tradition. As a lyrical novel,[33] *Trout Fishing* will reveal its secrets to us not by analysis of "story"—what happens and what happens next—but, if at all, by meditative casts into the individual chapters, each a small deep pool whose meaning might perhaps rise to our best lures. Like those trout pools, however, each section seems to conceal more meaning than any of our linear casts can catch. But we continue to cast, hoping no doubt to land the big one, a Moby Trout, a "great fish," like Santiago's marlin, that will draw everything together for us. Thus, the question about such a work always seems to be, do the vertical dispersions have a common center or offer a holistic meaning? In other words, how do we read such a book? One way is to begin with the genre conventions that seem to fit best. *Trout Fishing* seems most easily read through the conventions of the pastoral element of the oral/colloquial tradition.

One of the pastoral themes in the tradition is the concern with man's fate, his *telos*, or end—his *death*. Death appears as a theme even in the opening chapter. That the theme appears is not surprising, but that it appears in such a disarming prose style may well be surprising to many readers. The clues are in those vertical dispersals. But we as readers are forced to put them all together, by meditative casts, lateral drifts. We don't have a lot to go on: objectively, only the *Franklin* statue, *Washington* Square, *Adlai Stevenson*, and *Kafka;* and, ambiguously subjective and objective, the house *with stone furniture,* the tree *dark like a room,* and the door *like a huge mousehole.* A common reference point for the men whose names are here identified might lie in their identification with historic conceptualizations of America, but the common point of reference for the sequence of similes lies in the concept of domicile, and, though the salutation "welcome" on the statue points to the four axes of earth, not one place described seems finally comfortable or secure.

What we have so far, then, is a series of items and figures of speech that subtly associate America with something less than ideal places; this negative point may be validated in the vertices drawn by other details: the words of the statue, "saying in marble," *Presented By/ H. D. Cogswell/To Our/Boys And Girls/Who Will Soon/Take Our Places/And Pass On,* and the inscription over the church door "Per l'Universo." All these details suggest that this could be a sacred place, a world center, a universal navel. It could be that from which man emanates and to which he returns. But as it is presented to us here, every connotation is negative: here, at the beginning of *Trout Fishing,* the once-sacred place is a tomb, offering only a bare hint of renewal and sustenance—in the newspaper-wrapped sandwiches, filled on one occasion with spinach, Popeye's rejuvenating elixir— but little else. What we are left with, finally, is the traditional pastoral theme of *et in Arcadia ego:* even in Arcady or Eden—or America—there is death. *Welcome* to it, the statue says, "facing the directions of this world." Never has simplicity seemed so duplicitous.

Two sets of related themes that thread their way through the whole book are sex and violence, death and excrement. Or are they sex and death, violence and excrement, sex and excrement, violence and death? The question seems always, where do we put the emphasis? Ultimately, it doesn't really matter, for each of the book's forty-seven sections interweaves these motifs. The book is one of the most mortifying experiences one could imagine, and yet it manifests a remarkably subtle wit and humor, both so pervasive that only two chapters ("The Salt Creek Coyotes" and "The Surgeon") have almost nothing humorous. What Brautigan has recognized is the way that sex and violence energize the conventions of humor, turn scatology into eschatology. They appear together everywhere in the American naive tradition that he continues.

The combination of humor and grotesquerie that make the book so intensely ambiguous is well illustrated in the chapter "Worsewick." "Worsewick Hot Springs was nothing fancy," writes Brautigan. Persons unknown had put boards across the creek to dam it up at a point where hot springs fed into it. The narrator, his "woman," and the baby go there one day and bathe in the tub so created: "There was a green slime growing around the edges of the tub and there were dozens of dead fish floating in our bath. Their bodies had been turned white by death, like frost on iron doors. Their eyes were large and stiff" (p. 43). Playing there among the dead fish and slime, the narrator says he began "to get ideas," so his woman takes the baby back to the car for her nap: "It *really* was time," he insists, "for her to take a nap." He and his woman make love there in the water, but because she didn't have her diaphragm and he doesn't want to have more children, they decide upon *coitus interruptus*, so that when he ejaculates his "sperm came out into the water, unaccustomed to the light, and instantly it became a misty, stringy kind of thing and swirled out like a falling star, and," he says, "I saw a dead fish come forward and float into my sperm, bending it in the middle. His eyes were stiff like iron" (p. 44).

This is all incredibly grotesque and at least one critic, Neil Schmitz, has suggested that its demonic image of procreative sex is a complete "profanation." Such an unambiguously moral interpretation seems firmly based in a reading of other parts of this chapter. Focusing upon the image of the narrator having at his woman as the deerflies had had at her while getting from the car to the water and also upon the flat statement that he wanted no "more kids for a long time," Schmitz can turn the chapter into a bitter, Swiftian satire upon death-loving man. But Brautigan's tone just will not let it remain so, and if we turn to the crucial simile he employs to describe the "precipitous orgasm" (Schmitz's words) we can see how Brautigan's language gives another direction to argument: "Then I came, and just cleared her in a split second like an airplane in the movies, pulling out of a nosedive and sailing over the roof of a school" (p. 44). Agreeing not to bring children into an overcrowded world is not quite a profanation these days, and it is sex as recreation, not procreation, that Brautigan celebrates here (and in many of his

poems, despite the apparently contrary theme of "The Pill *versus*
The Springhill Mine Disaster"), at the same time he shows
graphically that much of the world has become a garbage dump or a
toilet reaching "down like an accordion into the abyss" (p. 101). It is
not a pretty world, but, Brautigan suggests, it's all we've got. So we
must make do with it.[34]

Because *Trout Fishing* is a popular traditional/lyrical novel, we
can drop a line into any of its pools and might come up with a clear
sense of the book's total meaning, a dominant theme drawing all the
vertices together. At any given point in the book its main theme will
be visible either in the text itself or in the activity that, implicitly,
always lies behind it. In other words, we can often take the text at
face value, or we can retreat to the transforming, metamorphic,
metaphoric process of imaginative creation that underlies it. Individual chapters will often be about the disjunction between "reality" and "the world," with specific images concretely manifesting
the grotesqueness of the world and other images illustrating the
impact of mind, imagination, and creativity upon it. In the "Worsewick" episode, for example, the "bathtub" pool with all the dead
trout, slime, and deerflies "says" one thing about the world, but
Brautigan's language and the narrative structure his art imposes on
the experience transform it into something different and not entirely repellent. The sheer playfulness of language conveys a rather
cheerful message ("the medium *is* the message"), and the whole
structure of the episode leads us from the most repellent-seeming of
mundane activities to an act (ironically, it is *coitus interruptus* that
achieves climactic revelation) that takes on cosmological significance, as Brautigan's similes take us from the age of the
dinosaurs ("I did this by going deeper and deeper in the water, *like a
dinosaur*, and letting the green slime and dead fish cover me over,"
he says of hiding his "hard on"), to the age of aeronautical technology ("like an airplane"), to the cosmic reaches of intergalactic space
("like a falling star"). Consequently, one would suggest that the
book is not about reality, or that manifestation of it called
"America," but about our knowledge of it, how we can cope with it
and finally must make do with it. The process is at best tragi-comic,
as the most profound pastoral art always is in its formulae of elegy,
ubi sunt, or *et in Arcadia ego*.

The meta-narrative component of *Trout Fishing*, in contrast to
most works in the tradition, we must extrapolate for ourselves from

the discontinuous sections, but in doing so we see clearly how tragi-comic becomes the whole structure. While the book has frequently been called a "quest," a search for the "real" America to replace all the sham dreams, all the corrupted visions, an America for *Amerika*, it seems less to provide a quest than images manifesting the development of the artist. In other words, it seems not the *Bildungsroman*, but the *Künstlerroman*. In a general way the book's meta-narrative (reconstructed) moves, like the simpler *Bildungsroman*, from childhood to youth to maturity. "The Cover of Trout Fishing in America," of course, is the invitational prologue to the book, so the fact of the narrator's mature presence there does not interfere with the development that actually begins in the next two chapters, "Knock on Wood (Part One)" and "Knock on Wood (Part Two)," both of which concern the narrator's childhood initiation to "trout fishing in America." Initiation is disillusioning in a particularly modernist way for him, since the first trout stream and the magnificent waterfalls he sees turn out to be nothing more than a perceptual error, a "flight of wooden stairs leading up to a house in the trees." Modernist, too, is the way the ritual charm that he enacts—knocking on wood—has the effect not of confirming "reality" or protecting his fantasy or desire, but of revealing their unreality and impossibility. So the boy does the only thing that any modernist youth can do: he internalizes his dream and his reality: "I ended up by being my own trout and eating the slice of bread myself" (p. 5). He becomes, in a word, the artist, and *Bildungsroman* metamorphoses into *Künstlerroman*, a portrait of the artist as a young (fisher) man.

"The Hunchback Trout" climaxes the series of episodes that includes the "Knock on Wood" sections, as well as "Grider Creek" and "Tom Martin Creek." These episodes show the various typal frustrations the young angler goes through before the glorious success of landing the hunchback trout. His success, however, is as much imaginative as sporting. Indeed, Brautigan's style intimates that the success is mainly literary, for the episode, more than most, is indicative of the role of style and language in *Trout Fishing*. The entire episode is controlled by a single metaphor—of the creek "like 12,845 telephone booths in a row" and the "kid covered with fishing tackle," "just like a telephone repairman," "going in there and catching a few trout" and keeping "the telephones in service," "an asset to society" (p. 55). Narrating the day the "kid" "punched in" for work at the creek and landed the hunchback, he is able to match the incredible physical energy of the trout with the verbal, imaginative energy of the artist: "The fish ran deep again and I could feel its life energy screaming back up the line to my hand. The line felt like sound. It was like an ambulance siren coming straight at me, red light flashing, and then going away again and then taking to the air and becoming an air-raid siren" (p. 57). In the book, one has the impression that this episode marks not an end of innocence but a discovery of the one effective potency man has in an otherwise impermeable world. That potency, again sacramentally ingested, is the artist's: "There was a fine thing about that trout. I only wish I could have made a death mask of him. Not of his body though, but of his energy. I don't know if anyone would have understood his body. I put it in my creel./Later in the afternoon when the telephone booths began to grow dark at the edges, I punched out of the creek and went home. I had the hunchback trout for dinner. Wrapped in cornmeal and fried in butter, its hump tasted sweet as the kisses of Esmeralda" (p. 57). Brautigan's Moby Trout, his great fish, turns out to be a hunchback in the Bell System.

In a lyrical novel such as this we might infer that "the kid's" actions contain all the message we—or the narrator—require, for eventually we do surmise that his sacraments are also incarnations. They are attainments of the dream in the only way possible, whether for artist or for man in general. Indeed, this is enough to go on in *Trout Fishing*, but we are impelled to read on, both because of the tremendous vitality of Brautigan's imagination and because we want to check our trout lines. Are there other manifestations of the theme, other avatars of the artist? There are. In "The Kool-Aid Wino" (a child who creates a "Kool-Aid reality"); the wine winos of "A Walden Pond for Winos"; the bookstore manager of "Sea, Sea Rider" (who introduces an adolescent narrator not just to sex, but to sex-with-imagination); old Charles Hayman, who lives his art, crotchety as he is (he's an aged, illiterate, child-loathing W. C. Fields of 1876), in "The Last Year the Trout Came Up Hayman Creek"; Lord Byron, memorialized in "The Autopsy of Trout Fishing in America"; and, finally, in the narrator himself in "The Hunchback Trout" (pp. 55–57).

There is a somewhat more extended "plot" structure than this suggests, however, for there appear to be three "transforms" of the basic narrative unit. The "Knock on Wood" and "The Hunchback

Trout" chapters bracket the first of three overlapping narrative sequences. The earlier chapters portray the narrator as a real fisherman before they spiral into fantastic verbal displays. Some of these chapters are as socially critical as anything elsewhere in the book, and so serve as a foundation for the shift that comes in the second of the three narrative sequences. In a general way, the second sequence focuses upon "the kid's" mature life. It shows more fully than the first his relationship with "his woman" and his friends, who are usually young couples, a pattern of socialization often following the period of male bonding, intimated in the first section, for example, in "A Walden Pond for Winos." The sequence also focuses upon the imposition of mundane reality upon the kid's trout-fishing mythopoeic vision.

One sort of episode in this middle sequence continues the more specifically social themes treated in the first sequence in, for example, "Prologue to Grider Creek" (on John Dillinger's home town), "The Message" (a young Hitler shepherd whose message is "Stalingrad"), "The Mayor of the Twentieth Century" (Jack the Ripper), "The Cabinet of Doctor Caligari" (on duplex realities), and "The Salt Creek Coyotes" (coyote poisoning associated with the execution of Caryl Chessman). In the middle section, these corruptions of the kid's trout-fishing vision are recreated in more humble figures. The obverse of the heroic criminals, these figures are avatars of the *failed* imagination, not the corrupted one. The terrified couple of "Room 208, Hotel Trout Fishing in America," fugitives from a murderous black pimp, are trapped in a bleak hotel room, drinking their lives away behind innumerable locks upon their door, and perpetually out in the world "on bail." The arch-conservative doctor of "The Surgeon," willing to give up practicing in any meaningful way the profession for which he is trained because people won't or can't pay their doctor bills, loads up his wife and kids in a camper and goes in search of an America the narrator confesses is "often only a place in the mind" (p. 72). Everything about the trout fishing *mythos* has gone awry in "A Note on the Camping Craze That Is Currently Sweeping America," an America aglow with the "unholy white light" of the Coleman lantern and so overcrowded with campers that one must wait for death among them in order to find a place to pitch a tent. And, finally, there are the narrator's friends in New York City—an unemployed burglar for whom he "fears the worst" and his cocktail-waitress wife—whose life he finds so depressing he feels he must strike out for Fairbanks, Alaska, as soon as possible: this in "A Return to the Cover of This Book."

What these episodes suggest, in contrast to the rather general themes of the earlier episodes, is the very personal dimensions of the failure of the imagination in the face of reality. These people are the narrator's friends or they are people whom he has actually met and talked to, and their lives make direct contact with his. Their problems—how to cope with the world—are his problems as well. These people have clung to the dream into their mature lives, too, but they have not made what Brautigan would consider adequate responses. Consequently, the narrator, with his woman and child, continues to seek streams beyond those where the uninitiated and the unaware have trekked.

Another sort of episode in this middle sequence describes some of these ventures; they involve the whole family now, and the roles of the woman and the child begin to take on increased thematic significance. In "The Teddy Roosevelt Chingader'," Brautigan recounts the efforts of the three of them to find a decent, undesecrated camping spot in Challis National Forest, at Big Redfish Lake, which had become "the Forest Lawn of camping in Idaho" or a "skidrow hotel" with "too many trailers and campers parked in the halls" (p. 61), and, finally, at Little Redfish Lake, almost empty of campers, clean and uncluttered. This episode, occurring earlier, is on the theme of "Camping Craze," but here involves the narrator himself. "The Pudding Master of Stanley Basin" introduces the woman and child as heroines. The woman finds a successful and humane way to catch minnows for the baby, and the baby, "too young" to kill, adapts her "furry" sound, which she makes for animals, to a "silver" sound and learns from the parents how to play with and take care of the minnows at the same time: "The children's game and the banker's game, she picked up those silver things one at a time, and put them back in the pan. There was still a little water in it. The fish like this. You could tell" (p. 65). In "The Lake Josephus Days" the narrator momentarily distracts himself with thoughts of the Andrews Sisters, the 'forties and zoot suits, but must admit that his main concern is the well-being of the baby, who, though ill from too much sun, soon recovers. The full significance of the baby becomes a bit clearer in "Sandbox Minus John Dillinger Equals What?" Though the narrator's own imagination may be corrupted to the extent that he can dream his daughter into the myth's violence as "the woman in red," the child herself *is* free, so the answer to the title's question, then, is a sandbox—or an imagination—without John Dillinger.

In the last sequence of sections, the child-as-hero appears—or reappears. In *Trout Fishing*, as in pastoral generally, the positive, beneficent potentialities of the unfettered, phenomenologically un-cluttered imagination belong to the child (or rustic or naif elsewhere in the tradition). Her anti-type here appears to be Trout Fishing in America Shorty. Shorty seems to be the emblematic, imaginative construct in the book who symbolizes all those other cripples—emotional, creative, psychopathic—who populate the book: "He was a legless, screaming middle-aged wino./He descended upon North Beach like a chapter from the Old Testament. He was the reason birds migrate in the autumn. They have to. He was the cold turning of the earth; the bad wind that blows off sugar" (p. 45). The embodiment of universal negation, Trout Fishing in America Shorty belongs to the unimaginative "naturalism" of writers such as Nelson Algren, so the narrator and a friend decide to ship him to Chicago to Algren, or, failing that, "if he comes back to San Francisco someday and dies," the narrator says, Shorty "should be buried right beside the Benjamin Franklin statue in Washington Square" (p. 47). In "Footnote Chapter to 'The Shipping of Trout Fishing in America Shorty to Nelson Algren,'" Brautigan says that Shorty has been taken up by the French "New Wave" film makers, who may be starring him in "Trout Fishing in America Shorty, Mon Amour," letting him in a dubbed voice denounce "man's inhumanity to man" (p. 63). "They'll milk it for all it's worth," he says, "and make cream and butter from a pair of empty pants legs and a low budget. But I may be all wrong. What was being shot may have been just a scene from a new science-fiction movie 'Trout Fishing in America Shorty from Outer Space.' One of those cheap thrillers with the theme: Scientists, mad or otherwise, should never play God, that ends with the castle on fire and a lot of people walking home through the dark woods" (p. 63).

The impotency of Shorty and the strength of the child in the book are both shown in the interesting episode in which they appear together. "The Last Mention of Trout Fishing in America Shorty" suggests that hope does exist for Brautigan's creatures, for the chapter shows the baby escaping Shorty's clutches, not by hiding behind garbage cans (as in the "first mention" chapter), but by scampering off to the very symbol of imaginative creation—a sandbox, one at the other end of the self-same park in which the book begins. When the Franklin statue "turned green like a traffic light, and the baby noticed the sandbox," she decided it "suddenly looked better to her than Trout Fishing in America Shorty" and the sausages he would give to her to eat: "Trout Fishing in America Shorty stared after her as if the space between them were a river growing larger and larger" (p. 97).

The child brings a fresh imagination to the world of *Trout Fishing in America*. That world is about as worn out as it can possibly be, but not merely because the landscapes are so depleted or trampled down or garbage-filled. It is worn out because the frame the angling Horatio Algering *mythos* has provided is now so inadequate. In its broadest configuration showing how the *mythos* can be replaced, the novel shows the narrator's becoming the creative, artistic imagination, not by denying the nugatory in our American existence but by transforming it. The always present and insistent dark vision accounts for much of the novel's length, for if the accounts of death and the epitaphs of one sort or another are eliminated, not much is left in *Trout Fishing*. The narrator here, as in any other pastoral work, especially one dealing with the theme of *et in Arcadia ego*, must simply adapt to the fact of decay and death even in Arcady, Eden, America—life itself.

Much of this adaptation appears in the plenitude of epitaphs, but much of it, too, appears in those "monuments" to man's physical being, scatology becoming eschatology in "Red Lip," "On Paradise," and "Footnote Chapter to 'Red Lip.'" Only a wryly mature imagination could present the abandoned outhouse of "Red Lip" as "a monument . . . to a good ass gone under," one announcing, "The old guy who built me crapped in here 9,745 times and he's dead now and I don't want anyone else to touch me. He was a good guy" (p. 7). Only an adjusted, comic imagination could create the statue in "On Paradise" that attests to man's physical transience; "It was a twelve-foot high marble statue of a young man walking out on a cold morning to a crapper that had the classic half-moon cut above the door./The 1930's will never come again, but his shoes were wet with dew. They'll stay that way in marble" (p. 49).

It is a literary imagination, as well as a healthy one, for there seems little doubt that the image of dew echoes the lines from Wallace Stevens's "Sunday Morning," ones that associate dew upon the feet with man's autochthonous origin and earthly *telos*. That origin—in earth—is powerfully, sadly attested to once again in "Footnote Chapter to 'Red Lip,'" for there the narrator, having, like Fitzgerald's Carraway, come home from searching for the dream America, retreats to the California bush and then sees it, too, become a refuse dump. They left the California bush, he says, when the toilet into which they had been dropping their garbage had become so full that it almost "became necessary to stand on the toilet seat and step into that hole, crushing the garbage down like an accordion into the abyss" (p. 101).

Everything in *Trout Fishing in America* deserves its memorial, even when it has passed its usefulness (as in the Byronic and the Hemingway heroes) or was never of any use to begin with (Trout Fishing in America Shorty) or was genuinely antithetical to use (Jack the Ripper, John Dillinger, etc.). Trout Fishing in America—the old pastoral, Walden, Algerian, Gatsbean, Nick Adams dream—deserves its memorial, too, and receives it in what most critics have acknowledged as the purest, most extravagant expression of imagination in the book: "The Cleveland Wrecking Yard" (pp. 102–7). This chapter brings us full circle back to the opening chapters, for the two parts of "Knock on Wood" have foreshadowed the transformation of trout fishing in America into the artifacts of industrial, technological America. The boy's waterfall staircase now shows up in the "used plumbing department, surrounded by hundreds of toilets" (p. 106). One can no longer market the myth as a fresh new product, but as an artist—a writer—Brautigan suggests that one can still find a way to use it: it can become the writer's medium and refresh his art: "I thought to myself what a lovely nib trout fishing in America would make with a stroke of cool green trees along the river's shore, wild flowers and dark fins pressed against the paper" (p. 110). It may be gone now, but it was good in its time. *Requiescat in pace.* Rest in Peace, Trout Fishing in America *Peace. Trout Fishing* is a book filled with memorials and epitaphs, and their insistent presences suggest just how thoroughly it is permeated with the spirit of the elegy, the *ubi sunt,* and the *et in Arcadia ego* themes of pastoral art. The big question seems constantly to be how to cope—with the fact of death, with the passing of a cherished dream, with the ambiguities that surround one always. The myth upon which trout fishing rests as a real activity begins to seem inadequate in a social structure shot through with violence, fear, cruelty, overpopulation, and ecological disaster.

Brautigan seems very much to be working a stream of American literature represented by many novelists, but in some ways his themes seem best represented by the poetry and philosophy of Wallace Stevens. Stevens worked in the world—in that most mundane of professions, the insurance industry; still, he wrote poetry that illustrated the potency of the imagination in transforming the world, not by denying it but by using it. In *The Comedian as the Letter C,* Stevens begins with a pale, unimaginative hero voyaging into a new world, "a world without imagination." The tension in Stevens and Brautigan is always between the external reality and the faculty of imagination, but the result in both writers is that the best art comes from the combination of a phenomenological reality and an idealistic imagination: "Nota: Man is the intelligence of his soil" becomes "Nota: his soil is man's intelligence." Both must interact if human beings are to bring order to chaos. Brautigan feels just as strongly as Stevens that reality must constantly be reinterpreted, the old myths replaced, revitalized, or stripped of their husks in order to lay bare the live core. But the job takes an artist's imagination, and we must all be artists. What *Trout Fishing in America* does, then, is to represent both the need and the expression of imagination, and Brautigan's portrait of a young trout fisherman thus becomes a portrait of the artist as well.

Notes: Phase Three

1. "The Life and Death of Literary Forms," *New Literary History: A Journal of Theory and Interpretation*, 2, no. 2 (Winter 1971): 214. My sequence of epigraphs is taken from Joe David Bellamy, *The New Fiction: Interviews with Innovative American Writers* (Urbana: University of Illinois Press, 1974).
2. Northrop Frye, *Anatomy of Criticism: Four Essays* (Princeton, N.J.: Princeton University Press, 1957), p. 103.
3. Nathan A. Scott, Jr., "The Literary Imagination in a Time of Dearth," in *Existentialism 2: A Casebook*, ed. William V. Spanos (New York: Crowell, 1976), p. 233.
4. Ihab Hassan, *Paracriticisms: Seven Speculations of the Times* (Urbana: University of Illinois Press, 1975), p. xv. See Hassan's discussions of what I call "sophisticated modern" in the chapter "Fiction and Future: An Extravaganza for Voice and Tape," pp. 97–117. The very tentativeness of this whole book is expressive of the problem—which Scott calls "dearth"—of the late-modernist fictional imagination, which has as yet no centers of authority it can continue to rely on.
5. Raymond M. Olderman, *Beyond the Wasteland: A Study of the American Novel in the Nineteen-sixties* (New Haven, Conn.: Yale University Press, 1972), pp. 5, 11.
6. Jerome Klinkowitz, *Literary Disruptions: The Making of a Post-Contemporary American Fiction* (Urbana: University of Illinois Press, 1975), p. x. Klinkowitz's use of the term "post-contemporary" may seem awkward—and indeed Klinkowitz himself has fun playing with the logical (or chronological) difficulties it involves; but his study is the successor to Hassan's *Radical Innocence*, whose focus on "contemporary" American fiction forces Klinkowitz to follow after with his term. One must be careful in dealing with all those essays and books since Irving Howe's *The Idea of the Modern in Literature and the Arts* (New York: Horizon, 1967), for no two critics necessarily mean the same things when they use the term *post*-modern. It may, for instance, be employed in the sequence of pre-modern, modern, and post-modern; or it may be employed in the sequence modern (divided perhaps into early, classic, and late) and post-modern, defining an epoch quite distinct from modern. Some of the problems of periodizing the modern are evident in the fine new journal *Boundary 2: A Journal of Postmodern Literature*, for I am not always certain that different writers/critics appearing in its pages—for example, Nathan A. Scott, Jr., and Robert Langbaum—construe modern and post-modern in the same ways. I would, nonetheless, regard *Boundary 2* as evidence for my argument that something epochal is afoot; the question is, What?
7. Philip Stevick, "Scheherazade runs out of plots, goes on talking; the

king, puzzled, listens: *an essay on new fiction,"* *TriQuarterly,* 26 (Winter 1973): 338. Further quotations from this source will be included within parentheses in my text whenever practicable.

8. Renato Poggioli, *The Theory of the Avant-Garde,* trans. from the Italian by Gerald Fitzgerald (Cambridge, Mass.: Belknap Press of Harvard University Press, 1968). For an excellent review of this work that puts it into the context of modernism/post-modernism, see Robert Langbaum, "On Renato Poggioli, *The Theory of the Avant-Garde,"* *Boundary 2,* 1, no. 1 (Fall 1972): 234–41.

9. Nathan A. Scott, Jr., "History, Hope, and Literature," *Boundary 2,* 1, no. 3 (Spring 1973): 599.

10. Charles Altieri, "From Symbolist Thought to Immanence: The Ground of Postmodern American Poetics," *Boundary 2,* 1, no. 3 (Spring 1973): 605–41, 607.

11. *Ibid.,* p. 608.

12. *TriQuarterly,* 26 (Winter 1973): 383–417.

13. William James, *A Pluralistic Universe* (New York, 1909), as quoted in *The Modern Tradition,* ed. Richard Ellmann and Charles Feidelson (New York: Oxford University Press, 1965), p. 437.

14. *On Modernism: The Prospects for Literature and Freedom* (Cambridge, Mass.: MIT Press, 1967), pp. 8, 9.

15. *The Physicist's Conception of Nature,* trans. Arnold J. Pomerans (New York, 1958), as quoted in *The Modern Tradition,* p. 446.

16. M. H. Abrams, *The Mirror and the Lamp* (New York: Norton, 1958), p. 6.

17. *Journal of Modern Literature,* 3, no. 5 (July 1974): 1072.

18. *Ibid.*

19. Robert Onopa, "The End of Art as a Spiritual Project," *TriQuarterly,* 26 (Winter 1973): 363.

20. Tony Tanner, *The Reign of Wonder: Naivety and Reality in American Literature* (New York: Harper, 1967), p. 10. Tanner's study focuses upon the transcendentalists, Twain, James, Stein, Anderson, and Hemingway.

21. *Ibid.,* p. 14.

22. My sense of these aspects in popular literature comes from Erich Auerbach's essay "Odysseus' Scar" in *Mimesis: The Representation of Reality in Western Literature,* trans. Willard R. Trask (Princeton, N.J.: Princeton University Press, 1953), Albert B. Lord's *The Singer of Tales* (Cambridge, Mass.: Harvard University Press, 1960), and Robert Scholes and Robert Kellogg, *The Nature of Narrative* (New York: Oxford University Press, 1966), the chapter "The Oral Heritage of Written Narrative." I have tried to pull together my own ideas in the section on popular narrative in *Four Modes: A Rhetoric of Modern Fiction* (New York: Macmillan, 1973). Of the relation between a writer, language, and the tradition, Jorge Luis Borges, in the parable "Borges and I," has this to say (*Labyrinths: Selected Stories & Other Writings,* ed. Donald A. Yates and James E. Irby [New York: New Directions, 1964]): "It is no effort for me to confess that he [Borges] has achieved some valid pages, but those pages cannot save me, perhaps because what is good belongs to no one, not even to him, but rather to the language and to tradition" (p. 246).

23. See Guy Rosolato, "The Voice and the Literary Myth," and Jacques Derrida, "Structure, Sign, and Play in the Discourse of the Human

Sciences," in *The Languages of Criticism and the Sciences of Man: The Structuralist Controversy*, ed. Richard Macksey and Eugenio Donato (Baltimore: Johns Hopkins University Press, 1970), pp. 201–15, 247–65. Derrida's comment near the end of his essay is quite revealing in connection with my sense of the two traditions of *tradition* in modernist literature: "There are thus two interpretations of interpretation, of structure, of sign, of freeplay. The one seeks to decipher, dreams of deciphering, a truth or an origin which is free from freeplay and from the order of the sign, and lives like an exile the necessity of interpretation. The other, which is no longer turned toward the origin, affirms freeplay and tries to pass beyond man and humanism, the name man being the name of that being who, throughout the history of metaphysics or of ontotheology—in other words, through the history of all of his history—has dreamed of full presence, the reassuring foundation, the origin and the end of the game" (pp. 264–65). Derrida himself deprecates the turn toward "ethnography" as a new means to a "full presence," but, ironically, structuralism itself has been turned into such a system, according to Robert Scholes, *Structuralism in Literature: An Introduction* (New Haven, Conn.: Yale University Press, 1974), p. 2.

24. Richard Brautigan, *In Watermelon Sugar*, bound with *Trout Fishing in America* and *The Pill versus The Springhill Mine Disaster* (New York: Seymour Lawrence/Delacorte, 1972), p. 138.

25. The realization that Brautigan works within a pastoral tradition is not original, but the following contextual discussion of earlier modernist writers and the analysis of *Trout Fishing in America* are quite outside the parameters of the one article-length treatment of the mode in Brautigan's first four novels: Neil Schmitz, "Richard Brautigan and the Modern Pastoral," *Modern Fiction Studies*, 19, no. 1 (Spring 1973): 109–25. Tony Tanner, in *City of Words: American Fiction 1950–1970* (London: Jonathan Cape, 1971), pp. 406–15, points to Brautigan's relationship to pastoral conventions, but he does not argue the idea since his concerns are directed elsewhere. In connection with this point, other published studies of Brautigan ought to be mentioned: Kent Bales, "Fishing the Ambivalence, or, A Reading of *Trout Fishing in America*," *Western Humanities Review*, 39, no. 1 (Winter 1975): 29–42; John Somer *et al.*, "Speed Kills: Richard Brautigan (and the American Metaphor)," *OYEZ Review*, 8, no. 2 (1974): 67–72; John Clayton, "Richard Brautigan: The Politics of Woodstock," *New American Review*, no. 11 (1971): 56–68; Terrence Malley, *Richard Brautigan* (New York: Warner Paperback Library, 1972); and Kenneth Seib, "*Trout Fishing in America*: Brautigan's Funky Fishing Yarn," *Critique*, 13, no. 3 (1971): 63–71.

26. See "Anderson and 'Winesburg': Mysticism and Craft," *Accent*, 16 (Spring 1956): 107–28, for a discussion of the folk/vernacular/popular/oral elements in Anderson's craft.

27. For a background to these assumptions about "authority," see these two essays: Guy Rosolato, "The Voice and the Literary Myth," and Jacques Derrida, "Structure, Sign, and Play in the Discourse of the Human Sciences," both with "Discussion," in *The Languages of Criticism and the Sciences of Man*, pp. 201–17, 247–72. Rosolato, a psychologist, emphasizes the Father, while Derrida, a philosopher, is more

interested in hermeneusis and the cultural methods of filling in the gap in the hermeneutic circle.

28. *Some Versions of Pastoral* (Norfolk, Conn.: New Directions, 1960), p. 11.
29. *Ibid.*, p. 14.
30. *Ibid.*, p. 10.
31. Max Schulz, *Radical Sophistication: Studies in Contemporary Jewish-American Novelists* (Athens: Ohio University Press, 1969), p. 22.
32. Richard Brautigan, *Trout Fishing in America*, bound with *The Pill versus The Springhill Mine Disaster* and *In Watermelon Sugar* (New York: Seymour Lawrence/Delacorte, 1972), p. 1. All further quotations from *Trout Fishing* are from this edition, which is a photographic reprint of three first editions. Brautigan's other published books of fiction include *A Confederate General from Big Sur* (New York: Grove, 1964) and *The Abortion: An Historical Romance 1966* (1971), *Revenge of the Lawn: Stories 1962–1970* (1971), *The Hawkline Monster: A Gothic Western* (1974), and *Willard and His Bowling Trophies: A Perverse Mystery* (1975), all published by Simon and Schuster (New York).
33. See Ralph Freedman, *The Lyrical Novel: Studies in Hermann Hesse, André Gide, and Virginia Woolf* (Princeton, N.J.: Princeton University Press, 1963) for a study of this concept in early modernist fiction.
34. Schmitz's excellent essay is cited in n. 25 above. One reason I cannot rely upon it more than I have is the conservative orientation Schmitz displays in his analysis of this episode in *Trout Fishing* and the whole of *The Abortion*. This latter novel is considered as a bitter, exceedingly ironic attack on the new sexual morality. I cannot finally accept such an interpretation of the novel, though I can see—in Brautigan's pervasive, traditional, perhaps "stoical" (Empson's usage here) ambiguity—a feeling that the world was indeed better in those old days before the need for Zero Population Growth. Obviously, either Schmitz or the flower children are misreading Brautigan, but the possibility for such misreading is typically an aspect of pastoral/performative art, where the very coolness permits a high level of audience participation and, thus, projection into the text/performance.

Conclusion

Conclusion

> . . . What we call a "literary period" is often
> not a period at all: its definition is not simply
> chronological but also typological.
>
> Ihab Hassan
> "Culture, Indeterminancy, and Immanence" (1978)

This history of the modernist novel in America is quite
provisional. I began with a notion expressed by Fredric Jameson, but
which is shared by most theorists of history, that a literary (or any
other) history is largely a result of the frame or model within which
a slice of epochal time is viewed.[1] The model employed has been the
all-purpose dialectic of phases called naive, critical, and sophisticated. As the Introduction explains, this dialectic can be applied to
any hypostatized series. It may be applied to a series of historical
periods (such as medieval, Renaissance, romantic), to a single
period's phases (for instance, naive romantic, critical romantic—or
Victorian—and sophisticated romantic—or modern), or to the
phases of a single author's career (the three phases, for example, of
James's *oeuvre*). It may be applied as well to a single genre's historical development, or used to historicize just one stage of a genre's
evolution. This last is what *The Exploded Form* attempts to do, for
the modernist novel in America is really only part of a third, or
sophisticated, phase of the history of the novel as a distinctive
genre. Although every period offers its exceptions, in general the
eighteenth-century novel is in a naive, the nineteenth-century novel
is in a critical, and the twentieth-century novel is in a sophisticated
phase.

The history of the genre of the novel, as the Introduction argues,
has resulted from the need felt throughout Western culture to imitate or represent nature or reality—at least what in each epoch
since the Renaissance has been regarded as reality. The novel's
generic form is predicated upon the same notion that underlies true

science: that a congruence or an isomorphism can exist between the frames of investigation (scientific hypotheses, paradigms, models) and the object investigated ("nature"), between the method of imitation (language, the generic form) and the object of imitation (life, reality, history). But even for science, reality has changed over the centuries, and as the model of reality has changed, so also has the form of the novel. After having been erected upon one model of the world in the eighteenth century, the novel was forced to exchange epistemes twice during the next two centuries. The first exchange came with the development of a romantic picture of reality; that picture was largely the result of the influence of idealist philosophy and art, and it was forced to compete with the picture given by modern, materialist, Newtonian science. This conflict gave us the prose romance that dominated nineteenth-century German and American fiction, but that also made at least a token appearance in England, in classic expressions by the Brontës. The second exchange of epistemes came with the exploding of Newton's materialistic universe by Einstein's theory of a relative, non-material cosmos of energy and forces.[2]

The new universe of relativity, post-romantic in time, has actually reinforced the forms of fiction created by romantic world hypotheses. Consequently, the relativity model of the universe has wreaked greater havoc on traditional, realist forms than upon romantic forms, and the "modernist" novel created by the epistemological cataclysm wrought by relativity theories remains a post-romantic genre in more than chronology.[3] It requires for its validating epistemic authority the notion of a transcendent subject, an "I" or a "Self," rather than a transcendent object—an a priori world. The modernist novel is no longer a single, nuclear, monolithic form; it is comprised, rather, of forms exploded from traditional novels as well as from romance, with any form, depending upon one's perspective, relatively as authoritative as another—and, more important, relatively as "realistic" vis-à-vis a putative "reality." But, in truth, the modernist novel generally seems uninterested in the "real" external world, for its philosophic grounding subsumes "reality" in human consciousness or in the objects studied by the human sciences, including language, myth, ritual, archetype, history, science, and any other semiotic system whose structure is a product of the human mind.

The modernist novel, then, belongs to a broad tradition of romantic idealism, and thus is constantly threatened by a solipsism that never accosts the traditional generic form.[4] This situation has meant that modernist fictions have been involved in largely epistemological enterprises, whereas the traditional realist novel, in reconstructing mimetic worlds, has been engaged in ontological ones. The traditional novelist seldom questions our assumptions underlying either the reality of the world or our ability to know it, but these are precisely the assumptions the modernist always doubts. The modernist is constantly engaged in finding out how we might know reality, but the traditionalist simply, even naively, goes about showing us what reality "looks" like to the senses. The realism associated with the traditional novel, therefore, has never easily been associated with modernist forms, and so the question always in need of answering is whether the modern actually represents the novel at all.

We have persisted in regarding modernist forms as novels, and have been enabled to do so by the exchanges among our definitions of "the real" described by Foucault and those who are concerned with *Naturphilosophie*—Whitehead, Weyl, von Weizsäcker, Teilhard, Heisenberg, and others. Because modern science is itself just about as indeterminate and relativist as modern philosophy, modernist modes of the novel have been able to meld the contents of romantic structures and traditional novels, and thereby to retain—however shakily—the label *realist*. But they are realist in quite different ways from earlier, naive realist forms, of course. As we have seen, reality has moved inside consciousness and become more or less indivisible from the forms—language, archetypes, myths, rituals, history, the models and paradigms of science—that conventionally structure it. The modernist tradition in fiction has simply reflected a paradigm shift—mirroring the "inward turn," in the phrase of Erich Kahler, that "reality" has taken during the past two or three centuries.[5] The modernist novel, then, ought not be regarded with any more concern than the prose romance of earlier centuries. And it is true that our perception of the antagonism of "the romance" to "the novel" has considerably altered during the modernist epoch—in large part, perhaps, because Richard Chase's thesis that American fiction is predominantly romance-oriented achieves a broadly based *ad hoc* validation in modernist American fiction.[6]

Still, in the last quarter of the twentieth century, many have begun to feel that the modernist novel has reached the end of its tether. Our modern consciousness of a world consuming the energy of a primeval explosion has become the sensibility of a universe overtaken by entropy—one where energy is used up and disorder is rampant. The third or sophisticated phase of the modernist novel is particularly beset by the feeling, as Tony Tanner puts it, that "everything is running down."[7] Or, as John Barth says, we have entered into a phase marked by the exhaustion of the possibilities contained in modernist forms, so fiction writers now are forced to find ways— as Barth himself has—to capitalize upon that very exhaustion.[8] But where the novel-as-genre is concerned, the only object that could be exhausted and thereby destroy the genre would be the destruction of the world itself. The novel's form, regardless of the interpretations played upon it during the modernist period, is not ultimately dependent upon mentation alone; it has always—even in its seemingly most solipsistic moments—required the world, nature, the external universe. The crisis the modernist novel faces, then, is brought about by all those assumptions, allegations, and hypotheses that it never has had anything to do with an empirically testable reality outside the forms of its representation.

II

The novel has always been the most comprehensive and ill-defined of literary forms. But today the novelist is faced with an unprecedented number of mutually incompatible choices, not merely of subject-matter and style, but between basic conceptions of what kind of world the novelist himself is living in and trying to depict.

Brian Wicker
The Story-Shaped World (1975)

I have tried to make the point that what we regard as novels must have some relationship to an ascertainable or posited reality apart from human consciousness. But the criticism which grew up with modernist fiction has tended, by its focus upon the autonomy of art, to separate the techniques of modernist fiction from the forms of reality it represented.[9] In fact, this result is one of the main features of the sophisticated phase of modernism itself; it makes the crisis necessary to define our late, or sophisticated, phase. This modernist crisis is precisely the object of Fredric Jameson in a recent essay, one that postdates both *Marxism and Form* (1971) and

The Prison-House of Language (1972). In "Beyond the Cave: Demystifying the Ideology of Modernism,"[10] Jameson begins by arguing that realism and modernism are actually two different *cultures*, the one following the other in a historical pattern. Much like my paradigm of naive, critical, and sophisticated, Jameson's pattern is dialectical, a model built on the well-known triad used by sociohistorians who label cultures as either "savage," "barbarian," or "civilized" types. Jameson uses this triad as a kind of "unified field theory" to describe primitive and modern cultures and everything in between. Using his modification of the paradigm, Jameson says that "in the passage from savagery to barbarism . . . we pass from the *production* of coded elements to the *representation* of them."[11] The stage known as civilization, according to Jameson, comes along to annul the second or barbaric, the "despotic and luxurious sign-system erected parasitically upon the basis of the older 'natural' codes."[12] This third stage is known in socioeconomic history as capitalism; in literature, as realism—particularly the realism associated with the novel-as-genre, and even more particularly with the "great tradition" of European realism in nineteenth-century fiction.[13]

Jameson's exemplary history brings us to the place where my history has begun—with the advent of "the modern." Jameson's model posits an identity between nineteenth-century capitalism and nineteenth-century realism, so, for Jameson, modernism in its entirety is a period of crisis. Although as a model his paradigm is synchronic, Jameson seems to prefer that it be relegated to a specific historical period. He does not redeploy the paradigm in order to analyze a second period—modernism itself. Still, his claims about the crisis of modernism, even as a diachronic period, seem consistent with the general claims of *The Exploded Form*. He says, for example, that modernism emerged as a result of the late nineteenth century's "fatigue with the whole process of decoding" its new, capitalist, bourgeois encodings, as well as the consequent effort to "recode the henceforth decoded flux of the realistic, middle-class, secular era."[14] But Jameson insists that "all modernistic works are essentially simply cancelled realistic ones."[15] Such exemplary modernist novels as Kafka's *Castle*, Robbe-Grillet's *Jealousy* and (I would add) Faulkner's *The Sound and the Fury*, Heller's *Catch-22*, and Brautigan's *Trout Fishing in America* are "apprehended . . . by way of the relay of an imaginary realistic narrative of which the symbolic and modernistic one is then seen as a kind of styliza-tion."[16] The reading of such works takes place in two stages: "First, substitution of a realistic hypothesis—in narrative form—then an interpretation of that secondary and invented or projected core nar-rative according to the procedures we reserved for the older realistic novel in general."[17] Thus, Jameson suggests, modernism offered no revolutionary rupture from traditional realism; it merely trans-formed realist values: "So the modern work comes gradually to be constructed as a kind of multi-purpose object, Umberto Eco's so-called 'opera aperta' or open form, designed to be used by each subgroup after its own fashion and needs, so that its realistic core . . . seems the most abstract and empty starting point of all, inas-much as every private audience is obliged to recode it afresh in terms of its own sign-system."[18]

With the process Jameson describes going on full tilt in contem-porary fiction, not much of a crisis should exist in the theory or practice of late modernism. And even Jameson intimates that the modernist novel is involved with reality, as individual "open forms" are recoded in the terms of given specific readers and their codes. But for Jameson there are two major problems: one problem remains the same as it is for many other critics of modernism: its hyper-subjectivity; a second problem is that "the reality" represented—or at least that which is known in literary history as "objective realism"—"no longer exists, because the dominant group has disin-tegrated upon which its existence depended."[19] Thus, says Jameson, although modernism "reinforces all the . . . presuppositions" of an "overstuffed Victorian bourgeois reality," it does so "only in a world so thoroughly subjectivised that they have been driven under-ground, beneath the surface of the work, forcing us to reconfirm the concept of a secular reality at the very moment in which we imagine ourselves to be demolishing it."[20]

An adequate modernist "realism" may not be possible for Jame-son, given his distinctive critical bias toward a Marxist historical paradigm. But, even so, what he concludes about the crisis of mod-ernist fiction in its late, sophisticated phase is emphatically uttered by others, too. His sense of crisis, therefore, is not likely to result only or even primarily from his ideological methodology. Jameson evokes our current crisis in no uncertain terms: "So we slowly begin to grasp the enormity of a historical situation in which the truth of our social life as a whole—Lukács would have said, as a totality—is increasingly irreconcilable with the aesthetic quality of language or of individual expression; of a situation about which it can be asserted that if we can make a work of art from our experience, if we can tell it in the form of a story, then it is no longer true; and if we can grasp the truth about our world as a totality, as something transcending mere individual experience, then we can no longer make it accessible in narrative or literary form."[21] One critic no less certain of the crisis than Jameson is Gerald Graff. In his essay "The Politics of Anti-Realism," Graff works from a critico-rationalist rather than Marxist position, yet he says much the same thing—or at least gives his critique the same severe ring Jameson has given his: "The formalist strategy . . . is really a renunciation and an adaptation. It exploits the incidental virtues of the homelessness, impotence, and marginality which capitalism thrusts on the artistic intellectual. The aesthetic affirmation of the spirit of 'play,' of the uninhibited exploration of the frontiers of consciousness, ignores the severely restricted boundaries within which this play and this exploration must take place. The play and the exploration presuppose the artist's dispossession from an interpretation that would permit him to master social experience."[22]

Besides the strong antipathy with which both Jameson and Graff regard the modernist crisis, they also share the initial assumption that must underlie any legitimate theory of the novel-as-genre. They both accept the notion that fiction (and all literature) still has the capability of mimesis. Jameson says at the outset in "Beyond the Cave" that any solution to the "problem" of the autonomy of the work of art requires only that it be headed back toward "the social and historical situations which form the absolute horizon of our individual existences."[23] Similarly, Graff, in a critique of certain forms of contemporary, presumably "post-modernist" fiction, says the "radical disorientation of perception and the cognitive estrangement brought about by self-reflexive fiction may result in a dulling of the audience's sense of reality or in a shell-shocked relativism suspicious not only of ideology but of truth."[24] For Graff, in fact, the referential aspect of literature is that element most crucial to its cognitive value. "There is no way," he says, "of determining the critical character of a literary work unless we know its disposition toward reality. If esthetic disruption and projection are not regulated by a rational respect for reality—that is, by a controlling realism—their critical value cannot be taken for granted."[25]

Jameson and Graff are eloquently, passionately assertive in their arguments about the crisis of modernism. Their concern is equally manifest in an essay by a third critic. In "Narrative Fictions and Reality," Roy Pascal carefully reviews one of the most important books available to a late-modernist theory of fiction—Frank Kermode's *The Sense of an Ending* (1967). In that book, Kermode outlines ways fictions are used in history, prophecy, and novelistic narratives.[26] A major premise of the work, Pascal points out, is that "no story is possible unless some fictional structures are used, but also that, as in other activities of the mind, understanding depends on the invention of fictions (of which language itself is an all-pervading one)."[27] The problem for Pascal that arises from Kermode's study is the relationship it posits between fictions and reality. Perhaps he is merely repeating faults existing in Kermode's earlier sources—Vaihinger's *The Philosophy of "As If"* and Nietzsche's *Beyond Good and Evil*, but Kermode seems to say that "narrative fictions are arbitrary or purely subjective"—at the very best simply "instruments of thought" that remain (as in Vaihinger) "contrary to reality."[28]

Pascal's concern is very much like that of both Jameson and Graff, for he insists upon a connection between fictions and reality; their "usefulness" as "tools" depends upon that connection. "The novelistic fictions are not," Pascal says, "'contrary to reality' or arbitrary deviations from reality; they are abstractions, projections of actual relationships isolated from some of the associations with which in real life they are bound, and which are thought by the novelist to be irrelevant to his immediate object. Thus there is no antithesis of 'truth' and 'effectiveness' in regard to fictions; their effectiveness, usefulness, depends on the fact that they embody an aspect of reality."[29] For Pascal, as reality is for modernist physicists in these post-Heisenbergian days, fictions are both subjective and objective, maintaining a deep connection to the mind at the same time they make a relation to external reality. Heisenberg himself has made a similar comment in one of his better-known books: "We know that any understanding must be based finally upon the natural language because it is only there that we can be certain to touch reality, and hence we must be skeptical about any skepticism with regard to this natural language and its essential concepts. . . . In this way modern physics has perhaps opened the door to a wider outlook on the relation between the human mind and reality."[30]

Jameson, Graff, and Pascal all recognize that the modernist novel is in a period of crisis, and they have their own ideas about the nature of the crisis. But each of these is an avowed antagonist to the underlying premises of modernism. We might rather expect them to provide the evidence for which I have used them. There are, however, evidences of the crisis elsewhere—from critics and novelists, in fact, who generally mean to be sympathetic to the aims of modernism or the post-modernism they prophesy. This evidence of crisis is seen in the enormous confusion of "paradigms" operating in current theory and criticism of the novel and prose fiction in general. At the moment, there are perhaps a half-dozen or more terms with their attendant models for what fiction either is, or ought to be, or soon shall be. These terms include *antifiction, metafiction*, the *nonfiction novel, transfiction, superfiction*, and *surfiction*—not to mention the new novel, the *nouveau nouveau roman*, and *structural fabulation*.[31] Most of these terms refer to approximately the same phenomena in the practices of recent fiction, but the primary emphasis of all is upon its deracination from conventional reality because of either an intense subjectivity or a self-reflexive concern with its own fictionality.

The model called "metafiction" can serve as one example of the crisis. William Gass apparently was the originator of the term. Both a critic and a novelist, Gass coined the epithet in an essay first published in a philosophy journal and later incorporated into *Fiction and the Figures of Life*.[32] As a modernist, Gass accepts the fictionality—and thus the subjectivity—of reality, and insists as a consequence that in the approach to the external world not even philosophy has a particular advantage over novels. Neither has much to do with "the world," and so nowadays fiction has often become appropriately "philosophical":

> The use of philosophical ideas in the construction of fictional works— in a very self-conscious and critical way, I mean—has been hastened by the growing conviction that not only do these ideas often represent conceptual systems of considerable complexity, they have the further advantage of being almost wholly irrelevant as accounts of the real world. They are, that is, to a great degree *fictional* already. . . . Then, too, the novelist now better understands his medium; he is ceasing to pretend that his business is to render the world; he knows, more often now, that his business is to *make* one, and to make one from the only medium of which he is the master—language. And there are even more radical developments.

There are metatheorems in mathematics and logic, ethics has its linguistic oversoul, everywhere lingos to converse about lingos are being contrived, and the case is no different in the novel. . . . Indeed, many of the so-called antinovels are really metafictions.[33]

Gass applies the label metafiction to works by such authors as Borges, Barth, Flann O'Brien, Coover, Nabokov, Barthelme, and others in whose works "the forms of fiction serve as the material upon which further forms can be imposed."[34] But following Gass, Robert Scholes has extended the conceptual model and applied it to three authors Gass named—Barth, Barthelme, and Coover—and to Gass himself, as well as connected it to a four-part model of criticism: "Metafiction assimilates all the perspectives of criticism into the fictional process itself," Scholes says. "It may emphasize structural, formal, behavioral, or philosophical qualities, but most writers of metafiction are thoroughly aware of all these possibilities and are likely to have experimented with all of them."[35] Despite these emphases, however, metafiction represents the efforts of these four authors to come to grips, according to Scholes, "with the problems of living and writing in the second half of the twentieth century."[36]

And yet the crisis that Jameson and others have observed can hardly be seen to have been averted in these efforts. Scholes's concluding remarks are as good an indication of the problems in the external reality as any of Graff's or Pascal's: "Barth and Barthelme are the chroniclers of our despair: despair over the exhausted forms of our thought and our existence. No wonder they laugh so much. Coover and Gass are reaching through form and behavior for some ultimate values, some true truth. No wonder they come on strong. All four are working in that rarefied air of metafiction, trying to climb beyond Beckett and Borges, toward things that no critic—not even a metacritic, if there were such a thing—can discern."[37] The socio-historical crisis is reflected in the formal problems of metafiction, moreover. Neil Schmitz, who also has analyzed Coover's metafiction, has concluded: "Emptiness, the hollow interior, haunts the writer of metafiction when he assaults ossified forms and exhausted language—an emptiness that is not necessarily the silence Beckett confronts."[38] Speaking of Thomas Pynchon's *V.*, Schmitz points out a debilitating result of metafiction: "An oppressive stylization occurs: writers who berate the 'lex of the game' find themselves confined to the cannibalistic forms of parody and farce."[39]

Scholes himself has identified the serious difficulties implicit in the metafictional model by pointing to its denial of both major functions, as Scholes names them, of fiction: of "sublimation" and "cognition." Metafiction suggests that not only is fiction incapable of realism, neither is it capable of *non*-realism: "The failure of realism as a faith," he writes in *Structural Fabulation*, "is balanced by another failure which has been much less considered. And that is the failure of fantasy."[40] The claims of fantasy to escape the world, Scholes says, have been as futile as the claims of the realist to represent it. "Thus, if we must acknowledge that reality inevitably eludes our human languages, we must admit as well that these languages can never conduct the human imagination to a point beyond this reality. If we cannot reach it, neither can we escape it."[41] In this matter, Scholes suggests, the failure of metafiction (which has generated, if not a metacriticism, then at least an "anti-criticism") has been its effort to have it both ways—to be a fiction "about the possibilities and impossibilities of fiction itself."[42]

There are other "fictional" paradigms besides metafiction that illustrate the contemporary crisis. As Scholes has noted, "If self-reflective fiction is one response to this dilemma, what has been called the 'new journalism' or the 'non-fiction novel' is another."[43] Mas'ud Zavarzadeh has written on the latter mode in *The Mythopoeic Reality: The Postwar American Nonfiction Novel*. Zavarzadeh sees the nonfiction novel as a distinctly post-modern response to the persistent demand for an adequate modernist or post-modernist realism. The nonfiction novel remains merely as additional evidence of the crisis of modernism, however, primarily because the form Zavarzadeh describes simply leaps off the horns of the dilemma in a direction different from metafiction's. True, the "totalizing novel" (Zavarzadeh's term for both traditional realism and the modernist subjective forms) seems "backgrounded," and certainly new forms have taken its place, but there is a logical contradiction at the heart of Zavarzadeh's analysis. He posits a form that avoids totalization, but that form is itself necessarily predicated upon a total view of reality—the view held by various modernist or existentialist commentators who habitually have regarded social chaos and moral entropy as all-inclusive of the world. Zavarzadeh's remarks on the opposed strategies of the nonfiction novel and "transfiction" (his generic term for such specific forms as metafiction) suggest the totalization which, early and late in the study, he extensively chronicles. He points out that both the non- and the transfiction novel share an epistemology in their noninterpretive stance toward external reality. But he seems to feel that there is some sort of real ontological difference between their points of view. "The nonfiction novel replaces 'interpretation' with a 'transcription' of naked facts. The various modes of transfiction employ a variety of strategies to avoid hiding the reality of chaos and the invading entropy in contemporary life under an imposed interpretive order. Metafiction, for example, uses a highly elaborate mock-interpretation and meta-commentary tinged with dark humor to reveal the absurdity of the contemporary totalizing novel's claim to a metaphysics of experience. And science fiction, another form of transfiction, operates with extrapolation rather than straight interpretation."[44]

Those works Zavarzadeh and others have treated as nonfiction novels are interesting in large part because they merely elevate conventional modernist aesthetic "objectivity" (which has both an objective and a subjective dimension) to an undeserved, unsubstantiated place of privilege. The problem of an adequate realism remains, however, just as much a problem for the nonfiction novel as for metafiction. This problem is clearly reflected in the almost naive innocence with which Zavarzadeh even claims an ontological difference between the "fictive" (or traditional, including the modernist) novel and the nonfiction novel: "Because of the nature of language, all attempts at objectivity are rendered subjective, but, nonetheless, there is an ontological difference between the nonfiction novel and the fictive novel. The reality which is mapped in a nonfiction novel is *not a staged reality invented by the narratist and patterned* in a way which endorses his interpretation of the order of the world."[45] It is not naive for Zavarzadeh to assume the reality of an external world, but it is naive to assume that any novel—traditional or nonfiction—can escape its fictionality.

III

I presume that the movement of fiction should always be in the direction of what we sense as real. Its forms are expendable. The novelist accommodates to the ongoing flow of experience, smashing anything that impedes his sense of it, even if it happens to be the novel. Especially if it happens to be the novel.

Ronald Sukenick
"The New Tradition in Fiction" (1972)

These responses to the crisis state of modernist fiction focus on the two major areas of controversy that exist in any debate over mimetic literary forms. Jameson, Graff, and Pascal are concerned with the world to be imitated. Scholes, Schmitz, and Zavarzadeh are concerned with the forms of representation. The former assume that there is an agreed-upon imitable world to be imitated; the latter assume that there are a variety of forms of imitation capable of representing the world however it exists. The former seem to have an inadequate sense of the ways in which history changes—or, as the structuralists would say, reveals the construction of models (or what Foucault calls *épistèmes*) of reality, the world. The latter seem to have an inadequate sense of the ways in which history changes—or displays the changes—in the one basis of literary representationalism that remains always visible: language. Thus, if one is not entirely satisfied by the claims of the realists, neither is one likely to be by the claims of the advocates of meta- or transfictions. And so we are left with the question, Where does the novel go from here? What will the post-modernist novel do?

One answer, which is very attractive in its simplicity, is that it will keep on doing what it has been doing all along. We must merely change the frame within which we have seen it. Such models of the novel as metafiction, surfiction, superfiction, transfiction, and the like can be put into a historical continuum this way, and no sense of alienation or rupture is necessary to accept this view: that the genre of the novel has always been conscious of its own devices. A critic/historian such as Robert Alter would say that the nonfiction novel is a non-problem for there is a clearly defined history of self-conscious fictions. Alter treats this history admirably in *Partial Magic: The Novel as a Self-Conscious Genre.* The study, Alter says, discusses novels that are "purposeful experiments with form undertaken . . . to draw our attention to fictional form as a consciously articulated entity rather than a transparent container of 'real' contents."[46] Alter's thesis is that there exists, so to speak, a "Great Tradition" other than the conventionally mimetic one F. R. Leavis identifies in his well-known book of that title. In this tradition, says Alter, the exemplary novels "systematically" flaunt their own conditions of artifice and thereby probe "into the problematic relationship between real-seeming artifice and reality."[47] As Alter demonstrates, this tradition in the novel has been around since the beginning, in Cervantes, Fielding, and Sterne, to name just three examples.

But, as Alter knows well, this tradition, though always visible to the critical eye, has never been the really dominant tradition until modern times—really, not until the triumph of what is understood as "modernism" itself. Such self-consciousness—by which we mean a consciously critical understanding of the fictionality of fiction—has always been present in the genre. It is only since the advent of modernism, however, that an entire epistemology has been predicated upon such fictionality.[48] Modernist notions of the world have at their core the idea that the reality we *do* know depends upon the ways in which we *can* know it. All these ways are metaphorical, analogical, tropological—*fictional*. Cervantes, Fielding, Sterne, and other early "metafictionists" were aware of the ways in which their genre's conventions determined their fiction's worlds; they were not aware, as the modernist has been, that there is *no* reality apart from those—or some other—conventions. Brian Wicker, in *The Story-Shaped World*, expresses a modernist's viewpoint when he says that "the relation of fact to fiction, of the real world to the world of story, is itself a kind of 'metaphysical pact,' a secret to which the narrator's art is the metaphorical key."[49]

A second answer to the question of what the post-modernist novel will do is that the genre's "realism" will be reoriented toward a relativism such as linguists associate with Edwin Sapir and Benjamin Whorf, and the structuralists with Saussure. This second answer merely encompasses the first, by acknowledging the limitations of our absolute pronouncements about reality, but without giving up on it absolutely, either. The view of the post-modern will, I believe, be called a "new" realism, then. David Goldknopf, in *The Life of the Novel*, positing a thesis I generally would support, suggests that in the traditional novel there are two basic conceptions of reality. One is "reality as a hard-rock donnée"; the other is reality as a "projection" of the imagination of the fantasist. Either of these "realities" must appear too naive for any post-modernist, post-Heisenbergian mentality. But, suggests Goldknopf, "there is an alternative to these two conceptions of reality." That alternative can appeal "to authors temperamentally disposed toward a hard sort of reality, yet unhappy with the dogmatism and naïveté of the orthodox variety." Goldknopf's alternative is "the concept of reality as a communal formulation. This concept is in the familiar empirical tradition which regards reality as a set of theories that have become facts through confirmation by experience." It has the advantages of both objectivity and subjectivity. "It meets science part way in that the objectivity, or externalism, of 'the world,' which is at the heart of any realism, is understood to be the result of activity, not the simple, passive exposure of the senses. The activity, however, is private only in its most primitive, and sophisticated, phases. In the broad reaches between, where the basic structure of reality is articulated, it is communal: the cooperative processing of experience by the individual and his culture." Goldknopf thus speaks of the "new realism" as one that goes beyond the old, though retaining its verisimilar, communal base. It will shape the virtues of the mimetic tradition "to a more far-sighted vision," for in it the author will be able to "take advantage of the fractures and pliancies in his subject matter," those "flaws induced by the heat of social change," as well as "the slackness which betrays the spent dogma."[50]

What sort of novel might actually embody the elements of an authentically new realistic fiction? I do not think it will be marked by the hippie-dippie, psychedelic, funky experimentalism that has characterized too much of our recent fiction.[51] It will have too great a problematic feel for lived-life for that. Robert M. Pirsig's *Zen and the Art of Motorcycle Maintenance* may well provide a paradigm for this critical new realism. Pirsig's book is perhaps an autobiography, but it is certainly "fictional" enough to be called a novel. An incredible publishing success, after having been rejected by more than a hundred publishers,[52] it has been so popular, I think, because Pirsig's experiences novelized in the book touch upon the central problem that has plagued the modernist mind—really, has plagued the human mind for centuries. The problem is the "split" between the subjective and objective aspects of reality, the issue that has been both a theme and a presupposition of technique in modernist fiction. But in *Zen and the Art of Motorcycle Maintenance* Pirsig's narrator argues strenuously that the split is the result of a false dichotomy, which can be avoided by our focusing upon "quality." Quality thus becomes his major concern in the work, subtitled "An Inquiry into Values." Quality, says Pirsig's persona, replaces the once-authoritative term *reality*. It becomes the third entity in a trinity of subject and object and the relationship between them. But quality is independent of subject and object and is anterior to both, so what Pirsig's narrative persona arrives at in the book is a "new" monism. This monism can, he believes, effectively reorient man in the modern world. Looking back on his musings of the obscure, Pirsig's self-reflective narrator reports: " 'The sun of quality, he wrote, 'does not revolve around the subjects and objects of our existence. It does not just passively illuminate them. It is not subordinate to them in any way. It has *created* them. They are subordinate to *it!*"[53]

Given this Copernican revolution in metaphysics, people can go about living life undivided by awareness of self and object, for the two, in Pirsig's system, become one in the event. Humanity can live life unbisected by the traditional separation of sensory awareness and intellectual awareness, sensation and intelligence, emotions and reason, art and science, religion and philosophy: "Quality," says Pirsig's narrator, "is the Buddha. Quality is scientific reality. Quality is the goal of Art."[54] Even that apparently unbridgeable gap between self and other—myself and the world, me and you—can be crossed; we share a common reality in the quality event:

> What guarantees the objectivity of the world in which we live is that this world is common to us with other thinking beings. Through the communications that we have with other men we receive from them ready-made harmonious reasonings. We know that these reasonings do not come from us and at the same time we recognize in them, *because of their harmony,* the work of reasonable beings like ourselves. And as these reasonings appear to fit the world of our sensations, we think we may infer that these reasonable beings have seen the same thing as we; thus it is that we know we haven't been dreaming. It is this harmony, this *quality* if you will, that is the sole basis for the only reality we can ever know.[55]

The main narrative drive of Pirsig's book—an "anatomy" combining a multitude of elements from many fictional conventions, especially the picaresque and the novel of ideas—is the resolution of a variety of dichotomies, explained in the narrator's "Chautauquas" and dramatized in the development of character and action. But the main image for the resolution that counts most—the healing of the split mind, the mending of the "broken heart," as R. D. Laing calls it, of schizophrenia—is the image of awakening from a dream. When Pirsig's narrator finally comes to terms with his son and with a second self called Phaedrus, he at last realizes that the dream he thought he once had dreamed had been no dream at all. It had been an experience shared by himself and his son, and it is the communal sharing of the experience that confirms it as real. At this point, at the book's climax, father and son achieve harmony, both within themselves and with each other, and so they emerge out of darkness into light, out of sleep into wakefulness. It is as if Pirsig's narrator had achieved the unity for which Saul Bellow's Augie—that *picaro* of critical modernism—could only continue to search. Augie is "still circling" at the end of *The Adventures of Augie March*, but Pirsig's narrator has broken the circuit—cracked the cosmic egg—and achieved repose within the world.

Pirsig's book is not the only significant new novel to suggest that we have begun to emerge from the nightmare of modernist irony into a cleaner, better-lighted place. *Humboldt's Gift*, the most recent novel by one of the masters of critical modernism, Saul Bellow, suggests a turn toward a new possibility for fictional realism, too. As with Pirsig's, Bellow's new realism is largely a reaffirmation of the transcendentalism one associates with the romantics. All modernism is a post-romantic movement, dependent upon many of the presuppositions of romanticism. But modernism has been marked by the despair of nihilism, the sense of the absurd of existentialism, and the disjunctions of relativism in science and philosophy. In fiction, particularly, the notion that novels could provide knowledge of the world was undercut by the tentativeness with which the modernist accepted the validity of subjective, as opposed to objective, knowledge. If post-modernism means anything, then, it means that we are finally beyond this particular rupture. So *Humboldt's Gift* would seem to point toward a new realism appropriate to post-modernism by its claiming—as Pirsig had—a congruence between subject and object. Says Charles Citrine, Bellow's hero, "I had the strange hunch that nature itself was not *out there*, an object world eternally separated from subjects, but that everything external corresponded vividly with something internal, that the two realms were identical and interchangeable, and that nature was my own unconscious being. Which I could come to know through intellectual work, scientific study, and intimate contemplation. Each thing in nature was an emblem for something in my own soul."[56]

Even more recent than *Humboldt's Gift*, *Going after Cacciato*, by the young writer Tim O'Brien, puts into practice some of the claims made for human imagination by Pirsig and Bellow. In many ways a successor to that exemplar of critical modernism, *Catch-22*, this National Book Award–winning novel treats the Vietnam conflict as a fusion of objective action and subjective, imaginative fantasy or fabulation. The two are hardly distinguishable. But O'Brien, as a product of modernist thought and, perhaps, a precursor of a post-modernist fiction, displays no particular anxiety about the fusion in the novel. In fact, it seems that O'Brien's protagonist, Paul Berlin, saves himself by means of this fusion or confusion or confluence—which may be nothing other than what ordinarily is called imagination. As a raw recruit just entering combat, Berlin endures his first battle zone march, firefight, and the humbling experience of extreme fear. Later he takes part in one of the more terrifying combat experiences in Vietnam—the searching of Vietcong tunnels; and, however ambivalently, he complies with his peers when his squad members agree to "frag" a lieutenant who insists on conducting the war "by the book," even when the book calls for the incredibly dangerous tunnel searches. Worst of all, he sees his friends and acquaintances die one by one.

So when Cacciato—a simple, pastoral naif, if ever there were one—lights out for Paris, as Yossarian's friend Orr had lit out for Sweden, Paul Berlin finds the solution to the problem *his* war was causing. Imaginatively, Paul sets out on the road to Paris, too, to that Paris where a negotiated peace was supposed to take place. This journey—which is what "going after Cacciato" represents—is the one that brings Paul Berlin to his "peace in Paris," though it never takes form in any other than an imaginative realm. From his "observation post," then, he performs the most crucial trick of all:

> He'd heard stories of how OPs were attacked: always during the darkest hours, whole squads blown away, men found days later without heads or arms. He tried to forget it. The trick was to concentrate on better things. The trek to Paris. All the things seen and felt, all the happy things. Average things. Peace and quiet. It was all he'd ever wanted. Just to live a normal life, to live to an old age. To see Paris, and then to return home to live in a normal house in a normal town in a time of normalcy. . . . To tell a few war stories—Billy Boy and Pederson, the bad time in lake country, the tunnels. And how one day Cacciato walked away, and how they followed him, kept going, chased him all the way to Paris.[57]

Paul Berlin's solution is not that of the soldier but that of the creative artist, and not just any creative artist, but one working in the tradition of pastoral literature that comprises so much of American fiction. In Cacciato, Tim O'Brien locates a naif whose simplicity and innocence link him to a more cheerful age and provide the novel with its more enduring values. In Paul Berlin, he locates the artistic temperament, the persona whose "flights of imagination" from his "observation post" finally constitute the novel itself. *Going after Cacciato* is not *Three Lives*, or *Winesburg, Ohio*, or *In Our Time*, or *As I Lay Dying* revisited, but it is a fine, funny, and, finally, tragic novel that shows once again the potentialities of a major strain of American fiction.

If such works as *Zen and the Art of Motorcycle Maintenance*, *Humboldt's Gift*, and *Going after Cacciato* mean anything, it would be that the new, truly post-modernist fiction will be a realistic fiction built upon the exemplars of the sophisticated phase of modernism. The new fiction, then, will offer a realism-beyond-"realism" and, therefore, a fiction-beyond-"fiction." But this is what any convincing realism in fiction has done. It has always had to become more convincing to critical readers than earlier realisms. So the question we might ask, instead of what will the new *realism* look like, is: What will the new, post-modernist episteme look like? Hassan makes some cogent suggestions—however "human and inconclusive"—in an essay called "Culture, Indeterminacy, and Immanence: Margins of the (Postmodern) Age."

"I had in mind," Hassan says of the essay, "only to note a certain cultural ethos, a certain epistemological shift, which I thought pertinent to the anxious order of our knowledge. I mean the order of indetermanence, a term finally no less uncouth than postmodernism itself, which I hoped to displace by a more precise token of our historical energies."[58] The major point of Hassan's essay, in fact, is borne in the portmanteau word, *indetermanence*, for it combines the two features—indeterminacy and immanence—whose play, says Hassan, "is crucial to the episteme of postmodernism."[59] Hassan gives traces of the themes of epistemological indeterminacy and the immanence of language from many fields, but the main one is science, whose spokesmen have persisted in transforming its mathematical symbols into natural language. His conclusion, advanced before his proof, is that ". . . relativity, uncertainty, complementarity, and incompleteness are not simply mathematical idealizations; they are concepts that begin to constitute our cultural languages; they are part of a new order of knowledge founded on both indeterminacy and immanence. In them and in other *Gedankenexperimente*—concept science seems to have preceded concept art—we may also discover models for our own historical moment."[60]

What this means, I think, is concentrated in "the new Gnosticism," "the dematerialization of existence." "Mental constructs—Nietzsche would say 'fictions'—become the primary resource of the earth; they are our knowledge. Mind insists on encompassing more mind in itself, on apprehending more and more reality im-mediately."[61] All of which is to say that our knowledge is always *im*-mediate, always, as Jacques Derrida insists, deferred and played off against difference—hence, Derrida's own portmanteau term, *différance,* suggesting that our knowledge is indeed both indeterminate and immanent, without either knowable origin or knowable end.[62] Finally, then, it is to say of art in general, of fiction, perhaps, in particular, that its "project" as an immanent system or field is "to generalize the condition of language and of art till the human environment itself becomes an immense signifier, till dumb matter begins to speak."[63] And, so we seem—in fiction, at least—to be back where we began, in the midst of an immense universe shot through with meanings, though no longer providential ones, just waiting for novelists to represent them to us. Considering the vast welter of objects now inhabiting that universe, we may legitimately believe that we are on the frontier again—awaiting the invention of a mode that will convey us securely into it. If indeed we are at the entropic edge of the modern, having gone as far as the energy of its primal explosion would carry us, then our only direction must be back toward those origins. We will have to wait and see if the novel will again spiral above its old realistic core in order to find its new realistic form.

CONCLUSION

Notes: Conclusion

1. See Jameson's *Marxism and Form: Twentieth-Century Dialectical Theories of Literature* (Princeton, N.J.: Princeton University Press, 1971), which has supplied me with a portion of the theory underlying my own historical model. See as well the following works, in addition to the continuing debates in the journal *History and Theory:* Harold Toliver, *Animate Illusions: Explorations of Narrative Structure* (Lincoln: University of Nebraska Press, 1974), which includes an excellent discussion, "Theories of Fiction and History," pp. 377–91, and a useful secondary bibliography, pp. 393–402; Hayden White, *Metahistory: The Historical Imagination in Nineteenth-Century Europe* (Baltimore: Johns Hopkins University Press, 1973), a book that demonstrates in massive detail ways in which histories are always informed by prefigurative models or tropological strategies of interpretation related to emplotment, modes of argument, and ideologies, as well as figures of speech such as metaphor and metonymy, synecdoche and irony.

2. Perhaps the most interesting account of all these developments is Michel Foucault, *The Order of Things: An Archeology of the Human Sciences* (New York: Pantheon Books, 1971), published originally in 1966 as *Les Mots et les choses.* The term *épistème* is Foucault's, whose three dominant *épistèmes*—Renaissance, classic, and modern—are consistent with my account of the development of the novel as a genre, except that his modern *épistème,* which begins with the emergence of the romantic movement, would, of course, embrace not only our current sense of "the modern," but also romanticism and Victorianism. My historical model, while generally in agreement with Foucault's, depends on our seeing several sub-movements or epicycles within the much more global definition Foucault gives the modern. One should also see the study of Foucault by Hayden White: "Foucault Decoded: Notes from Underground," *History and Theory,* 12, no. 1 (1973): 23–54.

3. I have made this claim before, but here I would offer at least two statements from others to support it: in *Fiction as Knowledge: The Modern Post-Romantic Novel* (New Brunswick, N.J.: Rutgers University Press, 1975), John McCormick says that "a version of historical Romanticism has not only survived but triumphed" (p. 7) in modern art, particularly, perhaps, in the novel, which is a form of knowledge predicated upon "impulses and practices of writers in the historical Romantic period" (p. 5). In "Culture, Indeterminacy, and Immanence: Margins of the (Postmodern) Age," *Humanities in Society,* 1, no. 1 (Winter 1978), Ihab Hassan writes: "On a certain level of abstraction, modernism itself may be assimilated to romanticism and its varied aftermaths" (p. 67).

4. Hayden White, in "The Culture of Criticism," an essay on three major advocates of representationalism in art and science (Erich Auerbach,

Karl Popper, and E. H. Gombrich), points out a major problem of modernism: "Now perception is subordinated to and made captive to the psyche, and the psyche itself is released from the control of tradition, which has always ultimately exercised some direction in previous literary movements, however much they were committed to the justifications of the claims of the imagination against both sense and reason. The surfaces of the external world, so laboriously charted over the last three thousand years, suddenly explode; perception loses its power as a restraint on imagination; the fictive sense dissolves—and modern man teeters on the verge of the abyss of subjective longing, which, Auerbach implies, must lead him finally to an enslavement once more by myth" (*Liberations: New Essays on the Humanities in Revolution*, ed. Ihab Hassan [Middletown, Conn.: Wesleyan University Press, 1971], p. 64).

5. See Kahler's *The Inward Turn of Narrative*, trans. from the German by Richard and Clara Winston, Foreword by Joseph Frank, Bollingen Series 83 (Princeton, N.J.: Princeton University Press, 1973). Another study that bears on this subject is Alan Friedman's *The Turn of the Novel: The Transition to Modern Fiction* (London: Oxford University Press, 1966); Friedman explores "the relation between the formal organization of experience in fiction and the ethical assumptions that guide the form," his main theme being "the existence in the novel of a gradual historical shift from a closed form to an open form" (p. xi).

6. See *The American Novel and Its Tradition* (Garden City, N.Y.: Doubleday, 1957). Chase, I might add, is also concerned to show the differences between the American novel (and its romance tradition) and the British novel (and its more realistic "great tradition"). Bernard Bergonzi, in *The Situation of the Novel* (London: Macmillan, 1970; Pittsburgh, Pa.: University of Pittsburgh Press, 1971), treats the subject in relation to contemporary American and British novelists.

7. Tony Tanner, *City of Words: American Fiction 1950-1970* (London: Jonathan Cape, 1971).

8. John Barth, "The Literature of Exhaustion," in *Surfiction: Fiction Now . . . and Tomorrow*, ed. Raymond Federman (Chicago: Swallow, 1975), pp. 19–33. The essay originally appeared in *The Atlantic* (August 1967).

9. Anyone interested in the development of modern criticism ought to look at the excellent brief survey by Murray Krieger in "Literature v. *Écriture:* Constructions and Deconstructions in Recent Critical Theory," *Studies in the Literary Imagination*, 12, no. 1 (Spring 1979): 1–17. Krieger is especially cogent on the reactions among contemporary critics to the New Criticism, a subject I have taken up in "Phase Two: The Critical" herein. For a more detailed study of the development of contemporary criticism—one using a model adapted from Thomas S. Kuhn's *The Structure of Scientific Revolutions*—see Grant Webster, *The Republic of Letters: A History of Postwar American Literary Opinion* (Baltimore: Johns Hopkins University Press, 1979).

10. *The Bulletin of the Midwest Modern Language Association*, 8, no. 1 (Spring 1975): 1–20.

11. *Ibid.*, p. 13.

12. *Ibid.*, pp. 13–14.

13. An interesting account of the shift in French fiction of the nineteenth and early twentieth centuries from objective to subjective realism is given in Richard Terdiman, *The Dialectics of Isolation: Self and Soci-*

ety in the French Novel from the Realists to Proust (New Haven, Conn.: Yale University Press, 1976). Like Jameson, Terdiman now advocates a Marxist materialism in criticism, but this study—which Terdiman would perhaps repudiate as naive—came before his conversion.

14. Jameson, "Beyond the Cave," p. 16.
15. *Ibid.*
16. *Ibid.*
17. *Ibid.*, p. 17. I have treated a phenomenon like this in "Faulkner's 'Golden Book': *The Reivers* as Romantic Comedy," *Bucknell Review*, 13 (December 1965): 19–31, and in "Modal Counterpoint in James's *The Aspern Papers*," *Papers on Language and Literature*, 4 (Summer 1968): 199–207.
18. Jameson, "Beyond the Cave," pp. 17–18.
19. *Ibid.*, p. 9.
20. *Ibid.*, p. 18.
21. *Ibid.*
22. *Salmagundi*, no. 42 (Summer–Fall 1978): 4–30, 23–24.
23. Jameson, "Beyond the Cave," p. 1.
24. Graff, "The Politics of Anti-Realism," p. 29.
25. *Ibid.*
26. Frank Kermode, *The Sense of an Ending: Studies in the Theory of Fiction* (London: Oxford University Press, 1967).
27. Roy Pascal, "Narrative Fictions and Reality: A Comment on Frank Kermode's *The Sense of an Ending*," *Novel: A Forum on Fiction*, 11, no. 1 (Fall 1977): 40–50. I should point out, in this context, that Wayne Booth and Wolfgang Iser in this same issue of *Novel* engage in a debate (which includes others) on the relative authority of authors (Booth) and readers (Iser)—a debate that, of course, involves the issues associated with the modernist crisis.
28. *Ibid.*, pp. 40, 41.
29. *Ibid.*, p. 49.
30. Werner Heisenberg, *Physics and Philosophy* (New York: Harper, 1962), pp. 201–2.
31. "Antifiction" is a term associated with Philip Stevick; "metafiction" perhaps "belongs" to William Gass and Robert Scholes, but the best discussion of the concept is in Gregory Galica, "Patterns of Experience: The Participatory Voice in Criticism and Metafiction," Ph.D. diss., Northern Illinois University, 1977, and "Nature, Perception, and Identity: The Participatory Self in the Post-Modern World," a paper delivered at the Sixth Annual Twentieth-Century Literature Conference (February 1978). The "nonfiction novel" is perhaps the invention of Truman Capote, but at least two books have been published on the subject: Mas'ud Zavarzadeh, *The Mythopoeic Reality: The Postwar American Nonfiction Novel* (Urbana: University of Illinois Press, 1976), and John Hollowell, *Fact and Fiction: The New Journalism* (Chapel Hill: University of North Carolina Press, 1977). Zavarzadeh also coins the term "transfiction." "Superfiction" comes from Joe David Bellamy, ed., *Superfiction, or The American Story Transformed* (New York: Vintage, 1975), while "surfiction" comes from Raymond Federman, ed., *Surfiction: Fiction Now . . . And Tomorrow* (Chicago: Swallow, 1975). The "new novel" and the *"nouveau nouveau roman"* are associated

with contemporary French fiction; see Stephen Heath, *The Nouveau Roman: A Study in the Practice of Writing* (Philadelphia: Temple University Press, 1972). "Structural fabulation" is from Robert Scholes, *Structural Fabulation: An Essay on Fiction of the Future* (Notre Dame, Ind.: University of Notre Dame Press, 1975). I really should mention here, too, the term "disruptive fiction," which is the concept underlying two books by Jerome Klinkowitz: *Literary Disruptions: The Making of a Post-Contemporary American Fiction* (Urbana: University of Illinois Press, 1975), and *The Life of Fiction, with Graphics by Roy R. Behrens* (Urbana: University of Illinois Press, 1977).

32. (New York: Alfred A. Knopf, 1970), p. 25. Since Gass, several essays—in addition to the dissertation by Galica—have appeared, including Robert Scholes, "Metafiction," *Iowa Review*, 1, no. 4 (Fall 1970): 100–115; Neil Schmitz, "Robert Coover and the Hazards of Metafiction," *Novel: A Forum on Fiction*, 7, no. 3 (Spring 1974): 210–19; Larry McCaffery, "The Art of Metafiction: William Gass's *Willie Masters' Lonesome Wife*," *Critique*, 18, no. 1 (1976): 21–35; and Barry Wood, "Malcolm Lowry's Metafiction: The Biography of a Genre," *Contemporary Literature*, 19, no. 1 (Winter 1978): 1–25.

33. Gass, *Fiction and the Figures of Life*, p. 25.

34. *Ibid.*

35. Scholes, "Metafiction," pp. 106–7.

36. *Ibid.*, p. 107.

37. *Ibid.*, p. 115.

38. Schmitz, "Robert Coover and the Hazards of Metafiction," p. 218.

39. *Ibid.*, p. 219.

40. *Structural Fabulation: An Essay on Fiction of the Future*, p. 7.

41. *Ibid.*

42. *Ibid.*, p. 8.

43. *Ibid.*, p. 9.

44. *The Mythopoeic Reality*, p. 224.

45. *Ibid.*, pp. 225–26; my emphasis.

46. Robert Alter, *Partial Magic: The Novel as a Self-Conscious Genre* (Berkeley: University of California Press, 1975), p. x.

47. *Ibid.*

48. Avrom Fleishman, in *Fiction and the Ways of Knowing: Essays on British Novels* (Austin: University of Texas Press, 1978), offers an interesting counterclaim on this point: "It is a paradox of our time, in which the 'fictionality' of fiction has become a watchword of literary pundits, that many currently approved fictional works have incorporated pieces of the real world in an increasingly self-assured way. . . . Theories which purport uniformity are usually suspect in literary history, but those of the novel's pure fictionality show up with high definition as prescriptive exhortations rather than as descriptive generalizations" (p. 10). Fleishman's study, I think, will be extremely fruitful in the future analysis of modern American fiction's adaptation of disciplinary "ways of knowing." Still, where realism itself is concerned, Fleishman comes down on the side of such critics as Jameson, Graff, and Pascal—none of whom wants to concede the epistemological gap posed in language by what Jacques Derrida calls *différance*.

49. Brian Wicker, *The Story-Shaped World: Fiction and Metaphysics/Some Variations on a Theme* (Notre Dame, Ind.: University of Notre Dame Press, 1975), p. 4.

50. David Goldknopf, *The Life of the Novel* (Chicago: University of Chicago Press, 1972), pp. 192–94 for all preceding quotations from this text.
51. An excellent collection of such experiments is included in *In the Wake of the Wake*, ed. David Hayman and Elliott Anderson (Madison: University of Wisconsin Press, 1978). Though such fiction is perhaps a dead end (appropriate for a wake), Hayman's introduction to this collection is excellent in explaining its techniques and philosophic groundings.
52. Tom Zito, "The Art of Metaphysical Maintenance: On the Road in Montana with Robert Pirsig," in *Writing in Style*, ed. Laura Longley Babb (Washington, D.C.: Washington Post Writers Group, 1975), pp. 37–43, 39.
53. Robert Pirsig, *Zen and the Art of Motorcycle Maintenance* (New York: William Morrow and Co., 1974), p. 240.
54. *Ibid.*, p. 276.
55. *Ibid.*, p. 268. Pirsig's explanation of quality here seems very close, on the one hand, to A. N. Whitehead's notions concerning the relation between the subject and the "event," presented in *Process and Reality* (New York: Macmillan, 1929), and, on the other hand, to Stephen Pepper's concept of the "purposive act." Pepper seems particularly relevant to a study of Pirsig: see Stephen C. Pepper, *Concept and Quality: A World Hypothesis* (La Salle, Ill.: Open Court, 1967), as well as his *World Hypotheses: A Study in Evidence* (Berkeley: University of California Press, 1948), where the fruitful concept of "root metaphors" is outlined.
56. Saul Bellow, *Humboldt's Gift* (New York: Viking, 1975), pp. 356–57.
57. Tim O'Brien, *Going after Cacciato* (New York: Seymour Lawrence/Delacorte Press, 1978), pp. 124–25.
58. *Humanities in Society*, 1, no. 1 (Winter 1978): 51–85, 84. Hassan has published two other essays that bear directly on the subject of the development of a post-modern episteme and art: "Prometheus as Performer: Toward a Posthumanist Culture?," *The Georgia Review*, 31, no. 4 (Winter 1977): 830–50; and "Desire, Imagination, Change: Outline of a Critical Project," *Studies in the Literary Imagination*, 12, no. 1 (Spring 1979): 129–43. See also his *The Right Promethean Fire* (Urbana: University of Illinois Press, 1980).
59. *Humanities in Society*, p. 51.
60. *Ibid.*, pp. 64–65.
61. *Ibid.*, p. 71.
62. For Derrida's discussions of the aesthetics and the metaphysics of *différance*, see *Of Grammatology*, trans. Gayatri C. Spivak (Baltimore: Johns Hopkins University Press, 1976), and *Speech and Phenomena, and Other Essays on Husserl's Theory of Signs*, trans. David B. Allison (Evanston, Ill.: Northwestern University Press, 1973)—among others of his works.
63. *Humanities in Society*, p. 80.

Index

early modernists, 72–73; and naive versus critical awareness, 73

Critical orientations: M. H. Abrams's schema for, 79n

Critical phase of modernist novel: several exemplary authors, 16, 19, 21; discussed, 85–124; and existentialism, 94; frames objectives of naive phase, 95; techniques of, bequests of naive exemplars, 95; patterns of modern existence in, 95–96; types of heroes in, 96–97; three variable fictional forms in, 97; melds fiction and a correlative philosophy, 97–98; and *mythos* of irony, 98; and ironic historical epoch, 98; and exploding universe, 98; and Christian Existentialism, 98; Nathan Scott, Jr. on, 98–102; and nihilism, 98–99; and Lionell Trilling, 99–100; and Saul Bellow, 100–102; and Norman Mailer, 100–102; eschatological idioms of, 101; concepts of authority in, 103; and Heller as exemplar of, versus Faulkner, 103; and the authority of consciousness in, 103–4

Cummings, E. E.: his poetic forms, 47

Darwin, Charles: and metaphor of evolution, 10; his *The Origin of Species* mentioned, 11; and "Social Darwinism," 46

Defoe, Daniel, 7

Derrida, Jacques: and the concept of the "signified," 140

Dewey, John, 15

Dialectical phases of literary history: Alastair Fowler's primary, secondary, and tertiary, 5, 23n3, 23n10; Schiller's naive and sentimental, 6; Northrop Frye's naive, sentimental, and sophisticated, 6, 23n10; *The Exploded Form*'s naive, critical, and sophisticated, 6–7

Donleavy, J. P., 94

Dos Passos, John, 16, 95

Dramatic narrative mode: in Benjy's section of *The Sound and the Fury*, 56–60; Percy Lubbock on, 56–60 *passim*; characteristics of, 56–60; and cinematic cutting, 57–58; and use of dialogue, 58–59; and objective point of view, 59–60

Dreiser, Theodore, 16, 96

Eliot, George, 11, 69

Eliot, T. S.: his "*Ulysses*, Order, and Myth," 40; his works as exemplars of shift from naive to critical phase, 88; mentioned, 87, 90, 101

Ellison, Ralph, 94

Ellmann, Richard, 46, 47

Empson, William: his *Some Versions of Pastoral*, 151

Entropy, metaphor of, 11–13

Epistemes: 176; Foucault's *épistèmes*, 177, 187, 195n; Ihab Hassan on postmodernist, 193–94

Evolution, metaphor of: and novel-as-genre, 10; and Charles Darwin, 10; and Hamlin Garland, 10; and metaphors of entropy and explosion, 11–13

Exemplars: in literature and science, 85; of modernist literature, 86–87; of naive modernism, 87; of shift from naive to critical phases, 88; of critical phase, 89

Existentialism: and critical phase of modernist paradigm, 92; the "crisis" of, 93

Exploded Form, The: governing metaphor in, 21; as a provisional history, 175; as result of three-phase dialectical model, 175; its view of modernist novel in America, 175; on the novel-as-genre's mimetic base, 175; on exchange of epochal epistemes, 176; on the modernist novel, 176

Explosion, metaphor of, 11–12

Farrell, James T., 16, 95

Faulkner, William: his *The Sound and the Fury*, 15, 19, 21, 54–72 *passim*; explodes novel-as-genre, 49; explores epistemological problems, 49; his *As I Lay Dying* and epistemological modes, 49–50; his *Go Down, Moses* and narrative *mythoi*, 50–52; his *Go Down, Moses* and gaps of indeterminacy, reconstruction of narrative, and biblical rhythm, 51, 51–52, 52; his *Absalom, Absalom!* and modes of narration, reconstruction of narrative's history, and evolution of historical modes, 52, 53, 106; his experiments with epistemological and ontological modes in *Light in August, The Unvanquished,*

conflict between presentation and interpretation in, 42; his *The Sacred Fount, The Spoils of Poynton, What Maisie Knew, The Wings of the Dove* mentioned, 42; tension between author and reader in, 42; "modal counterpoint" of myth/romance and realism in his *The Aspern Papers*, 43; fusion of epistemological and ontological modes in, 43; narrative authority in, 44; his splitting of the novel-as-genre, 44; as precursor of modernist fiction, 44

Jameson, Fredric: dialectical model of literary history of, in *Marxism and Form*, 4, 178–79; on existentialism as projection of modernism, 92; discusses modernist "crisis" in "Beyond the Cave: Demystifying the Ideology of Modernism," 179–80; on cognitive engagement of modernist fiction with "reality," 180

Jones, James: his *From Here to Eternity*, 17

Joyce, James: his *Dubliners*, 46; Faulkner compared to, 53; use of poetic modes of narrative in, 56; his *A Portrait of the Artist as a Young Man*, 60, 61; works of, as exemplars of shift from naive to critical to sophisticated phases, 88; mentioned, 15, 19, 39, 86, 87, 89, 101, 109

Jung, Carl: and relation of "collective unconscious" to archetypal criticism, 91; archetypes of, in *Catch-22*, 117

Kahler, Erich: on the "inward turn" in literature, 15, 29, 54–55, 177; his *The Inward Turn of Narrative*, 29

Kennard, Jean: on existentialism in modernist fiction, 92–93, 128

Kermode, Frank: on *What Maisie Knew* (by Henry James), 42; his *The Sense of an Ending*, 182

Kern, Edith: on confessional forms in modernist fiction, 89

Klinkowitz, Jerome: on disruptive fiction as "post-contemporary," 128

Knowledge, the problem of: and relation to generic, modal, and archetypal conventions, 18. *See also* Mimesis, problem of

Kosinski, Jerzy, 132

Kuhn, Thomas S.: his concept of paradigms in science applied to literary history, 39, 85, 127; his *The Structure of Scientific Revolutions*, 39; his "Postscript" to *The Structure of Scientific Revolutions*, 85

Lacan, Jacques: on the "signified" and the voice of the Father, 140

Langer, Susanne K.: her *Philosophy in a New Key*, 14

Lawrence, D. H.: and poetic narrative, 56

Leavis, F. R.: novels as "dramatic poems," 60

Lewis, R. W. B.: his *The American Adam*, 3–4

Lewis, Sinclair, 16

Literary history: models of, by Fowler, Frye, Jameson, and in *The Exploded Form*, 4–8, 12, 20–21, 23n; metaphoric models of, 5; protometaphoric models of, 5, 12; the probelm of, 175

Litz, A. Walton: on *Ulysses*, 15

Lubbock, Percy: on dramatic and oral narrative modes in *The Craft of Fiction* 40, 56–60, 65

Lyrical narrative mode: in Quentin's section of *The Sound and the Fury*, 60–65; and stream-of-consciousness, 61–62; and subjectivity, 62; and lack of narrative progression, 62; musical use of language in, 62; domination of visual imagery in, 62–63; thematic associativeness in, 63–64; dream work in, 64–65

McCullers, Carson, 94

McGuane, Thomas, 149

McLuhan, Marshall, 39

McMahon, Thomas: his *Principles of American Nuclear Chemistry: A Novel*, 12

Mailer, Norman: his *The Naked and the Dead*, 17; Nathan Scott, Jr.'s discussion of, 100–102; mentioned, 94

Malamud, Bernard: as critical phase exemplar of performative mode, 152–54; and pastoral mode, 153; Max Schulz's view of, 154; mentioned, 94

Marx, Leo: his *The Machine in the Garden*, 4, 41

Masterman, Margaret: on Kuhn's concept of paradigms, 86
Masters, Edgar Lee: his *Spoon River Anthology*, 46
Medawar, P. B.: on Herbert Spencer and evolution, 11–12
Melville, Herman: his fusion of epistemological modes in *Moby-Dick*, 41
Metafiction: as expression of late modernist crisis, 183–84; William Gass on, 183–84; Robert Scholes on, 184–85; Neil Schmitz on, 184; difficulties in, 184–85; relation of, to nonfiction novel, 186; mentioned, 20
Metaphors: epochal, 10–13, 21; of exploding universe in science, 39
Miller, J. Hillis: on death of God in nineteeth-century literature, 35
Mimesis, problem of: in novel-as-genre, 175; in relation of frame to object, 176; and cultural epistemes, 176–77; and the modernist crisis, 186–87; and realism-beyond-"realism," 193; in modernism, 195–96n; and "fictionality" of reality, 198n48
Models. *See* Literary history; Paradigms
Modes. *See* Dramatic; Lyrical; Oral; Pictorial; Frye, Northrop
Modernism: two strains of, 144–45, 147; in context of other period concepts ("contemporary," "post-modernism"), 169n
Modernist crisis: and "inward turn," 15; and Newtonian crisis, 15; and Darwinian crisis, 15; relativity and indeterminacy in, 15; as aspect of sophisticated phase, 178; Fredric Jameson on, 178–80; and Jameson's dialectic of savage, barbarian, civilized, 179; problem of realism in fiction in, 179; Gerald Graff's view of, 181; Roy Pascal's view of, 182; confusion of fictional paradigms in, 183; metafiction in, 183–85; nonfiction novel in, 185–86; and transition to post-modernism, 186–87
Modernist epoch: nature historicized in, 37
Modernist fiction. *See* Modernist novel
Modernist novel: as tertiary phase of novel-as-genre, 7; synchronous with ironic historical epoch, 10; rooted in

"traditional" novelists of nineteenth century (Melville, Twain, James), 16; indeterminacy and reader's imagination in, 18; and formalist criticism, 18–19; fusion of novel-as-genre and romance in, 22; epistemological problems in, 36–38; perception and modes, models, paradigms, genres, types, archetypes in, 38; entropic edge of era, 39, 194; reflective of late nineteenth-century crisis of "inward turn," opening-up of nature, art, philosophy, 54; its use of fiction's modes, subsuming of reality in consciousness, idealism, solipsism, and epistemological enterprises, 176–77; definitions of reality in, 177; reflections of "paradigm shifts" in, 177; the crisis situation of, 178; viewed by Jameson, Graff, Pascal, 181–82; problem of mimesis in, 181; confusion of paradigms in, 183–86; at end of epoch, 186–94. *See also* Critical phase of; Naive phase of; Sophisticated phase of
Morris, Wright: his *The Territory Ahead*, 95

Nabokov, Vladimir, 133
Naive phase of modernist novel: beginnings of, in late nineteenth-century and early twentieth-century fiction, 16, 19, 41–53; use of genre concepts in, 17; pastoral/elegiac modes in, 17; *The Sound and the Fury* as major exemplar of, 54–81; shifts of, to critical modernist phase, 88–89; paradigmatic forms of, in Faulkner, 103; authority of consciousness in, 103–5; archetypal forms in, contrasted to critical awareness in Heller, 105–6; aspects of, characterize American literature, 130; and novel-as-genre's shifts in authority, 138–39; American vision in, fused with experimental forms, 143; and two senses of "tradition," 144–46; pastoral/performative modes in, 149–52; aspects of, revived in Malamud and Brautigan, 152–54, 155–68; development of, reviewed, 175–78. *See also* Critical Phase of modernist novel; Modernist novel; Sophisticated phase of modernist novel

Nature, concepts of: novel-as-genre and, discussed, 29–39; and "spiritual authority," 30; and changing forms of novel-as-genre, 30–31; in Classical, Renaissance, and Puritan eras, 31–33; in Romanticism, 33–35; in modern period, 35–39

Naturphilosophie: and epochal metaphors, 12; texts illustrating, 25*n*; mentioned, 177

New Criticism: corollary of critical phase of modernist novel, 91

New fiction: Philip Stevick's concept of, 129–32; "axioms" of, 131

Nonfiction novel: as expression of modernist crisis, 185–86; Mas'ud Zavarzadeh on, 185–86; and "transfiction," "totalizing novel," and modernist aesthetic of objectivity, 185–86

Novel-as-genre: in relation to historical determiners, 7–8; modernist transformations of, 9; and modernist modes, 9; relation to Frye's historical modes, 9; and metaphor of evolution, 9–10; and pre-modernist crisis, 15; mimetic form in, 29; concepts of nature and "spiritual authorities" in, 29–39; and Newtonian science, Augustinian theology, and rationalist philosophy, 30; and modern science's exploded world, 30; formal problem of, 30; empirical realism in, 31; nature and mind in, 31–32; and inward turn of spiritual authority, 33–34; romantic idealism in, 34–35; entropy and relativity in, 35; epistemological problems in, 35–37; relation of, to history, 37; congruence between epistemological and ontological modes in, 41; oral, dramatic, lyrical, and pictorial epistemological modes of, in a naive phase exemplar, 54–81; impact of early modernists on, 72; modernist modes of novel contrasted to, 134; modernist novel as sophisticated phase of, 175, 178; problem of mimesis in, viewed by recent critics, 178–82. *See also* Critical phase of modernist novel; Modernist novel; Naive phase of modernist novel; sophisticated phase of modernist novel

Novels, types of: realistic, 16; naturalistic, 16–17; manners, 17

Oates, Joyce Carol, 53

O'Brien, Tim: his *Going after Cacciato* as possible post-modernist exemplar, 191–92; his novel mentioned, 22

O'Donnell, George Marion, 104

Olderman, Raymond M., 128

Onopa, Robert: on art as religion, 142–43

Oral narrative mode: in Jason's section of *The Sound and the Fury*, 65–68; narrator's self-awareness in, 65; imitation of direct address in, 66; colloquial style in, 66; narrative emphasis in, 66–67; treatment of theme and character in, 67–68; epithetic figures of speech in, 68

Paradigms: metaphoric and protometaphoric, 3–4; and models of literary history, 4–8, 12, 20–21; Kuhn on, in science, 85; defined, 85; and concept of exemplars, 85–86; the three dialectical phases of, 86–93

Pascal, Roy: on mimesis in novel-as-genre, 182

Pastoral mode: in modernist fiction, 21; and the performative mode, 149–54; in Brautigan, 149; in Anderson, 149–50; in Hemingway, 150; in Fitzgerald, 151; in Malamud, 152–54; in O'Brien's *Going after Cacciato*, 192

Performative mode: discussed, 142–54; versus artifactive strain of modernist art, 144–45; and authority of creative process, 146; Brautigan as sophisticated phase exemplar of, 146–49; naive phase exemplars of, 149; epistemological and ontological modes in, 153–54; *Trout Fishing in America* as example of, 155–68 *passim*

Pictorial narrative mode: in Dilsey's section of *The Sound and the Fury*, 68–71; as normal mode of novel-as-genre, 68; pictorial presentation in, 69; conventional moral perspective in, 69; authority of novel-as-genre used in, 70; authoritative style in, 70–71

Pirsig, Robert: his *Zen and the Art of Motorcycle Maintenance* as possible exemplar of post-modernist novel, 22, 189–91

Play, concept of. *See* Game, concept of

Poggioli, Renato: on avant-garde literature, 132

Poirier, Richard: on the concept of performance, 140; his *The Performing Self*, 142

Post-modernist novel: and a "new realism," 22, 188–89; and link to modernist novel, 187–88; Pirsig's *Zen and the Art of Motorcycle Maintenance*, Bellow's *Humboldt's Gift*, and O'Brien's *Going after Cacciato* as possible exemplars of, 189–92; episteme of, 193–94; likely return of, to origins in novel-as-genre, 194

Pound, Ezra, 11, 15, 39

Proust, Marcel, 109

Pynchon, Thomas: his *Gravity's Rainbow*, 12–13

Rankine, W. J. M.: and entropy, 11

Realism, a new: its relativism, 188; David Goldknopf on concept of, 188; combination of subjectivity and objectivity in, 188–89; illustrated in novels by Pirsig, Bellow, and O'Brien, 189–93

Richardson, Samuel, 7

Richter, David: on *Catch-22*, 106–7; and critique of naive existentialism, 107

Robbe-Grillet, Alain, 104

Romanticism: Northrop Frye's view of, 6; in relation to Wordsworth, the Victorians, and modernism, 7. *See also* Modernist novel; Nature, concepts of; Novel-as-genre

Salinger, J. D., 94

Sartre, Jean-Paul, 107

Schiller, J. C. F. von: on naive and sentimental art, 6

Schmitz, Neil: on metafiction, 184

Scholes, Robert: on metafiction and problem of mimesis, 184–85

Schulz, Max: on Malamud and Jewish American fiction, 154

Scott, Nathan A., Jr.: his *Three American Moralists: Mailer, Bellow, Trilling*, discussed in context of the critical

phase of modernist novel, 99–102; mentioned, 94, 128, 155

Smith, Henry Nash: his *The Virgin Land*, 3

Sophisticated phase of modernist novel: exemplary authors mentioned, 16, 20, 21; self-consciousness in, 20; discussed, 127–68 *passim*; crisis in epochal metaphors in, 127–28; and post-modernist fiction, 128–29, 186–94; relation of, to early modernists, 129; relation of, to Stevick's "new fiction," 129–32; concept of play in, 132–33; concept of game in, 133–35; performative mode in, 133, 142–54; and artifactive mode in, 133; centers of consciousness in, and indeterminacy in, 135–36; problems of knowledge, mimesis, the critical field, and authority in, 136–38; myth, archetype, language, act of writing in, as authorities for modes, 138; relations to naive and critical phases, 138–39; concepts of performance and "voice," 140–41; *Trout Fishing in America* as exemplary novel of, 155–68. *See also* Critical phase of modernist novel; Modernist novel; Naive phase of modernist novel; Post-modernist novel

Sound and the Fury, The: four modes of ontological organization in, 51; explosion of narrative in, 51; impact of, on the novel-as-genre, 55; epistemological modes of presentation in, 56–71; as exemplary, paradigmatic modernist novel, 86–87. *See also* Dramatic narrative mode; Lyrical narrative mode; Oral narrative mode; Pictorial narrative mode

Spencer, Herbert, 11, 12

Stein, Gertrude: as modernist experimenter, 45; mentioned, 16, 39, 73

Steinbeck, John, 16

Sterne, Laurence: his *Tristram Shandy* as potential dead-end for novel-as-genre, 88

Stevens, Wallace, 139, 168

Stevick, Philip: on a "new fiction," 129–32

Structuralism: as a formistic metaphysics, 93

Styron, William, 16, 94
Sukenick, Ronald: "Interview," 127;
"The New Tradition in Fiction," 186;
mentioned, 133
Superfiction, 20, 183
Surfiction, 20, 183
Swados, Harvey, 94

Tanner, Tony, 12, 142, 143
Teilhard de Chardin, Pierre, 12, 29, 177
Texts: as modes of being and knowing, 3
Thompson, William (Lord Kelvin): and
entropy, 11
Thurston, Jarvis: on oral formulaic tradi-
tion in Anderson, 149
Totalizing novel, 186
Tradition: the oral, 143–44; two senses
of, in American literature, 144; Brautigan and the pastoral/performative, 149,
155–68; the concept of "voice" in,
149–50; Milman Parry and Albert B.
Lord on, 150; Empson on pastoral, 151
Transfiction, 185
Trilling, Lionel: discussed by Nathan A.
Scott, Jr., 99–100
Trout Fishing in America: as exemplar of
sophisticated modernist phase, 155–
68; in pastoral/performative tradition,
155 ff.; point of view in, 156; style in,
156–57; as subtle lyrical novel, 157;
and oral/colloquial tradition, 157;
death as theme in, 157–58; sex and
violence as themes in, 158–59; grotesque humor in, 159–60; metamorphic
style and playfuless in, 160; formulae
of elegy, *ubi sunt,* and *et in Arcadia
ego* in, 160, 168; meta-narrative struc-

ture in, 160–67; shift from *Bildungsroman* to *Künstlerroman* in,
161; typal frustrations of artist in,
161–62; three transforms of basic narrative unit in, 162–67; trout fishing
mythos in, 163; theme of imagination
in, 163–67; the child-as-hero in, 165;
in thematic context of Stevens's *The
Comedian as the Letter C,* 168
Twain, Mark, 41

Ulysses: as exemplary, paradigmatic text
of modernist novel, 86–87
Updike, John, 12, 21, 53

Vonnegut, Kurt, Jr., 16, 21, 73, 149

Wain, John, 113
Walcutt, Charles C., 36
Warren, Austin, 65
Weizsäcker, C. F. von, 12, 177
Weyl, Hermann, 11, 12, 177
Wharton, Edith, 16
Whitehead, Alfred North, 12, 13, 29, 30,
31, 177
Whitman, Walt, 11, 47
Wicker, Brian: his *The Story-Shaped
World,* 178
Wittgenstein, Ludwig, 16, 25n21
Wolfe, Thomas, 16
Woolf, Virginia, 86, 87
Wright, Richard: his *Native Son,* 17

Yeats, W. B., 15

Zavarzadeh, Mas'ud: on nonfiction
novel, 185–86